HOLY SHIFT!

EVERYTHING'S A GIFT

A Spirit-Led Journey through Illness to Wellness

LAUREN LANE POWELL

CS Crystal Spectrum Publications, LLC

Asheville, North Carolina

Library of Congress Cataloging-in-Publication Data

Names: Powell, Lauren Lane.
Title: Holy shift! everything's a gift : a spirit-led journey through illness to wellness / Lauren Lane Powell.
Description: Asheville, NC : Crystal Spectrum, 2017.
Identifiers: LCCN 2017935640 | ISBN 978-0-9911532-6-8 (pbk.)
Subjects: LCSH: Ovaries--Cancer--Patients--United States--Biography. | Cancer--Psychological aspects. | Attitude (Psychology) | New Thought. | Spirituality. | Biography. | BISAC: BIOGRAPHY & AUTOBIOGRAPHY / Personal Memoirs. | BIOGRAPHY & AUTOBIOGRAPHY / Women. | BODY, MIND & SPIRIT / Healing / General.
Classification: LCC RC279.6.P69 A3 2017 (print) | DDC 616.99/465--dc23.

Editor's note: Text selected and reprinted from Facebook is printed as originally posted on social media. No attempt to alter spelling and punctuation has been made. Some photos included from snapshots and do not meet the minimum standards for clear printing.

The photos of Paris and Lauren Lane Powell featured throughout the book were taken by Larry Powell.

Printed in the United States

Published by

CS Crystal Spectrum Publications, LLC

Ashevile, North Carolina
www.crystalspectrumpublications.com

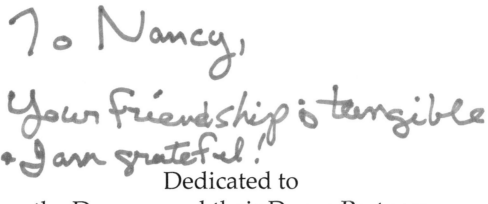

To Nancy,

Your friendship is tangible + I am grateful!

Dedicated to
the Dancers and their Dance Partners

To the dancers who lose their hair and endure unending fatigue, but keep on dancing anyway.

To the dance partners who care for us in all ways, and keep on dancing with us.

In Joy ♥!

Lauren Love Powell

To Nancy;
Your friendship is tangible
& am grateful!

TABLE OF CONTENTS

ACKNOWLEDGMENTS

From the Easter morning when I was twenty–one, Unity, a denomination of the New Thought movement, provided me with a strong, growth–oriented spiritual foundation. Since then, Unity principles have guided my every step, especially from the diagnosis of cancer to now. My Dad and Grandmama discovered Unity and introduced me to it at a time in my life when I needed direction. They deserve much gratitude for their loving guidance of my spirituality. Through Unity, I learned a benevolent God is everywhere present, including within everyone and within me. I learned about love and fear, joy and pain, forgiveness and misjudgment, and about my relationship with my emotions. Through Unity, I embraced meditation as a form of prayer. When I invited my sister to sing with me, she fell in love with Unity, as did our mother shortly thereafter.

Other positive influences affecting me include the writings of Leo Buscaglia, Scott Peck, John Bradshaw, Neale Donald Walsch, Thich Nhat Hanh, Deepak Chopra, and Eckhart Tolle. My family's immersion in metaphysics, the Law of Attraction, the Power of the Mind, *A Course in Miracles*, *Emotional Intelligence*, *Brain Gym*, and *HeartMath* also opened me to new worlds and offered me a roadmap to the workings of the universe.

My mom at the piano surrounded by me and my friends.

This book would not be possible without the consistent love and support of my mom and my sister Kristen, my co–creators. I owe my love for music to my mom, who made singing an integral part of every celebration or trial from my early childhood until her passing. My sister continues to sing with me in perfect harmony.

In addition, my stepmom MaryAnn played a key role in the birthing of this book. She held me accountable during a difficult five–year process for she saw me as an author long before I could. The first question she'd ask after we hugged hello was, "How's the book coming?"

Alongside my family of origin, my spiritual family promoted the completion of this book. Cheryl Commer, Pat Coughlin–Mawson, Shirley Stallings, Phyllis Wickliff, Maryann Heaton–Holden, Cecilia St. King, Mary and Ernie Perry, Pam Chappell and Pete Whele, Francesca Bowling–Kemper, Jody Soland, Jim Sanders, Jeanie DiCarlo Wagner, Monica Breen McNamara, Dr. John Miller, Rev Olivia Crystal, Armand and Angelina, and many more who lifted me up in prayer, sent me Reiki, visited me, called me, and visualized my healing before it became real. My virtual support team shone through Facebook, sending me healing messages and cheering me through my successes and setbacks.

Facebook's platform allowed me to share my journey and furnished me with an amazing outlet for my creativity. I thank Facebook for giving me a place to share my pain, my joy, my music, my artwork, and my pleas for prayer and healing in real time.

My eternal thanks go to the doctors, nurses, and techs at IU Health, especially the chemo crew who allowed me to create the experience I created.

My best friend, life partner, and husband, Philip Long, supplied the main anchor I needed in the swirling waters of surgeries, self–care, and surrender. His clear head and willing hands made sure I was fed and comfortable during chemo. That nurturing gave me time and strength to heal and write. Phil has witnessed my journey and encouraged me to write a book that may aid many. I am grateful beyond words that our lives are entwined.

I wish to express appreciation to the staff at Crystal Spectrum Publications for their work in creating a shape and structure for this book. In addiiton, their editorial guidance helped me clarify the telling of my story in certain, more challenging sections.

Lauren Lane Powell

FOREWORD

$\mathcal{H}$ ow does one begin to introduce a book so unique, so honest, so full of wisdom…a book that bursts with joy in the midst of pain, harnesses the collective compassion of hundreds of people and explores not only an individual journey towards healing but the Source of that healing itself? Within these pages swirl both the raw emotions of a human being and the raw power of a spiritual being. It is these intense emotions and transforming power that one feels throughout Lauren Lane Powell's recounting of her encounter with ovarian cancer (which she so delightfully calls cAnswer) and her remarkable way of creating an experience for herself and her team of co–creators that is filled with faith, authenticity and humor.

Lauren graciously gives us a behind–the–scenes look at how she consciously chooses to apply spiritual principles to a potentially devastating set of circumstances. We are allowed to intimately witness how she decides to treat her body and soul, including the tumors and the painful procedures required, with compassion and gratitude. The use of positive affirmations and beautiful sounds are at the heart of Lauren's approach to regaining her health. Chemotherapy, once feared and detested, becomes her best friend and is given the loving moniker of "Chemo/Dreamo"; the bag containing the chemicals is greeted with a kiss. Friends are invited to sing, chant, and read with her during treatment, transforming the chemo room into a space of peace and support. Her colostomy bag becomes Lucy, as in "I Love Lucy," and in spite of the misery involved, is treated with respect. The thin, exhausted features that greet her in the mirror each day are the recipient of her words of encouragement and love. Nurses, visitors and doctors are regarded as angels, and the words of her Facebook community become a holy text through which she fortifies her mind and body. In this way, Lauren's experience becomes a practice of not only mind over matter but heart over matter.

I found myself in tears at many points along the way in this story, but they were tears of tenderness for the greatness of spirit I sensed in Lauren and in the community that rose up to surround her in her time of need. I was awed at how this radiant, beautiful woman, who had lived a dynamic and independent life leading workshops as a sound healer and vocal performer, was able to reveal her vulnerability and ask for help. It was for her an "All hands on deck!" moment when she put out the call for backup support. "I get to heal from ovarian cAnswer," she declared, "and I need you with me." Help came both from the macrocosmic and the microcosmic expression of the Divine —that is to say from her highest concept of God and from ordinary people like you and me—and she accepted it gratefully. This, I believe, is the secret behind her strength: Lauren recognizes the essential unity of all souls, and because of this recognition she was able to draw upon the collective energy of her spiritual community.

The story of this community is one of the many reasons this book is so fabulous. Not only is the reader introduced to Lauren's own spunk and courage but to the insights of many others as well. As she says, her Facebook log became a type of journaling and as it expanded, thousands of comments, advice, prayers, jokes, and encouragement poured in. Those many voices are prominently featured in this story, a testimony to Lauren's mindset of inclusion. I became part of that Facebook team, eventually interacting with Lauren and her sister on a more personal level. Lauren also began including me in her daily inspirational meme texting, a gift unasked for and given faithfully in grace. No matter what she was going through, Lauren found time to send that meme to all of us, determined to do as John Wesley said,"…all the good you can by all the means you can, in all the ways you can, in all the places you can, at all the times you can, for all the people you can, while you can." In addition to these memes, Lauren began posting a "Song for the Day" from her repertoire of original music to inspire others. Sometimes she couldn't get it there until midnight, but it always appeared—a beacon of light sent forth into the world as a symbol of gratitude for the support she was receiving.

This is the glittering diamond in the cavern of Lauren's experience—that she is ready to offer the best she has without assurance of receiving anything in return. She is one with the principle of reciprocal harmony. She plants seeds in people's hearts but does not ask to gather the flowers herself. She finds great joy in knowing they will one day gather them for themselves. Because she has been able to immerse herself so fully in this flowing stream of love, losing any sense of where it begins or ends, unconcerned with ideas of gain or loss, she has found herself the recipient of everything she has offered. This, as the great ones have taught us, is the way the Divine operates. We see this in the words Lauren uses to describe her reaction to hearing her diagnosis: I asked "Why me?" and I heard, "Why not you? Now you get to change the way cAnswer looks and feels for multitudes of people!" To me, this is the true mark of wisdom—when one is capable of releasing the ego that defines a certain sense of identity to embrace what presents itself in the eternal now. Lauren allowed herself to face things as they are, envision things as they could be, and infuse that vision with the highest vibrations she could muster.

Lauren answered many calls when she wrote this book. The first call was to apply all the wisdom she had accumulated in her own life to her situation. The second call was to share what she had to offer in the form of a public journal. The third call was to accept the waves of healing energy sent her way in the form of both a virtual and hands–on community. The fourth call, challenging beyond comprehension, was to use all that she had learned to walk both of her parents through their own illnesses and transitions in 2015 and 2016. And the fifth call was to offer the world this transparent chronicle of the entire process. By rising to the occasion each time she was called, we now have this incredible account which is exactly what it claims to be, "a spirit–led journey through illness to wellness."

I believe this story gives readers a formula for living, a formula that has wide application to life in general, even if it does not involve illness. It is a formula that takes the ordinary and through the power of love, faith, and community makes it extraordinary. It is an account that will invite you to reframe the challenges you may be facing, no matter what they may be. It is a healing balm emerging at a time of conflict and confusion in our world, and true to form, it is offered as a surprise wrapped in ribbons of hope. You will be very happy when you unwrap it. Talk about a gift—holy shift!

In joy,
Frances Key,
Author of *The Team Books: A Mother's Wisdom from the Other Side*
Jacksonville, Florida

Chapter One
The Diagnosis

*I*n late March 2012 I participated in a wonderful Healing Arts Festival in Navarre, Florida. For two days, I demonstrated the relaxing effects of singing bowls combined with the human voice. I sang with the bowls for individuals who sat across from me on chairs while placing their feet inside a larger quartz crystal singing bowl. I usually stay very relaxed during this process. This time I felt burning in my gut. *Could this be a hernia?* I do lift a lot of weight on the road. *Could it simply be a really bad case of indigestion?* My body's not used to antibiotics and I had taken two rounds recently. I looked back three months, to when the discomfort began. Any number of things could have caused it.

The following week after the workshop I visited Ft. Walton. My hostess, Jennifer, suggested I see her naturopath so the next day Dr. Hendricks examined my fingernails, my urine, and my eyeballs. He pushed, poked, and prodded. When he found a little nodule just above my pubic hairline, he chose his words carefully. "This could be digestion challenges, as you suspect. But to vanquish any other suspicions, I would like to have you take this test to rule out ovarian cancer." My heart dropped, fell through the floor and, at that moment, I became a witness to my life. I began to watch and wait to see what I would do next. I became a fascinating study to myself.

The office building housing the lab for my blood draw sat at the back of a lot a few blocks away. I kept driving past it. My frustration turned into panic the third time I passed it. The fear of being lost cast an unusual dark sinister cloak closing around me. I was shaking when I finally parked near the door to the lab. The evangelical angel lab tech swept me up in prayer at my first sign of permission. I had now opened myself to receive all prayers from anyone, anywhere, at any time! With fury in her voice she asked that the demon of cancer be driven out . . . if it was indeed cancer. I felt just a little bit lighter.

I became a witness to my life at that moment, watching and waiting to see what I would do next. I became a fascinating study.

FB Post March 29, 2012
Calling all healers! Always in the right place at the right time, now in Ft. Walton Beach, saw a naturopath who found a suspicious something in my lower abdomen. Blood test shows high levels of whatever signifies cancer. It could be something else, but I will know more when I see an OB–GYN and have a biopsy...soon, I pray. Please pray for me and hold me in the light. Thank you for your healing work!

CHARLOTTE: I see your victory as healed and whole!

MELISSA: What we know is there is healing happening in your body right now. Every cell, every atom is in complete alignment with Divine perfection. I see the light moving in your lower abdomen and throughout your body now. All is well. All is heathy in you right now. Peace to your mind, and health, health, Divine Health in your temple. And so it is!! GOD LIGHT SURROUNDING YOU AND PERMEATING EVERY CELL OF YOUR BEING....LOVE YOU SISTER!!!!! I AM CALLING ORI AND A.R.E. NOW...

SCOTT: And we know Lauren, as a representation of the Source, is Whole and Perfect. And so it is...

LITTLEHAWK: Namaste ~ Sending you much Love and Healing Energy. Love and Miss You. Many Blessings

SIDNEY: I am not a healer but I am sending my love to you. Be well my dear friend.

JAMIE: You are filled with the healing light of all that GOD is...Health is your natural state of being and this suspicious something has no power of the TRUTH of who you are in BODY, MIND AND SPIRIT...You are here in service to the world and the Universe loves, nurtures and supports you in all areas of your life...HEALTHY AND WHOLE I AM, I AM...

ALLIANA: Lauren...how easy to hold you in your natural radiant health and well being!

MARTHA: Lauren....You are healed and whole... And you are so open and healthy that cancer does not stay in you...it flows continuously and affects you not!! Your optimism and joy for living keep everything flowing and moving and completely healthy

LISA: Ernest Holmes says it is as easy to cure cancer as it is the common cold. Your healing is complete as you claim it so. As my guides, angels, and healers in spirit tell me, all is well. Know that, and call on Archangel Raphael for the healing you desire.

LINDA: Lots of healing coming down the line from everyone for you. Cancer is a physical fungus, get working with the bicarbonate of soda and the thick black oil made from cannabis, a little bit of MMS wouldn't go amiss either and eat raw live food. We are spiritual beings in a physical body.

PATRICIA: Your body has already begun to heal itself. That is the normal, natural process. I hold this as an immovable truth!

OLIVIA: My continuing prayers go with you, my dear...sending light and healing energy to every cell of your body and seeing them responding in this now moment. Thank you, God.

JO M: Lauren, we will add you to the Healer's list in Sarasota and add you to our Reiki Box as well. Om shanti shanti shanti…Jo and Patricia

MARILYN B: I see you whole and healthy…radiant and beaming as you are and have always been. Sending love and healing for body, mind and spirit! It is done.

LAUREN LANE POWELL: You are all such wonderful friends. I got an appointment Monday morning with an OB–GYN. I will keep you posted of my continued perfection!!

I practiced meditation and prayer for the next 48 hours while I waited to hear the lab results; and I worked to stay in peace. When fearful emotions overwhelmed me, I wept them out, spending equal time experiencing serenity and despair. I also spent hours just around the corner from my hostess's home in a no–kill cat shelter, a little piece of heaven for those of us who are naturally cat crazed. So many cats. So much love. So comforting.

Dr. Hendricks finally called the next morning and asked me to come in.

"You can't tell me over the phone, huh?"

That wasn't a good sign. Jennifer went to the doctor's office with me as moral support. For two days I had practiced being okay with whatever happened next and, that helped a little when Dr. Hendricks told me it still could be digestive. But the numbers looked like ovarian cancer.

Breathing came hard. I sucked a big breath deep into my body as my whole world shifted.

The normal CA–125 test reads anywhere between 0 and 35. My number was 2,679. At that time, I purposely did not want to know how strongly the tests indicated the cancer possibility. I knew that a biopsy was required to confirm the diagnosis. *What if it really was cancer? Could it all be a dream? When can I wake up? I am so healthy! I'm fit! I'm in the best physical shape ever! It can't be cancer! It just can't be! As intuitive as I am, I would know if there was something growing inside me, wouldn't I? As well as I know my body, I could feel it if there was something nasty like cancer growing in it, couldn't I?*

In shock, Jennifer and I both sat and cried in her car before we drove away from the office. It didn't make sense. I was so healthy. Then I drove to the Ft. Walton Beach Florida Unity Church to pack up my things from the events that past weekend.

On arrival, I walked into the minister's office visibly upset.

I think it was you Lauren, who taught me to own it first, then love it and then let it go.
—Judith Simon

"I may get to heal from ovarian cancer," I cried.

Instantly, angels Rev. George and his wife, Rev. Barbara, surrounded me and allowed me to express my deep black despair. Cradled in their arms, I bawled for every pain I ever felt, for every pain I ever caused, and for every pain I might yet experience. Held in the light of their compassion, tears of fear flowed out of my eyes and evaporated in the glow of the sanctuary window. Each wave of wailing released pounds of panic. These precious people actively opened their hearts and poured love, everything I needed, upon me. In that eternity, Grace descended.

Staying in the present moment proved close to impossible. My whole being wanted to dwell in the land of "what if?" As I focused on right here and right now, I saw more clearly the beauty of life all around and within me. If I was to enter a dark place of illness and suffering, I was bound and determined to love it all! Sweet Spirit, show me how!

Usually, business occupied my life—preparing for the next workshop, sending and answering emails, booking the rest of the year, etc. But today was different. Today, I might have cancer.

A day or so before the ultrasound needed to confirm the presence of cancer, my good friend Rev. Shelley Heller called from Oklahoma City to ask, "Why do you get all the fun transformational experiences?"

She said this in love and with tongue in cheek. It made me realize this experience had already been transforming, only a few days since my possible diagnosis. I hadn't spoken to a doctor yet about the diagnosis or treatment, yet my transformation had already begun. My priorities had changed instantly with the chance of having cancer. Whatever it is, I am bound and determined to love it all. Sweet Spirit, show me how!

I looked for blessings in this monumental upheaval and I found them. If this was cancer, life as I knew it would change forever. I tried to find blessings in the here and now. I felt physically strong. I had no symptoms except the tummy cramps. I attempted to look forward to the adventure as this was all new territory. I would get the opportunity to experience another side of life. I tried to be excited. I would be able to take some time to rest, to stay home for a change. I went back and forth between terror of the unknown and bemused anticipation of something wonderful about to happen!

Something Wonderful is Going to Happen

April 2, 2012 FB Post

Great Good Morning to you all! At 10:30 I see the OB-GYN, to insure that the numbers were high because of digestion stuff. I am dancing in the light of your healing. BIG HUGS of gratitude for holding me in the light and for continued healing energy!! I feel so blessed to have such a network of friends! I'll keep you posted!

MARY ANN P: The Lord is my light and my salvation, so why should I be afraid? The Lord protects me from dange, so why should I tremble? Psalm 27:1 Remember what you taught me. Breathe.

SHARON: Thoughts and prayers are with you, Lauren. I try to remember that even diagnostics are an opinion.

DEANNE: You are a wayshower, and with all you know, I am sure you will heal beautifully and help others heal, too.

NANCY: Wellness is your natural state—seeing you healing and restored in God's care

MONICA: Mom just said she agrees with you about healing and learning together (so do I). We are praying for you.

DONNA: It's all been said already. Just know you are in our hearts. You know what to do and that is an awesome advantage. Thank you for your openness. We love you.

JOY: Seeing this experience passing you quickly with physical, emotional, material, spiritual renewal, bringing even greater inspiration and connectedness. You are right, you have a massive support system and you are embraced in love.

DIANE: Oh! I do so so love you, Beautiful Light Lauren. So much love from so many from all over the world—coming to you at your home in Indiana. You are whole, you are healed…and so it is… Amen.

KATHLEEN: You are and have always been since our childhood very much like a flower needing sunshine to grow. Let our love and light fill you with peace and healing. Keep some of that energy that you are so easy to bestow on others to do a bit of something for yourself. (I'm sure your mom would agree with me on that!)

DOE: Healing songs are being sung for you. They are and will continue to be filled with love and light, sweet sound sister.

CAROL: I love your positive attitude. No fear. Don't own it. I am in agreement with you that nothing is amiss. You are perfectly whole. I'll be speaking that for you, my sister! Bless you!

PAM: Lauren, I speak healing to you right now. Take time to be there for yourself. You have sung songs of healing for others and it is time to honor Lauren with your own special song. Sending you a very special request from the UNIVERSE. Sing the greatest love song from all of creation and you complete your own special song. Because love is all there is.

MARC: Hi, Lauren, and I KNOW you have a powerful KNOWING and healing consciousness. I will keep you in my thoughts and prayers, KNOWING healing is already done in Mind and you are in perfect alignment with the love and wholeness that YOU ARE!

AMY: Lauren, I'm sending you all of the love and prayers that are in my heart for your healing. Your love and healing of others comes back to you in all of our voices. Love you.

CHARLES: YOU are on my Prayer list Lauren, and I will pass it on to a number of prayer lists I'm a part of…Angels are watching over you.

JANE: Welcome to the healing club! What's wonderful about it is, life takes on a whole new meaning, as we release anything that doesn't support perfect health and love! It really puts everything in perspective! Sending lots of love and healing your way.

My step-brother Mike sells medical equipment and computer programs designed to aid physicians in diagnoses, treatment, admissions, etc. He continually deals with doctors and hospitals all over the country. He warned me about doctors' typical language.

"If it is cancer, they will try to put the fear of God in you."

He wasn't kidding!

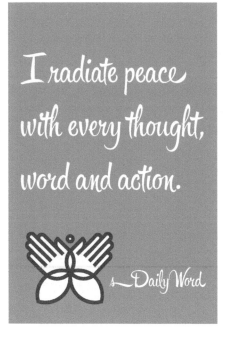

I radiate peace with every thought, word and action.

—Daily Word

Thanks to the administrative assistant at the Unity Church, I found an OB-GYN in Pensacola. When a technician did the ultrasound, I could see large masses that I didn't recognize on the screen. The technician wouldn't tell me anything saying that was the doctor's responsibility.

I don't remember the doctor's name, but Mike was right! Upon meeting him for the first time, the doctor said, without blinking, "You have ovarian cancer and you will die if you don't get it all out of you soon."

I paid $400.00 cash to learn that news! I thanked him, stood up and walked out of his office in a daze. No tears yet. I was stunned.

It really is cancer. Holy Shift! I sat in my van and tried to breathe, my breath caught in my throat. I became still and sighed a long, low tone. The next breath in went deeper. I pushed a different tone out on the exhalation. My belly breathed for me the third time. As I sang a strong, solid, whole "ooooo," I relaxed and closed my eyes.

This is the photograph I sent to John of God, a healing place in Brazil. Asking for assistance takes on a whole new meaning at this level.

"What do I do with this?" I asked God, the Universe, the angels, Holy Spirit, or anyone listening.

Then I heard, "Do it differently. Change the way cancer looks and feels by doing it differently."

The Diagnosis

April 2, 2012 FB Post

OK, just got back from the Doc's. It appears that I get to heal from ovarian cancer. Breathe. I have a powerful support system. I have angels everywhere. I'll do my part in taking care of myself medically and with my diet, meditation, and sound healing. With my community and with my God, healing is at hand. I am open to receive! This, too, shall pass! Thank you all for continued prayers. I love you!

JEAN: Seeing your angels surrounding you and sending you healing

KATHIE: Lauren, you have a wonderful connection with your body. Listen for any clues as to what it needs right now. All will be well. Sending hugs and prayers your way.

KALAR: Always pray for you and hold you in the the light, beautiful sister of mine!

AMY: Lauren, you are the most wonderful healer I know. I pray for you to be your healthy self soon! Sending you hugs and love.

COLLEEN: Darling Lauren…you practice Truth hourly, you know Truth and I know everyone is truly wrapping you in the purest of love–thoughts. Love flows between us

MARY ANN P: Dear Lauren, I know you will be well very soon, because you have so many kind and loving friends in your corner. We will put you on our prayer chain at Peace. Love and Hugs

JOHNNIE BETH: If I can beat lung cancer, (with God's help), you can beat this, too, with your powerful belief and faith system going for you already. Prayers are up and I see you developed in the White Light of God, already healed.

JOY: Seeing you in your absolutely true state of wholeness and love.

SHELLY: So glad to hear your voice this AM. Got you on a couple prayer lists and sending you bunches of love. If you need me, I'll come down.

SUSAN: Gentle Woman, Reiki on it! Blessings to you now and every moment.

UNITY DRUM CIRCLE:You are a Healthy, Wealthy Child of God. I see your healthy body breathing in all that is good and breathing out all you no longer need.

SUSANNE: I am sustained by Divine Light. I am protected by Divine Light. I am surrounded by Divine Light. I am ever growing into Divine Light. -Swami Radha

CRYSTAL INTENTIONS: My bowls sing to see you as whole and perfect.

ERNIE: Asking for help is being in Community!

LiIVE PEACE WOODSTOCK: Pray for you, Lauren, today at the church on the mount in Woodstock, NY.

CHRISTINE M: Holding you in God's Love & Light, Lauren! There is only vibrant health in Divine Mind. Blessings of Healing, Support and Guidance to you!

After the ultrasound, I drove back to the hotel in shock. *I must tell my family.* I lingered in the sun beside the pool for as long as I could. I wanted to give my loved ones a few more moments of life without cancer. I knew it would change our lives forever. I sat by the pool when I made the calls.

Mom first. Breathing deeply and consciously, trying to stay in peace, I sighed the words I knew she never wanted to hear. "I get to heal from ovarian cAnswer, Mommy."

"Oh, sweet angel! I wish I could hold you right now!"

"I can feel your arms around me, Mom. Don't worry about that. We're gonna get through this, you know!?"

"Of course we are. I'm just sorry you're gonna have to go through this."

We had a good cry together and I reminded her that everything was perfect or it wouldn't be.

Then I called Dad. I told him the same thing. "I get to heal from ovarian cAnswer."

"Yes, you will!" he said without a pause. No doubt in his mind. I wish I could be that sure. I told him I'd call him after I asked my step–brother what hospital to contact first. At once, he reminded me to watch the thinker. I was able to tell him that I had been, and will be, the observer on purpose through this. What a wonderful place to be, watching what goes on inside my mind and body without judgment. Speaking with Dad, I saw myself rock slowly back and forth, feeling him mentally cradle me like I did Mom moments ago. Through my palpable and beautiful anguish, I felt every emotion intentionally and saw them laid out before me.

Kristen is not only my sister, she's my prayer partner. Because she was vacationing in Mexico on Spring Break with her family, I decided not to tell her until she came home. No need to trouble her mind immediately. I prayed she wouldn't see it posted on Facebook before I could talk to her. Miraculously, she did not.

At noon, I deliberately soaked up and sweat out the bright hot Pensacola sunshine ceremoniously as I purged my emotions. Each time I said "I get to heal ..." I felt stronger, more empowered.

Later, I asked each person with whom I spoke to practice speaking those words back to me. "Lauren gets to heal from ovarian cAnswer." Not "Lauren has ..." or "Lauren is sick with ..."

Finally I called Phil, my husband, my best friend. "Honey, I get to heal from ovarian cAnswer."

"Oh, babe!" His voice broke. I heard long silence as we just breathed. "What now?"

We started talking logistics about where, what, and how. No questions were answered.

In the stillness, I learned that I have the opportunity to use every single tool I've collected the first 50 years of my life to heal whatever this is, in order to get on with the second 50 years of my life. Tools like: GRATITUDE; SURRENDER; FORGIVENESS; PRAYER; ASKING "SHOW ME A DIFFERENT WAY TO SEE THIS;" LOVING "WHAT IS"; GRACE; GOING WITHIN; MEDITATION; MEDICATION; LISTENING TO MUSIC; SINGING; HAVING FUN WITH IT; CHANGING THE VIBRATION; ATTITUDE IS EVERYTHING; GRIEVING; GOING DOWN THE RABBIT HOLE; ALLOWING; ASKING FOR BLESSINGS; RECEIVING BLESSINGS; WILLINGNESS; HELPLESSNESS; TRUST; AVOIDING NEGATIVITY—INCLUDING LISTENING TO NEWS AND VIOLENT ENTERTAINMENT; LISTENING TO YOUR INTUITION; FOLLOWING YOUR INTUITION; RELEASING; REFRAMING; RECREATING; REMEMBERING THAT EVERYTHING'S A GIFT; ASKING "SHOW ME THE BLESSINGS IN THIS"; EMBRACING CHANGE AND HOLY SHIFTS.

I'm sure there are more!

I feared how the changes in our lives would upset him and me. My life on the road was over, at least for now. Phil's quiet and uncomplicated life alone was over, at least for now. I knew we'd make the best out of it but, *Holy Shift!* Even amongst our tears, we both knew the ride would be interesting. We prayed for guidance, to be led to the right and perfect doctors, at the right and perfect time. Nothing else mattered right now.

I have taught others how to live life more fully by embracing "what is" and releasing all that no longer serves them. I have given lectures on the power of really feeling the feelings in order to release them. I have spoken to hundreds of audiences across the country about positive prayer and the use of the authentic voice for healing. My own words come back to me now.

April 2, 2012 FB Post

Thank you all! I know it feels like "bad" news…but what if we reframe it and just let it be "news?" "Good" and "bad" is so…defining. And what if, through this healing, the love and light that gets me there is the same love and light that helps the planet heal, because of all we learn through this together!?

MARTHA: What a wonderful opportunity for you, Lauren, you beautiful soul!! I am here for you any time. Your positive attitude will take you where you need to be.

LAUREN: Martha is right. This is an opportunity of a life time! I told everyone to please remember to use the language "Lauren gets to heal from cAnswer" when you talk to other people. Beyond my family, Facebook quickly became another support system. I knew I was not going thru this alone. As you can see, the prayers I received are heartfelt and numerous!

CECILIA: It's okay to cry, too. Sometimes things just feel scary. FEEL it and allow yourself that and then FEEL the LOVE.

LAUREN: Thank you sweet angel Cecilia for reconfirming my own work! I do FEEL everything. When the fear comes up, I embrace it! I feel it totally, I use it! I purge it! THEN I find my way back to this excited anticipation as quickly as possible! ! What a ride!!…a wondrous ride!

ROBERT: Ah ha…the chance to heal. Perhaps you'll also create a few new chants to do it. Love and healing to you!

JOLEEN: Safely surrounded on all sides by love.

DEBBIE: We never met, but I heard you speak and sing and play at Unity. My heart goes out to you. I can tell you are just an angel in disguise. I send you peace in your healing process.

JOHN: Lauren—will sing a healing song for you today. You are so loved

SHANNON: Love you, Lauren. Holding you in the light of Divine radiant health!

LESLEY SMITH: Lauren! Knowing you are in perfect health and will be guided to everything you need on every level. My friend just successfully dealt with this and is taking great care of herself on every level.

PAT: You absolutely know we see you in perfect health. We are sending you healing long distance Love thru Reiki and the sound of the bowls.

Robert's words "chance to heal" became the title for my new CD, but spelled "Chants to Heal!" Thank you, Robert!

DOROTHEE: Dear Lauren, I pray for you, seeing you whole and perfect. Sending you healing sounds.

GLENDA: Dear Lauren, you are a shining presence of light and healing. Your healing is blessing so many others, too. Easter week is a wonderful week to feel the supportive energy of Divine Overcoming. Lifting and supporting you—knowing you're surrounded by angels.

DOVE: Dear Lauren, I see you full of Light and Love, receiving your answers from this opportunity to dive in, even deeper.

ALIANNA: Yes, Lauren!! With the breathing system of all of us, you are already victorious!! Much love and deep appreciation

SPIRITUAL TOOL
PRAYER
SHOW ME HOW TO DO THIS

My first prayer was: "Sweet Spirit, show me how to do this?"

I heard loud and clear, "Do it differently. Change the way it looks and feels."

How do I do that?

"By first having fun with it."

Yeah right! How do I have fun with cancer?

The first directive I received was to "change the spelling."

"Cancer" rhymes with "Answer" so I added a lower case "c" and it became "cAnswer!" Immediately I noticed how different the word feels when I read it!

I have noticed that creativity is born out of chaos, that birth and rebirth follow contraction. If this is truly my reality, I can hardly wait to see what glorious, colorful, mystical, magical, inspired masterpiece will come from this contraction I call cAnswer!
~ Lauren Lane Powell

The repeated instruction I received when I prayed was to stay creative. I had finished a rough draft of a yoga video for a good friend the previous month. During the week I spent alone I plugged in and refined it. The act of editing reminded me of the fun we had during the taping and the love I felt for my friends. Spirit was right! Working creatively was an excellent distraction! The video turned out great and my friend loved it, and now had a product to sell and share with her students. I found, however, that it wasn't enough to stay busy. I also needed to create.

Aside from the video, I immersed myself in music. Being a composer, expressing myself in song is as natural to me as breathing. Songs of fear and forgiveness, surrender and trust, and hope and healing began to pour out of me. My little digital recorder stayed with me at all times.

"At the deepest level, the creative process and the healing process arise from a single source. When you are an artist, you are a healer; a wordless trust of the same mystery is the foundation of your work and its integrity."

Rachel Naomi Remen, MD

Prayers came pouring in on Facebook. And all I had to do was ask!

LISA LYNN: Lauren, my precious friend, I refuse to see you any way other than beautiful, harmonious, and free. You have been such a source of healing for me and I know your healing well is full and taking beautiful care of you I see you surrounded by your light and the lights of all you have brought healing to and those you will share your healing with in the future. We are so bright that only love can survive in us. I love you and look forward to hearing about your healing.

LISA M: We put you in the center of our circle in my Science of Mind class—and we are a powerful group! All is well!

KELLY: Lauren, I just heard about your new challenge! Please know you're in my heart, and healing Light and Love are being sent your way. I know you are held safely, and the Truth of who you are is Health and Wholeness!

PATRICIA L: I do not know you but have enjoyed following your wonderfully uplifting posts and insights...thank you...I am holding you in light seeing you as the whole healthy and happy child of the one who made you...Namaste'

ON DAD'S TIMELINE FROM HIS MINISTER: O Lord my God, I cried to you for help, and you have healed me! Gracious God, You are the healer. You are the One who makes bodies whole. Though You often heal through various means—doctors, medicines, surgeries, loving friends—You are the source of all health and healing. Dear Lord, continue to heal Lauren. Heal her fears, her sadness, her cancer. Be with her family as they support her during her strong battle against this tumor. Make her the whole person You have created and saved her to be. May we all discover more of Your wholeness each day. It's in Your name we fervently pray...Amen.

I have everybody everywhere praying for me and my health!

Feeling Fear
Accepting Prayer

Unity's Daily Word is a consistent source of inspiration.

I let go of concern and let God be God in my life.

~ Daily Word

You shall eat the fruit of the labor of your hands; you shall be happy and it shall go well with you.

~ Psalms 128:2

Chapter Two
No Distance Between Us

The Wheatland Music Festival falls on the weekend after Labor Day in Remus, Michigan. Phil and I attend regularly as our last hurrah before autumn falls.

The festival features music of all kinds on three stages, a world class juried art show, great healthy food, camping in a pine forest, and workshops covering everything from banjo to clog dancing. The first year I attended, I noticed no workshops offered for singing among the many other wonderful choices. So I submitted an idea for a vocal workshop in 1993.

The following year, I conducted my very first *Sing For Your Soul!* workshop. When over a hundred people showed up to learn how to sing, I knew that this was what I wanted to do for the rest of my life!

Phil and I at Wheatland

April 3, 2012 FB Post

I feel your arms around me now. There is no distance between us. Thank you!

People ask me, "How is your husband taking this?" I affirm that Phil is okay. When we spoke, he felt numb. We both agreed that he would serve me best by staying home and taking care of our sanctuary. What would he do in Jacksonville without his fuzzy family? Visit with me for a while and then what? We are used to being apart so this feels normal. I asked him to *not* let it "sink in;" rather to forget about cAnswer altogether and see me as he always sees me, whole and healthy. That is how he can support me best.

We will, of course, stay in touch and he is willing to come if I need him. My mom, dad, and maybe stepmom will be with me for the actual surgery. My sister may come too. She comes home from her vacation tomorrow.

I have angels everywhere! I ask now that the love you send me is extended to my husband and all of my family. Thank you again for continued support! I accept!

RENELLE: Holding you in great love, Lauren, and visioning you well.

ALIANNA: I have my vast international harp therapy community playing "Somewhere Over the Rainbow" for you. Great choice for Phil, too. You are so right in that he really can serve you best right now by being Present at an apparent distance.

P KAY: Lauren, I support you. I am seeing you whole and healthy. Send love to you, your husband and family. You are such an inspiration, with your beautiful openness to receive your highest good. I love you!

STEPHEN: Lauren, God is watching over his beautiful star both of this world and the next in his world. He has protected you throughout time to know and will forever. I am praying for you selfishly, as we all are, but we know that you are ours for now and his forever and he is yours.

JENNIFER R: Me, too. 4 am. I don't know what woke me. Was it you? I picture myself in a bubble, like a snow globe, and swirling within it is what I need. Today, I see you, Lauren, inside that globe and the light of healing and protection swirls around you with every bump. As life jostles you, you're bathed in fireworks of healing light. Be well, you are loved.

CATHERINE GD: Touch the hem of my garment, sister! I am here to guide you through. Love you and always see you in perfect health. Call me.

STEPHEN: After reading your Post, I am so glad you found a man like Phil. You two fit each other so well. I believe you could never have lived your life so well without him. I believe he has been your rock and you have been his daily sunrise and vision of what heaven is all about.

April 3, 2012 FB Post

WOW! I can feel the outpouring of love from everywhere! It is palpable! Especially from my sweet husband. He will, at some point, come to Jax to be with me after all. His decision. I am so blessed!

THERESA: Hi, Lauren, you make such a difference in the life of so many. I know that you will be well before you know it! Sending love, light, and many, many blessings of perfect health!

STEPHEN B: Lauren, out of bed, getting ready for the day. First thought was prayers for you. Glad to see Phil is going to make it to Jax. As I said yesterday, he is your rock and foundation, your port in the storm you always return to. He is your personal lighthouse to guide you home, both figuratively and literally.

JO and PATRICIA: Lauren, Lauren, Lauren…we sing the chant of your name. We see you whole and sweetly healed. We see you filled with Divine Mother's sounds of love. We see you in the precious joyousness that you share with others. We see you in that vibrancy and we sound your loveliness...om shanti om shanti om shanti…Jo and Patricia

PATRICIA: Dearest Lauren, we're sending this news out to the Sarasota Healers Network (a 50+ person prayer and Reiki circle). I've told them you're planning on dancing this cAnswer away. We see you as you truly are, filled with Light, Love and Bowl–Soul Music. Big Love and Hugs from your Sarasota Family.

That evening, I presented my Body by God workshop at the Pensacoloa Unity Church in which I talk about how I lost weight using forgiveness and self–love. I wonder now, if I lost weight because of my inner and outer work, or because of the cAnswer. I decided the messages were strong enough either way, and that it didn't really matter. Losing weight may or may not have had anything at all to do with it. I had reached a level of tangible self–love. That love would now help heal my body.

A positive gal in the workshop, Hennie, gave me yet another way to talk about cAnswer. "I CAN–CER-tainly heal from this!"

How awesome! Then she gifted me with a book by Denise DeSimone called "From Stage IV to Center Stage." Denise healed from head and neck cAnswer by employing the medical route and Spiritual techniques; as well as social media, by calling upon her support team for prayers, and assistance. This book covered everything I was already doing. My mom and dad bought it. When Dad downloaded the book onto his Kindle he called me.

"My God!" he said. "This is your story."

I read slowly, a blessing from my dyslexia. I read a chapter at a time, then put the book away and meditated. After breathing in the words and writing down each "aha" insight, I shared my insights on Facebook. Denise exemplified the very feelings I had just expressed.

Along with added prayer work and yoga, I changed my diet on the first day of the "scare." Because I learned that cAnswer feeds on sugar, I decided to eat no carbs at all. I also learned that cAnswer cannot live in an alkaline body, so I started juicing, drinking a mixture of baking soda, molasses, and water (yuck!).

Dr. Hendricks prescribed the supplemental "cAnswer killer," graviola. That regimen provided all the nutrition, in addition to the Isagenix protein plus shakes taken twice a day. No more coffee! Talk about big life changes!!

Kristen came home in the morning. To my relief, she had not looked at Facebook. She and her family—husband, Jeff, and sons, Steven and Ryan—had been in Mexico on Spring Break for Ryan's senior trip. When she called, I told her, "Kristen, I get to heal from ovarian cAnswer."

We cried and talked about possibilities, from surgery to recovery to death and rebirth. When we considered the possibility of her growing old without me, we decided that wouldn't happen.

Earlier that day, Mom had a vision of a woman standing in a meadow with arms up, and sunlight on her face, wildflowers all around. She said she knew this future me had healed from cAnswer, because my hair was short and curly, not long and straight. *How interesting!* She said it gave her peace.

April 4, 2012 FB Post

Here's the scoop! On Monday morning at 7:30 a.m. I go to Jacksonville, to Shands, a very good teaching hospital. Since I have no health insurance after my husband's layoff, I will fill out forms, etc. Someone told me it will be a grueling process. I believe we can change that. Please see me attracting the right and perfect administrators, doctors, surgeons, anesthesiologists, everyone I need to support, nurture, and heal myself. Then . . .

Please see a beautiful, bright, quiet room with smiling faces. Please see everyone in my presence possessing the highest consciousness, knowledge, skill, and having an openness to sound healing.

Please see me continuing to be playful. Thank you all!

Everything seems surreal. I am watching myself as if from afar. I would love to stay in this place, seeing the big picture—much easier from this perspective.

Today I have decided to be Playful with Everything

On April 4, 2012, Louise Davis of Blossom Yoga hosted my final workshop in Florida before I went home to face a new reality. I walked into a beautiful studio in Ft. Walton Beach—softly lit, warm, and cozy. Twenty–five or more people filled the room. We circled around the singing bowls and I played and sang with my whole heart.

Near the end of the evening, I spoke my new truth. "I want to share with you something I just learned about myself." Choosing my words carefully, I said, "I get to heal from ovarian cAnswer."

When I heard a gasp I said, "Please, when you speak of it to anyone, use these words: 'Lauren gets to heal from ovarian cAnswer.'"

Immediately, they put me in the center of the circle. Every hand was lovingly, gently placed somewhere on my body. Then they sang for me, chanting my name, and the words "heal" or "healing." Some sang the word "love" to me. Some sang "peace." I soaked it up! I felt embraced, cradled in the precious arms of God, uplifted, and healed at depth. In fact, "healing" took on a new meaning. I knew that everything was going to be all right.

SPIRITUAL TOOL
RELEASING CONTROL

Sweet Spirit, I am conditioned to having my life lined up months in advance. Sweet Spirit, I know where I will be, when I will be there, and what I will do there ...up until now. Sweet, Sweet Spirit, I choose now to trust. I don't know exactly what that means. Show me.

Show me how it feels to let go of all control and trust in Divine Protection.

Show me how to love not knowing what is coming next. Show me how, Sweet Spirit. Show me how!

Singing songs about healing with words like "You can–cer–tain–ly heal from this" made me feel uplifted. I didn't care that my loud singing must have been heard through the thin walls of my hotel. I created songs about releasing control while flinging my arms around wildly, as if to let go of everything I knew to be true and safe. Songs about trust and surrender poured out of me and I danced as I sang them to my body. My sweet precious body. What are you in for!? NO! Do not worry! SING!

April 5, 2012 FB Post

In my meditation yesterday, I saw happy little fishes of light swimming around inside my body consuming every cAnswer cell. They turned black upon digesting, and then shook a little. The light within turned brighter! If you are willing, please picture with me, a few moments a day, these sweet little fishes happily devouring all imperfections. Thank you so much!!

In the middle of singing, I had another big "Aha!" After touring for twelve and a half years, I now knew I reached only the people who showed up at my level in my spiritual journey. I had known for a long time that my intended work was bigger and more vast than I was able to express in this way. Previously I was not willing to slow down to make a change. How could I? I loved touring! But that love was holding me back. Now I had the opportunity to *stop* completely—to heal and see what magic God offered next. I'd be able to reassess how I did everything—how *not* to work so hard all by myself. I appreciated the upcoming rest. I would ask for help from every source … a new learning experience for me. My gratitude poured out for all of the continued prayers I received every day and my new understanding. Here is where the rubber meets the road. I remember thinking, *"For the last 29 years I may have been preparing myself for this experience. Holy Shift!"* I kept hearing, "Congratulations! You have graduated. You're ready now!"

STEPHEN: I am sitting here thinking about you and thinking about where you are. I can't seem to concentrate on studying for my classes. It all seems so trivial. Life is what is important and the people in it. I seem to be realizing that more and more every day. It has been so easy to get stuck in the whirlpool of the rat race. Anyway, I will pray extra hard for you throughout the night and in the coming days, in hopes of preparing you for the journey and the amazing gifts and experiences God has in store for you in the near future.

LAUREN'S: Thank you Stephen, my long–time friend. You are so right. My thoughts went in this direction: "From here, I get to recognize, at a deeper level, what is really important. Everything else drifts away. Right here, right now the only thing that matters is my healing…whatever that means. I know that there is healing in dying and that not all healing means "curing." I get to feel this wholly. I get to meditate on this. I get to be with this by myself, alone, for a good long time. This alone time is so very valuable." In meditation, I kept hearing:

"Be with death as if she were a friend. Make friends with dis–ease. Love the cAnswer."

> "Whenever you are confronted with an opponent, conquer him with love.
>
> —Mohandas K. Gandhi

April 8, 2012 FB Post

Twenty-nine years ago on Easter, my Grandmama took me to my first Unity Church service. My father had suggested I find some Spiritual support in 1983, when I was addicted to poverty, living on the edge, and basically angry at God. Having lived through Mom and Dad's horrific divorce, and then Mom's next relationship with an abusive boyfriend, I was 'living it up" in Sarasota, Florida all by myself for the first time. In fact "big-by-self" was the badge I wore from age 8. That Easter Sunday I found a home and a community, in Unity—one that I have served and that has served me ever since. That Easter so many years ago brought to me a sense of belonging I had never known. Now it brings me deep understanding. I feel totally prepared to walk this walk in Faith and Grace.

Thank you, God! Thank you, Unity!

I traveled back to an awesome, healing church community, Unity of Ft. Walton Beach, to celebrate Easter and my 29th Unity anniversary, and to say my goodbyes to a life I loved. As I surrendered tears washed over me and I felt baptized by the Holy Spirit. In my mind, everything Easter stood for was exemplified in my mind and my body. *I have cAnswer. I will be cut open. Parts of me will be cut out. Life will never be the same. I wonder what the resurrected me will be like?* I received many hugs and wellness wishes from everyone at Unity, especially after Rev. George announced my longstanding attendance and my immediate sabbatical due to my opportunity to heal from ovarian cAnswer.

The long and uneventful trip across the top of Florida to Jacksonville afforded me time to process the present moment and my feelings. I played the cassette tape my mother had given to me at Christmas time. *Jesus Christ Superstar* allowed me once again, as it always had in childhood, to emote, dance, wave, stomp, and otherwise express myself. I sang along with Ted Neely at the top of my lungs, "I'll Die! Just Watch me Die! See how I Die!" In my understanding of death and rebirth, the Christ Spirit within me is strengthened when the flesh is tested. *"OK God!"* I knew if I survived this dis-ease, something precious would be no more. A layer of innocence had been stripped away.

As I sank down deeper into the music, each character became a part of me in the dance with cAnswer. Simon wanted to fight the cAnswer! Herod laughed at me—the Healer! Pilate reminded me that I could have chosen differently. My body symbolized Judas, by betraying me. The Jesus part of me accepted: "My time is almost through, little left to do. I will drink your cup of poison." I thought about chemo. I know I was dramatic (maybe theatrical?); but this kind of drama, of driving down the open road while I spilled my guts out in the form of song, sweat and tears, could only be good for me.

April 9, 2012 FB Post

Dad and I met last night in Jacksonville. We are moving in a deliberately peaceful way through our day. We will get to Shands at the right and perfect time. Every step of the way, we will meet angels who will show us what's next, how the money will be worked out perfectly and how happily healing happens. Thank you for your love and for your continued vision of my wholeness!

ALLAKARA: Powerful. Thank you. Transition is the highest form of awakening.

(ME): This IS a transition! From a life of HARD work to one of allowing life to be easier. Thank you God!

SHIRLEY: I affirm health and wholeness as you continue to be filled with the healing love and light of the One. It would be my honor to be there with you in person to support you at Shands.

PAT: The people you meet on this journey will be blessed by YOU. Someone need to meet you. Someone needs to feel your energy and love. And you have said "Yes! I will share my love with All!"

LARRY POWELL (My dad): Hi, Pat. This is me using Lauren's computer. I am sitting in Shands Hospital. Charles Garmond got us here! Thank you for your words of sweetness. I know you're right. I sure feel a lot of love and know I have plenty to share! She is sitting right here beside me!

MARY: Amen to that! We have been blessed to share time and music and full—moon howling on the beach with Lauren!

My Dad and I stayed the night at my friend's house, and Daddy fell in love with Cheryl's "Easy Button" from Staples. We drove to Shands the next day where, by late afternoon, we learned the procedure would not be done in Florida, but back home in Indiana. Dad left to go back to Clearwater and I spent another night at Cheryl's. By the time I arrived at her house, she had bought two more "Easy Buttons", one for my dad and one for me. All through the coming months, we referred to that button. When I was weak from the meds causing me to walk very slowly around the hospital, we would look at each other and proclaim, "That was Easy!"

That evening, Cheryl offered to do whatever I needed, but neither of us were guided to do anything more than sit there with each other in the stillness.

CONGRATULATIONS!

You have graduated

You're ready now

Some people

receive a cap & gown. . .

I received cAnswer

April 9, 2012 FB Post

Amazing! By my willingness to do all of this in Jacksonville, by my friends' willingness to support my family's travels to Jacksonville, by my family's willingness to hop a plane at any moment, and by willingness itself to do what needs to be done, we don't have to do it! Sometimes just by being willing to do…whatever, I don't have to do it! I just had to be willing. What I mean is I *get* to *heal* at *home!* Hot Damn!

After spending the day with Dad at Shands, we learned I have to be a resident of Duval County to receive health care without insurance. I guess they did at one time have federal funding for out–of–state cases, but they no longer do! After the tiny moment of panic subsided, I realized what that meant. I get to go home!

I will find the right and perfect healthcare in Bloomington. I will stay in trust! Meanwhile, I get to sing my Happy Little Fishes song, keep up with my naturopath's recommendations, and keep my mood and my alkaline level HIGH! I truly expect that, by the time they do surgery, they will have a lot less to remove, or it will be benign.

I have no idea what's coming next and I am open. I really do feel physically good.

This trip home means so much. Thank you again for all you do to help my Happy Healing!

PHYLLIS: No place like home and we love you here. We are praying. IN CHRIST

KAYE: Lauren, I know all will be well and all will be well and all will be well.

NAOMI: "I thank God no one told me that it couldn't be done,
I thank God no one told me learning new things wasn't fun,
I thank God no one told me parts of me were missin',
If they did, I thank God I didn't listen!"- *Lauren Lane Powell*
(Pssst…I think you're one of the best kinds of people. You have been one of my role models since we first met at Wheatland when I was very small, and I love you.)

ARMAND and ANGELINA: We just heard of your powerful healing process. All the best from us. We know you will stay in truth no matter what appears to be showing up.

SALLY: I'm sending you prayers and positive energy on your healing path. What wonderful messages you are receiving from your friends. Keep your incredible spirit strong.

I am Open to Receive

The world is mine when I drive across the country. I rarely listen to the radio. My CDs go unused. My satellite radio is also silent. I keep my mind on the road, and keep my body, my center, and my Spirit fully in charge. In the sanctuary of my van, prayers are spoken, inspirations are felt, and questions are asked. I get great answers when I'm rolling down the highway. Fabulous "ahas" have sometimes come as feelings rather than thoughts.

Traveling is a time of reflection and resurrection. When I review my story honestly and own all of it, I often find the painful events to be the most pivotal in my growth. Those experiences have shaped and molded me more than others less traumatic. I have formed lifelong beliefs based on single, dramatic occurrences, all of which have served me well. I wonder how this cAnswer Dance will serve me?

An example of one such occurrence happened when I was eight years old. My family went camping. and took along my first two–wheeler, a bike I loved. I felt independent and grown up when I rode it. On an errand, I peddled down the hill to the camp store for a bag of ice. The ice fit into my basket, but proved too heavy for my young body to ferry up the hill. I kept falling over on my way to the campsite. With bloodied knees and elbows, I was in hysterics by the time I reached the top of the hill. I said aloud through my tearstained mouth, "I'm not a big girl! I can't do it by myself!"

Something inside me snapped and said, "Watch me! I *can* do it *big–by–self*! I don't need anybody!" That single shift colored the rest of my life. While being self–sufficient and independent have served me well many times, my "big–by–self" idea often stood in my way of receiving assistance of any kind…until recently. My new mantra is, "I am open to receive".

A large part of my inner work in 2010 and 2011 was wrapped around this big–by–self stuff. I've worked on this many times before, and it still bubbles up from deeper and deeper layers. In January of 2010, I asked my dad for help to organize my paperwork, computer, billing system, etc. The same day, I asked for my stepmother's help in drawing "Behold the Face of God" on the tops of mirrors I was using in my Forgiveness Workshops. She added beautiful designs around the rim of the mirrors. They are lovely!

I realized again how damned uncomfortable it felt to ask for help, but the more I practiced, the easier I asked. The discomfort was worth recognizing and honoring. In a meditation, I saw that when I asked for help as a child, I often did not get it, and the consequences were scary. So asking for help equalled fear at some level. Driving home from Florida, I loved and reassured that frightened little girl. I told her that it's safe now to ask for and accept help. And yes, another song was born!

I include this story because, for the last two years, I have been consciously working on opening myself to ask for help and allowing myself to receive assistance. If I had been diagnosed before this self–exploration, I may not have been in the place to accept the right help during my healing. I may not have chosen to accept allopathic medicine. I might have chosen to keep it all very private and try to heal myself by myself…big–by–self. I've been in humility boot camp for two years for a reason! Now I choose to use *everything* available to me for my healing.

Everything includes whatever modern medicine can provide. It includes prayer from everyone and anyone who cared to pray for me. It includes more willingness to be open.

On My Way Home

Adventure filled my life on the road, along with the unknown, movement, light, and laughter. I was "on" all the time and I thrived. Activity seemed essential and I embraced it lovingly. Then, after all the excitement, I would travel home to peace.

Being an extrovert to the extreme, I only recently grew to enjoy the solitude and sanctuary provided by my home. To go home was to reinvent, regroup, and rest in a familiar, comfortable, and totally predictable place. Phil would be taking care of the house, cutting felled trees for firewood, and feeding the wild and tame critters. Going home meant coming in from the cold to an electric blanket, with a cup of hot cocoa and a cat on my lap. For seven to ten days every month of the year, I rejuvenated in this place of peace and comfort. Then I went back out on the road.

For the first time in twelve and a half years, going home was not a joyful, anticipatory event. It took three days to make a trip that normally spanned a day and a half. I knew that our life with my new challenge would never be the same; that my going home would disrupt my husband's treasured solace. In fact, he was the one that taught me how to love my own alone time.

Our Sanctuary

Early in our relationship, I felt pretty insecure having just come from another less–than–healthy relationship. I can imagine how Phil must've felt with this clingy, needy bundle of emotions. He told me that he needed some alone time.

"What do you mean you'd rather be alone than be with me?"

He calmly stated that it wasn't a matter of loving me *or* his alone time. He loved us both equally. While that fact may have taken some time to sink in to me, eventually it made sense. I learned to feel valuable when we were apart. What a blessing! I cultivated a relationship with myself that I would not have had, allowed by my life on the road and with Phil. I love being alone. Truly! The word "loneliness" is not in my vocabulary. Thank you sweet husband. So naturally, I wondered what life at home would be like now. We haven't been together 24/7 for almost thirteen years. How is being home all the time going to feel? How will I feel when depending upon Phil for everything? Will I lose my independence? For the first time in my life, I was afraid to go home. I was afraid to go home with my body unhealthy.

Those were the longest three days in my memory. Yet I reveled in the muck and the mire of the darkest of emotions, discovering love and joy at the same time. I nurtured myself each moment by asking, "What would feel the best to do right now?" Sometimes the answer was "sing!" so I warmed up my voice and sang as long and as loud as I could. Other times I heard "dance!" at which point I would pull over, clear a space in the back of the van, crank up the speakers, and boogie for a bit. When I reached my evening destination, I would walk on the treadmill in the hotel, do yoga, drink tea, and write. A hot soaky bubble bath became a daily luxury that I knew I would have to give up temporarily after surgery.

Because I was in no hurry, I could have stopped to visit any number of people and see any number of things, but I was too busy counting the moments of peace and comparing them to the hours of panic and tearful release. I drove for a couple of hours at a time and took longer breaks than usual. I stopped driving at around 7:00 each evening, instead of my usual habit of pushing through into the night. I wallowed in whatever luxury I could afford in the way of a hotel room and asked for a later check–out time. Then I would drive again from 1:00 to 7:00.

I nursed each moment, every single precious second of being on the road, knowing it very well could be my last trip…at least like this. I kept feeling like everything had changed. When I healed, (and I did intend to heal!), life as I had known it would be no more. So I grieved more for my old life. Sweet tears poured out of me like a sprinkler system gone mad. My glasses became so dewy they needed windshield wipers on the inside. I discovered a long time ago that when I cry on purpose, my eyes don't show it like they do when I try to hold back and am forced to cry.

So I cried on purpose, with direction and determination. I cried to drive out the toxins that accompany negative energy. I cried to release wave after wave of feeling out of control. I cried all the way home—when I wasn't singing. Most of the time, I sang and cried at the same time. I must've been a sight! I should have recorded it. It would have been worth documenting wailing of this magnitude. Maybe I was getting the need to emote out of my body before I arrived home as Phil wouldn't know what to do with all these tears. He would be frightened enough on his own. I wondered what he was going through with time and space to think between the news of my diagnosis and the time when I walked in the front door. As I neared home, my feelings became more polarized.

On one side I experienced the approaching peace of the familiar, the serenity of nature, and the love of family. On the other hand, the fear of the future, the ugliness of the unknown, and the grief of letting go of my life as I knew it loomed in front of me. Both equally compelling sides, lived simultaneously within me.

April 12, 2012 FB Post

I am home now. HOME! Feels quite wonderful and very strange. I have never lived at home. I mean when we moved to Bloomington in 1999, I went on tour and have lived on the road ever since. At the longest stretch, I have not spent more than two to three weeks at a time at home in twelve and a half years! My personal challenge with this is knowing that I'll be sucking up my husband's precious alone time. We are both so used to being alone and loving it. I know we'll be okay. I know we love each other deeply. We are best friends first and foremost. It's just an adjustment...
Sigh!

JOY: It's an adventure...something new to experience every day. I know it will be an easy and insightful transition.

MARY: I hear you...and trust you both have the deep wisdom and love to do all that is to be done.

JOHN: Take this time to re–experience each other!

SOPHIA: Relax and enjoy all your blessings to the fullest. Continuing to send love and prayers your way.

MARTHA: Another great opportunity for growth!

LAUREN LANE POWELL: I just love and bless those FGOs!! (freaking growth opportunities!)

MONICA: You and Phil will get to be quiet and peaceful together!

TERRA: I call them "FOGs" (F*ing opportunities for growth) You are in the hands of your deep and inner knowing/God, sister. All is perfect. You are perfect. I will continue to hold this high watch for you.

April 12, 2012 FB Post

Tomorrow morning is my biopsy. I know that all the prayers received, the new diet, the toning, the wonderfully tasting baking soda/molasses mix, the happy little fishes, and my Christ Spirit within will find the tumor contained, smaller and removable in its entirety! Thank you, God! It is done!

JOHNIE BETH: God's pocket of miracles is very deep. Keep digging and you will have the miracle of healing with your faith and trust You are so ahead of the game. Go Girl. Go God!

The most painful events in my life were the most pivotal in my growth

Holy Shift. April, Friday the 13th and my sister's birthday proved to be auspicious. "Happy Birthday! I have cAnswer!" On that day, I saw my own OB–GYN. I have had a female gynecologist for as long as I can remember. It never made any sense seeing a man about a woman's parts. I feel the same about priests counseling couples on married life. In fact, the only male "female doctor" I've seen was the guy in Pensacola who told me I was going to die if I didn't have surgery right away. I don't think a woman would have informed me in that manner. In fact, what Dr. Wendy Corning did tell me was that for her to take a biopsy would be too dangerous and might make the cAnswer spread. Upon the exam, my own doctor did indeed say, "Yes, it is cAnswer."

She said she could perform the surgery in Bloomington, but would rather refer me to a good friend and colleague, a specialist, Dr. Jeannie Schilder. She recommended Indiana University Simon Cancer Center in Indianapolis. We cried. "But I'm so fit and healthy," I argued again, to no one in particular. Then came the big question: How in the world would I pay for this—whatever "this" winds up being? My mind was pulled in too many directions to focus. *Everything* was unknown. I knew nothing about this area in the unknown. Most of my life has had some structure, sometimes loosely woven. I have been the weaver. I chose the colors and the textures to create the fabric of my life. Now they were chosen for me. My new journey, never imagined, just began.

Dr. Corning confirmed what my step–brother had previously told me, that a teaching hospital could not turn me away. Also, I could pay as I was able. I sobbed in the waiting room and waited in the sobbing room while she called Indianapolis. As I practiced deep breathing, I gained some composure. She set up a consultation for the following Monday. There would be no waiting around! She described my future, a total hysterectomy and probably chemotherapy. *My hair!*

April 13, 2012 FB Post

And the fun begins! My OB–GYN told me that to take a biopsy from an affected ovary was not safe. I'll go to Indianapolis on Monday for a consult. Then probably to surgery quickly thereafter. I am so blessed to have the angels that I have around me. I know everything that needs to be removed will be, and that I will thrive in my healing afterwards because of all of your prayers. Please keep them coming.

ALLIANA: Our continuous rhapsody of song flows in, through and around you always, dear Lauren.

SOPHIA: Continuing to send you love and light form GA, Lauren. We see you whole, cancer free and in radiant health! Love and hugs!

THERESA: I know that you will emerge from this experience healthier than ever! Many prayers for your perfect health on all levels!

Saturday and Sunday offered some semblance of normalcy. Providing daily care and loving the animals helped me stay in the moment. At that point, immediacy was all that I had. Tending to "the flock" helped keep things in perspective. I was so grateful for our fuzzy children!

April 15, 2012 FB Post

Pondering in meditation upon what amazing opportunities lie before me, many truths become clear'

In the past two months I have reached new heights of discipline.

I've learned that I must have fun with everything!

I have been asking for assistance from the universe in a big way, not too small a task for a former "healer–who–wants–to–save–the–world." I mean, what's a codependent supposed to do? (Kristen and I have a song with that title!)

New original healing songs are already evolving and the biggie:

God sees something so much better, so much bigger, so much grander than even touring for twelve and a half years. The people in my workshops, those who follow me, who listen to my music, those I reached face to face, were in my audiences. Now I am ready to reach more people. Doing it the way I was doing was not allowing me anything beyond what I have gotten. Duh...

God knew that stopping short, not just slowing down, was the only way I could make a change. I look forward with playful anticipation to what Divine order has in store for me next!

Phil had attended the consultation with me. I knew better than to go alone, as I would hear detailed explanations as, "Blah blah blah." My better frame of mind than I was in on Friday in Dr. Corning's office allowed me to be more at peace with "what is." Each day, things that I thought once so bloody important drifted away. By now, meeting Dr. Schilder was less traumatic than it could have been. She told me that she would cut me across, from hipbone to hipbone, right below the bikini line. I asked about my abdominal muscles and told her I use them in my singing. She assured me that minimal damage would be done to the muscles. The procedure should take a couple of hours. Recovery would take a few weeks, then we would talk about chemotherapy.

SPIRITUAL TOOL
TRUST

I am learning to trust at a deeper level the closer I get to the surgery. I really have no choice but to trust.

Trust —the definition changes daily. The more unknown that is present in any given situation, the more trust is required. It becomes a relinquishing of power, a letting go of any perceived control I had. This kind of trust, blind faith, if you will, is something I have never known at this depth. I allow myself to trust the doctors. I allow myself to trust modern medicine. I allow myself to trust the process. I don't know what that means!

As I sit with the word "trust", intuitions and inspirations come forth.

To trust—to surrender—is to give it all away to a power higher than myself. All the fear, all the anguish, all the judgment, all the despair, anything that is not love, peace and joy, in this deep place of trust, in this space of surrender, I give it all to You. Sweet Spirit, show me how.

Divine Orchestration: The Right Place at the Exact Right Moment
Kristen Lee Hartnagel

I attended my first big motivational speaking event in Nashville with my new company while I waited to hear where and when my sister would be having surgery to remove the cancer. As a sales performance coach, I met with attendees who wanted to go over their business action plan, and to determine whether or not coaching was a fit for them. But my mind was not comletely present.

After I received the call and understood the plans, I stood there with very vivid and clear thoughts about what options lay before me to proceed. I could look into flights…trains…or a bus. I could rent a car to get to the hospital.

Before I made a decision, my colleague and friend, Neal, walked up to me and said, "I think I'm going to go back and visit my friend."

"Where is your friend again?"

"He lives in Bloomington."

"Could you give me a ride? I need to go be with my sister."

He chose to tell me of his plans at that very moment—*not mere chance.* Two minutes earlier, it would have gone down like this, "I think I'm going to go back and visit my friend."

"Great! Have a good time. Drive safe." Hug and bye.

Not only was divine timing at work, but also divine placement because lots of people milled about during a break in between speaking sessions in this very large hotel.

I love living in that flow.

April 17, 2012 FB Post

Surgery is set for Thursday at 11:00 am—total hysterectomy. "Letting go of what no longer serves me" reaches a whole new level! Dr. is very optimistic. I am ready!

My sister is already here in Bloomington. Mom will come down tomorrow. We will all drive to Indy and meet Dad there. The operation is two hours long. I asked my sister to sing me through surgery. "No problem!" She replied. So sing a song between 11:00 am and 1:00 pm. I will feel it! Love you all!

(111 comments within the first two hours—all positive. I am so blessed!)

Kristen's friend dropped her off at the beauty college as I was walking to my van. This first of many demonstrations of effortless grace made our heads spin. Back at the farm, a whole day and a half

permitted us to play, relax, release, and just be with each other. We sang in harmony. We danced on the deck. We were both giddy, as if we were embarking on some grand adventure together. We memorized that feeling. That emotion soon became my choice. "Fear and excitement are the flip–side of the same coin," I teach in my workshops. "And I can choose which I want to feel." I choose excitement. I combine music, movement, and meditation, in any combination to maintain excitement. Kristen *gets* it. She's there, too. Together our light shines so brightly that halogens have to wear shades!

Dance, together with song have combined to create joy and an integral part of our lives. A day never passed when Kristen and I didn't dance or sing, or both. We choreographed and harmonized our lives with our bodies and our voices, often at the same time. When we danced and sang, we lived in a world of our own creation. When we danced and sang, we became the dance and we became the song. We couldn't fight. God bless Ann Dunn and Bonnie Baxter for the gift of dance. Thanks, Mom, for seeing its value in our lives!

"While I dance
I cannot judge,
I cannot hate,
I cannot separate myself from life.
I can only be joyful and whole.
That is why I dance."

— Hans Bos

April 17, 2012 FB Post

Dancing the cAnswer away with my sister.

JO: I'm holding the radiance of your profile picture and know the doctor's optimism will prevail. Singing your song tomorrow. Love the women's meditation circle.

KATHY: Will keep you in prayers and will sing!

DOROTHEE: I am going to play the flute and Tibetan bowls for you. Sending you all the love and blessing for a successful operation.

ELIZABETH: Lauren, you are in my heart and my prayers. I see the revitalizing Presence of Whole Life flowing freely through you and the Power of the Great Physician does its wondrous work.

REV. LAUREN: Holding you and all who are attending you in the light of your own perfection and asking all the angels to be present. Singing away between 11:00 and 2:00 (just in case they get started a little late) on Thursday. THINGS ALWAYS WORK OUT FOR YOU!

DEANE: I'll sing you a song and if you hear someone way off key—that would be me. You are so loved. With all that loving energy, I have no doubt that you will heal perfectly.

CINDY: Sending love and light and healing energy your way! Don't forget to blow some bubbles!

KALAR: Love you converting cancer to cAnswer!!!! How wonderful is that transmutation!

After silence, that which comes closest to expressing the inexpressible is music. — Aldous Huxley

Kristen helped me to process my feelings some more. Having her support on the phone, although from afar, is always a blessing. Her physical presence beside me, walking with me, provides incredible support. I wrote a directive that I asked her to implement upon my entry into surgical slumber.

My Request

I want you all to sing me through surgery.

Now breathe. Take your time.

Kristen, remember when you and I were outside of Mom's procedure room many years ago and we were singing? I'll ask the nurse where you can go in private to do this.

All I want from you is song and laughter. As long as you're together and as long as I am under the loving care of the angel doctors, I want song. Phil, my love,

sing along with any that you know and enjoy listening otherwise. Between the four of you, there will be plenty!

They don't all have to be our songs, for goodness sake. Any song you know will work! Just keep singing! When you're not singing, play music. I want to "hear" "Inspire Me" in it's entirety.

I'll see you as a much healthier Me very soon! Love you all!

Keep singing. Keep singing. Keep singing. Keep singing.

I prepared for surgery since April 2nd. How can we prepare ourselves for the unknown? Is there any preparation? Everything felt like it had been put on hold—my life and that of my family. It reminded me of that phone call where you never get through to your party, but rather listen to the

Muzak, hoping eventually you'll get to talk to a real person. My life seemed to be accompanied by Muzak. "Enjoy your wait" was the message I heard. Enjoy my wait! Hmmm. Anticipation… Fear or Excitement…My Choice!

Kristen and I sang *Every Need is Fulfilled* in the waiting room to keep ourselves centered. Mom came in for awhile, trying hard to hold her smile in place. She then traded places with Daddy, who videotaped Kristen and I singing. When they left, Phil came in. Everyone said goodbye. I said goodbye. "Goodbye." It felt strangely peaceful to me. I knew my family was going through their own shift! That's why I wanted them singing, to keep them in their peace. I had one last look as they wheeled me into the operating room. The anesthesiologist reintroduced himself and asked me some questions. I asked my surgeon if she would play my CD while I was under and she agreed. I heard Kristen's voice on the first track of my *Natural Affirmations* CD as I was fading away. "I have no limitations. I have all that I need. I have great expectations. I will succeed."

REV. OLIVIA: My sweet Lauren, I have been silently praying all day for you as you have undergone your surgery. I know you were surrounded by angels and that your surgeon and medical care givers are Divinely guided for your best care. Sleep well, my friend. Rest and recuperation are all you need now. Everything else is assured Well! I love you. Rev. O.

Let Go and Let God

Chapter Three
Learning to Love

I woke up to the same song that was playing when I went under, "I have no limitations. I have all that I need. I have great expectations. I will succeed." The music still floated through my body; the surgery was over. I thought, *"I'm still here."* Kind of. The haze around and within dissipated as I tried to smile. *"I wonder what comes next?"* Then I remembered.

"Have fun with it."

"Stay in the now moment."

"Love what is."

These first three directives from when I asked upon my diagnosis, "How do I do this?" remained the same. Well, I danced, sang, and laughed my way into surgery. I would be able to dance, sing, and laugh my way out of surgery—or not.

The incision formed a big smiley face from hipbone to hipbone. So maybe no dancing.

"The wound is the place where the Light enters you."

— Rumi

April 19, 2012 FB Post

My family wanted everyone to see that I was smiling. I knew everything was perfect! Not only did I have my family singing me through surgery, but many of my prayer partners, healer friends, and extended family were all singing, too!

I wanted to cheer, to applaud, but It hurt when I laughed. So when I couldn't dance, sing or laugh, at least I could *smile!*

When I cannot sing for myself, I know others will sing for me. I only need to ask.

JO: Been singing to you all day and sending you Light & Love!

PAT: We are singing and dancing with you, Lauren. Feel our positive vibrations all through your body!

JULIE: My mom and I are sitting here thinking of you. Sending lots of love your way!

JOANNE: I sang and loved you today, more than normal, Lauren! How are you doing?

JOHN: Breathing with you.

MIKE: Love and Light. Positive vibes thrown your direction all day. Love You

LEX: Thinking of you and sending positive thoughts your way.

OLIVIA: SO MANY ANGELS SINGING AND PRAYING!! LOVE YOU!

MARY: Affirming only Good, Light and Love for you today. Thank you for inspiring me and so many others!

WANDA: All the love in the universe surrounds you now. And for all the love you have given so and so bountifully and so freely, it returns to you now a gazillion fold.

PATRICIA: Dear Lauren, I think of all your many wonderful and uplifting songs and know you are unlimited and will succeed, one day at a time. Take it slow, breathe, let others do for you now. Love you lots.

These are just a handful of the comments that were posted on the day of my hysterectomy.

KC: Sending out healing for the beautiful soul—Lauren Lane Powell

Lauren and her Vocal Vibration Meditation

The woman in the picture above seemed like a stranger to me, but who I used to be. I was no longer that woman. cAnswer had changed me forever. In less than a month's time, I had moved from singer, teacher, and healer to patient. At that time, in that moment, patience engulfed my full being. Patient was all I needed to be. Patient was all I could be. Patient.

April 21, 2012 FB Post, Larry Powell

Today is the second day after her surgery and she is eating, walking and laughing. She is a miracle. The operation was a success and she goes home to Bloomington tomorrow! The doctor says following chemotherapy, she can expect a complete recovery. She will most likely be posting herself tomorrow. Thank you for your continuing prayers.

ALIANNA: Lauren, how lovely to know you are recovering so very well and will be home soon!! Much love to you, Radiant one.

JOHNIE BETH: Praise God! God is Good All the Time. Thanks, Larry, for the update.

KALAR: Thank you so much, Larry, for letting us know how she is. As always, through the dark she shines like a star! As much as I could, I sent my spirit to stand beside her during the surgery, and I will always be here to offer support, hope and faith, as her spiritual sister.

JIM: HI, LAUREN. SENDING POSITIVE HAPPY THOUGHTS YOUR WAY.

MERRILLEE: Just heard on Oprah from Depak Chopra, M.D. that it's okay to receive a diagnosis, but skip the prognosis! You are in charge of your recovery. More people do recover best without chemo. I just read about canned asparagus as a rejuvenator. Also check out fresh and raw drinks. Fresh fruit before other foods and do not cook the fruit. There are so many remedies. We can just google and find so many. I have a file full for my mother. We are doing many of them. We are open to the best comfort in palliative care. Namaste.

KAY: You continue to be in my thoughts and prayers, Lauren. Missing your positive FB posts and looking forward to hearing from you in the perfect timing.

Weakness plagued me after the surgery and I couldn't eat much. Although limiting, I wanted to stay on my "cAnswer Diet" as long as I could. I managed to push the little light that signaled available morphine so most of the time I was pain–free. In spite of all the positive stuff, I couldn't sleep. Someone came in every three hours to take vitals, give me meds, and stick me for more blood, leaving my arm black and blue with failed attempts. Thankfully, I would be going home soon.

The day of my diagnosis, I had started a cAnswer Diet after reading pages upon pages about nutrition for healing. I found a few things in common with all of them. The more alkaline my body, the better. Since I already ate for health, I simply eliminated the most acidic foods. These included coffee, dairy, and meat. I became a vegan overnight. I did anything I could to help myself and gain back a little control. I squeezed lemons into my water to make it alkaline. I received my best nutrition from Isagenix Shakes, a whole food product that I had originally consumed for weight management.

Before surgery, the scales showed 117 pounds. After surgery, I weighed three or more pounds less, just from the removal of the infected ovaries, etc. Excess weight had bothered me my entire life. I never liked my body. In my twenties, I taught aerobics which kept me fit with a lean, hard body. I also smoked. The harder I exercised, the harder I judged myself. That self–judgment continued into my thirties and forties, when I railed against the idea that as we age, our bodies change, and weight is harder to lose and to maintain. My attitude was, "Watch me!"

I came into cAnswer below my ideal weight because I had worked my ass off to be "perfect" by the time I reached fifty. So I arrived at fifty with a perfect body. Now I was sliced open, wounded, hurting, too thin, swollen, weak, and pissed off!

I worked hard to love my tummy. In so doing, I got rid of the pooch through diet and exercise, only to regain a permanent pooch inserted by way of surgery.

Before I went into surgery, I met the hospital chaplain, Lorraine. She visited me the next day too. Each time she asked me if I wanted prayer, I just nodded and cried. I guess my behavior was okay.

If you can't cry during prayer, when can you cry? I asked her if she was comfortable singing to me. She was and did with a sweet voice. I felt love flowing out with her song, "Lord, be with me in times of trouble." She also practiced "healing touch," an energetic healing technique I requested. Lorraine visited me every day that I stayed in the hospital. Such a blessing!

My other request was, "No TV in my hospital room." At home, we only have three PBS stations. I don't enjoy babble in the background from 500+ stations. This silence allowed me to listen to my company with little to no distraction.

My dad's IPAD or my MAC Book provided a diversion from the hospital routine and my conditon. Beyond the messages and videos he shared, my own family of Facebook Angel Friends remained present. I only needed to look at the day's comments to feel the love and hear the prayers.

The nurses and doctors set walking as a priority to prevent blood clots. I couldn't believe how much effort was required to take baby steps outside the hospital room door. I exhausted myself walking the hallway around the nurses' station. Doing anything exhausted me, so besides visiting and walking, I slept anytime quiet prevailed.

I suspected it might be too early to go home when the doctors released me on Sunday, four days after the surgery. Although I wobbled around, I held a pillow across my tummy, and bent over at the waist. Still in excruciating pain, I was sent home. However, I trusted the doctors. A tablet I could take every three hours, if needed, replaced the morphine drip. Dulcolax (a laxative because the morphine would stop me up) and Lovenox (a blood thinner) rounded out the meds. Additionally, Phil would have to administer a shot in my tummy every day for ten days to prevent blood clots. Yow! No fun at all. We practiced that routine a few times before we left the hospital.

My laundry list of dos and don'ts included no lifting, no sit–ups, no yoga, and no gymnastics for at least two months. The doctors would let me know when to start chemo. Sweet Spirit, Show Me how to do get through that!

Among four days of mail, this certificate waited for me when I arrived home. How ironic!

April 28, 2012 FB Post

It's been awhile since I've been online. I did get home last Sunday night. Monday and Tuesday were great. Eating well, sleeping great, and feeling good to be home. Wednesday was very different. I woke up feeling well beyond "plugged up." Phil gave me some magnesium citrate, which only made me sicker. I mean really sick! According to the surgeon's notes, simply loosening the bowels should have done it. At long last they did flow, but I was sicker than ever, with no relief in sight. I was beyond nauseated and in a great deal of pain.

I don't mind admitting I was scared. Phil had our neighbor sit with me while he went to get yet another laxative, but before he even got home I had called 911 and the ambulance met him at the door. Getting the gurney through the mobile home was no small feat. Somehow, six paramedics, our neighbor, my husband, and I all fit tightly into our bedroom. They lifted me onto the gurney because by this time, I couldn't hold my head up, let alone get from one bed to the other. They wheeled me out across the lawn and into the ambulance. The 20–minute drive into town seemed like an hour. They gave me all kinds of pain meds, but nothing helped.

The pressure in my gut and chest never did lessen. Because the original surgery was performed in Indy, I needed to go back there. The most expedient way? Med–Evac! A ride in a shiny helicopter would have been a lot more enjoyable and exciting had I been able to breathe!

Divine Order was all over this—my original surgeon "happened" to be on call and she whisked me back into surgery. Using the original incision, she opened me back up again! Somehow, when she took the cancer out the week before, part of the big bowel was weakened. Luckily, only liquids seeped out, because the small intestine held everything else back.

The second surgery, from 2:00 to after 5:30 am, led to a temporary colostomy. A long tube was inserted into my nose and down into my tummy to suck out the fluids. None of this led to any relief in my breathing at all. All day Thursday, my breathing was painful and shallow. For a singer and a breathing teacher, this would *not* do! My heart rate was high as well. All night long, I felt very tentative. All of my abdominal muscles, from stem to stern, were tighter than a drum.

This morning, the doctors decided that my entire torso, including the lungs, is filled with fluids. No clots, no solids, praise God! x–rays today confirmed all of this. So tomorrow they drain me. My sister drove all night Wednesday from Grand Rapids, Michigan to Indy, picking up Mom on the way. My dad and stepmom joined us shortly thereafter, and Phil, of course. My whole family arrived before I was out of surgery.

I am feeling so much better now. I know your continued prayers have been heard, honored, answered and welcomed! *All is well!* Holy Shift!

SURRENDER

JOHNIE BETH: Somehow the 5th day is the worst day to go through. I'm glad things are better for you. Bless your heart and the courage it took to keep breathing, even tho it was the hardest thing a singer has to go thru. BREATHE! Thank you, God, for you!

JANET: I just knew there was a reason to keep you in my prayers. Still won't let up. God hears our prayers. Sending love your way!

GLENDA: Loving you every step of the way—so glad this is behind you and knowing perfect health for you. Great love, Glenda.

MICHELLE: You have been on my mind the past few days. So glad to hear the worst is over and the healing continues in its perfect way.

MARTHA: I've been wondering about you, sweet Lauren! Thanks for your update. Glad you are getting drained!! All is well, indeed!

DEEDEE: I've loved your positive outlook through it all. You have many who are pulling for you. Be Well.

SHANNON: Aww..geeze, wish you didn't have to go through all this. Keep up the positive attitude and Feel Better SOON!

MICHELLE F: I am sending loving hugs. I surely know the anxiety of not breathing well. Hint, breathe in through your nose and out from your mouth, with pursed lips. You, my lovely friend, will breathe out with joyful melody.

MARY: I am so glad to hear you are doing better. You scared me. I am sending lots of hugs and positive thoughts your way. Heal and rejoice in that!

SHADDIA: May Love surround you on your journey.

LAUREN M: The best we can do is love you through it, Lauren. You are loved by all those you can see and thousands you can't. This, too, shall pass and we will all still be loving you. Deep healing energy and Angel visits to you and Phil, as you iron out the kinks together.

.
CHERYL: Amazing Journey! Amazing Healing! Amazing Lauren!! Love you!

OLIVIA: Angels and Guides surround you, waiting for you to ask for help. Do it now and feel them working with you and Spirit for healing. Prayers affirming that this is so are going out now. Feel the Love.

SHERRIE: You are blessed and highly favored! You are in our prayers and Chuck says to feel the angel wings wrapped around you, keeping the warmth of the healing energy firmly in place where it can do its highest good. Chuck said he sent his greatest and most powerful spirit angel to be with you during this great time of healing. All our love.

AMY: I continue to pray that you get better each day. Hugs.

SANDRA: Dear Angel, Ommmm, all is well.

ELIZABETH: Universe, please give her a break!

Friends and acquaintances posted these and many more comments. It thrills and amazes me how little fear they hold. Everyone is *so* affirmative, exactly what I needed. What I learned from that night, from that helicopter ride, I hope never to have to practice again. I am grateful for knowing how deeply surrender can be felt.

> **LAURA: I've been following your journey. What a gift to everyone and to yourself. Legions of angels surround you. Amen. Healing is now taking place.**

Little did Laura know I was flying through the air at the moment she posted this on my timeline on April 25th at 10:48 PM. My own prayer chanted in my head throughout the flight.

"If it's my time, I'll go. I'm ready. Just take care of my mommy, because she's not." While many people would grieve my passing, my mom would fall apart. I tried to send her peace. I went in and out of consciousness throughout the flight. In the emergency surgery, I saw nurses, techs, and doctors hovering around me, all in white—many more than I thought could fit in that room. More still appeared and their images went to the ceiling. I then understood these were not nurses, techs, and doctors. These were angels. They lifted me up, nurtured me, cradled me, and loved me. My body wept.

> **The best we can do is love you through it, Lauren. You are loved by all those you can see and thousands you can't. This, too, shall pass and we will all still be loving you. Deep healing energy and Angel visits to you and fill you up as you iron out the kinks together. ~Rev Lauren McLaughlin**

As they loaded me into the helicopter, I asked Phil to call my sister and my mom. Mom was changing back out of her nightgown, putting her clothes on, and grabbing her purse to leave, when Kristen called her and told her to stay put, that she was on her way. She also called Dad on the drive. In two and a half hours, she picked up Mom. For another three hours, they sang all the way to Indy—in part for me and my healing, in part for their sanity, and in part to keep them both awake. Dad returned to his cousin's home in Indy, where he had stayed during the previous surgery. They all greeted me when I woke up the next morning.

What just happened? I was alive but in pain. I didn't die after all. What did I experience the night before? I still felt the peace of letting go, so I knew dying won't be bad when it comes. I'm happy to be alive now!

In the midst of the storm, peace must come from within.

Lauren Lane Powell

My deja vu reflected my family around my hospital bed. When a moment of clarity broke through, I remembered that I had given up during the flight. A hot rush of shame washed over me. I had to confess and my dad was the closest.

"Daddy," I said with tears in my eyes, "Last night, I gave up. I can't be brave anymore."

He said, "You don't have to be brave, sweetheart. Let us be brave for you."

We wept together. Slowly, I realized the seriousness of my condition from last night. My doctor came in smiling on her rounds, happy to see me awake. She explained how lucky I was to be alive. During the hysterectomy, the prying off of my very large infected ovaries from the bowel had weakened the intestines. The intestinal wall tore and feces had filled my body. To save my life she took out all of my intestines and other organs, rinsed them off, cleaned me out, and put them all back. During the surgery, Dr. Schilder went through the same incision as the previous hysterectomy leaving me only one doozy of a scar.

MARY ANN: Hi, Lauren. St. Peregrine was working overtime last night, as we saw two hawks hunting at dusk on our way to South Bend! And today you are feeling better. I sure do miss you and am sending love and positive thoughts hourly. Keep up all your positive affirmations because it is working. Love & Hugs.

SPIRITUAL TOOL
DOWN THE RABBIT HOLE

I learned early in my Spiritual quest not to give energy to unwanted outcomes, to stay positive and to focus on the good.

That is the healthiest place to be. However, allowing myself the luxury of feeling the feelings that my lips dare not utter—the big, bad "What ifs?" releases more toxins from my body than holding it all in. To pre-grieve a negative outcome or even a past possibility removes those chemicals from the body of doubt, fear, and anxiety. Release of this kind is a cleansing neccesity. To admit out loud that I am/ was terrified is an act of humility. If I announce that I hate what is happening to me with all the rage that's in me, then I can let it go. So, down the Rabbit Hole I go.

This emergency surgery in the wee hours of the morning saved my life but gave me a colostomy. Huh? OK, God, what do I do with this? Once again, I heard "Have fun with it." You're kidding right?

Upon hearing the command a second time, I took a deep breath. It came to me *how* to have fun, kind of, sort of. At least to make friends with it, kind of, sort of. I named her "Lucy."

I don't know why I chose that name, but the minute I personalized "her," I became less attached. I found it easier to deal with a her instead of an it. So now I pooped through a hole in my tummy. I could see it, and smell it, both of which appalled me. The pain dismayed me. Grossed out and pissed off, I deferred to "Sweet Spirit, Show me how to do this," second nature to me now. In recovery they drained my lungs which were full of fluid. A sweet orderly wheeled me down into the basement, where a very large German male nurse spoke in broken English. "Vee vill steek zis pipe into zee back and zin vee shall push it down past your ribs and drain." I was so thin that I could feel each rib catch the hard plastic tube and painfully resist its passage. Once it reached its destination, I waited, with my arms at right angles to my body and out in front like a zombie. I listened to the sucking sounds as I felt my back, ribs, sides, insides, and tummy ache. It wasn't over yet. I expected more poking and prodding to get me back to whatever my new normal would be.

The uncomfortable catheter stayed in place. At least I didn't have to worry about wetting the bed. They took forever getting the tube out of my throat—a really nasty part of all this. Of all the tubes I had in and on me, the one down my throat felt the worst. I pushed away hard any fears of not being able to sing again because of this stupid hard plastic tube down my throat. They kept me on oxygen for the longest time, especially at night because my levels indicated below safe too often. IVs stuck into each arm were attached to the lovely morphine pump. It delivered just enough to take the edge off of the pain and help me sleep. Every time its red light came on signaling an available dose, I pushed that button.

With all this help I expected to be free of pain, but it still hurt to breathe. I remained weaker than ever. I walked at a snail's pace and I had to be severely encouraged to try at all. Fluid formed around my lungs, so they stuck a long hard plastic tube into my upper back that scraped each rib as they pushed it down. They filled two bottles and started a third. Eventually, I breathed more easily and the pain lessened. I chose to keep using the oxygen at night as it made me feel better.

Three different people—a colostomy nurse, a dietician, and a doctor—gave me confusing dietary instructions:

"Don't eat nuts."

"Do eat nuts."

"No milk."

"Yes milk."

"Soft foods only."

"You'll need roughage to help it work well."

On and on.

The colostomy nurse made the most sense. "Start gently and see how things flow. Then test foods one at a time to see how they digest."

The thing I didn't want to know was how to change Lucy. The colostomy nurse appeared three different times to show me. I already knew more than my healing head could handle. Besides, I feared that as soon as I learned how to babysit Lucy, they would dismiss me and something else bad would happen.

During this hospitalization, trying to get any sleep at all seemed downright comical because the nurses kept coming to my room all during the night. I asked Chaplain Lorraine if she'd come and see me. Her beautiful chant, that she later told me she learned in the Catholic church, soothed me. "Be with me Lord when I am in trouble. Be with me Lord I pray." What a blessing!

The day after the emergency surgery, April 26th, Kristen's father-in-law passed away in hospice. My brother-in-law, Jeff, lost his dad while his wife stayed with me. The timing couldn't have been more strained. Imagine her struggle, "My husband, my sister." So, as soon as she knew I was going to be okay, she went back to Michigan to her family. Mary Ann, my stepmom, stayed for a few days and provided more love and light than ever. She brought me such pretty things to set up in my room. She adds color to life wherever she goes. I loved having the entire family together, even under those circumstances. Because Dad and Phil were able to stay with me, Mom went home on Wednesday. Until then, she had spent every night next to me on an amazingly designed chair that unfolded into a bed.

I spent all day Thursday and all day Friday with the two men in my life. The month before, when I first learned of the cAnswer, I had arranged with Dad to read me a book that he had first read to me when I was five or six years old. *The Wonderful Adventures of Nils* is about a nasty little boy who was shrunk down to the size of an elf. He was forced to get along with animals he had abused. It contains wonderful history and geography of Sweden. Each day in the book provided a new adventure. Each day I fell in love with my father's voice again. The nurses and techs enjoyed the bits and pieces they heard, too.

I started feeling better day-by-day. With more fluids releasing, I became comfortable. A wonderful nurse removed the catheter as gently as possible. In comparison, my only other catheter experience happened with a horrible "Nurse Ratchet" type in the early 90's during a tubal pregnancy. That surgery proved much easier than this one. But, in preparation for removal of the catheter, I tried to explain to Nurse Ratchet how I would like to proceed. "I'll breathe deeply. When I exhale, I will loosen my inner grip and you can *slowly, gently* take it out." As I was speaking, she ripped the cord out of me with as much force and downright anger as she could. I hurt for two weeks.

This nurse listened to me. She heard my horror story and promised she could do it better. She made up for Nurse Ratchet and then some. I knew it could be done gently. That blessed night I got out of bed twice to pee by myself. (Sorry if that is too much information, but little things blessed me every day.) At that time, I slept very well when left undisturbed.

They kept me in the hospital for ten days this time. I was afraid to leave. I didn't want to be released and then need to be whisked away again with another emergency.

Going home. Really? Am I ready? It feels too soon. I thought they might keep me through the weekend. The doctors told me that the way I was recovering indicated things were improving enough and indicated that I was ready to go home. So Dad had to shlep ten days worth of stuff, medical supplies, another blow–up mattress pad that they otherwise throw away, the plastic breathing tester thingy, pillows for the ride home, and Lucy's wardrobe. It took him eight trips back and forth to fill the car all by himself.

Lucy's wardrobe included flanges to be glued to my body, the glue itself, tape to help the glue, powder to help the tape affix to the glue, adhesive barrier wipes to protect my skin, alcohol wipes,

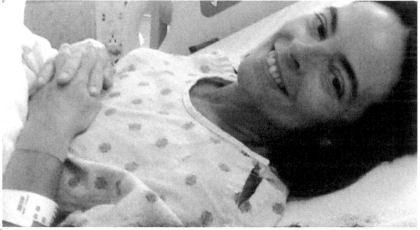

Q-tips, gauze pads, deodorant spray bottles, and five different styles of bags with their respective hard plastic closures. After that, Dr. Schilder called me at home the next day and asked why I left the way I did. When I questioned her, she said I had skipped some release protocol. Who knew?

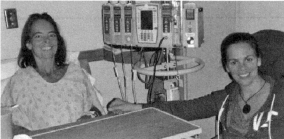

Chapter Four
I Love Lucy

We drove home for an hour and a half through the fog. I surrounded myself with pillows: one underneath me, one behind me, and one on the dashboard where I stretched out my bony legs and rested my feet. Holding another pillow against my tummy, I tried to carry on a conversation, but I don't think I was much company. I faded in and out of sleep until we arrived home. Phil met us at the car. I slowly and deliberately waddled into the house clutching my security pillow. I shrank away from the affectionate greeting from our two dogs that I usually received well. That night I gave them one pat each. I noticed worry in their eyes.

Dad poured me into the recliner and propped me up with a multitude of pillows. Then he and Phil unloaded the car. Dad, eager to be home, decided to drive four more hours back to South Bend. I so appreciated those few days and nights with him.

I remember one night in the hospital I awoke around 3:30 AM. Dad lay asleep in the chair/bed next to me. At once I felt like a small child amused with wide–eyed wonder by the blinking and steadily glowing little lights in different colors positioned all around the room. Red, blue, green, white, and yellow lights. The sounds of beeps, bells, whistles, chimes, and buzzes captivated me. But all of them totally annoyed my sick adult self. But the little child I turned into when I saw my daddy curled up and sleeping transformed those bells, beeps, whistles, chimes, and buzzes into something captivating and became music to my ears. I heard rhythm from the beeps and buzzes keep time with the bells, whistles, and chimes to create melody and harmony. Because my daddy is and always has been a lover and a teacher of jazz, I thought maybe his very presence in the room ignited that fanciful moment.

Home

What an adventure! I now rested on a throne of pillows in a chair that swallowed up my body. Phil gave me a shot of Lovenox in the tummy every day for ten days to prevent blood clots. I bore the injection itself well, but the stinging afterwards lasted for fifteen long minutes. Lucy was a trip and a half! During my first trek from the chair to the kitchen for a glass of water, I felt something warm trickling down my leg. I grabbed the end of the bag and waddled quickly to the bathroom. I discovered I had forgotten the plastic clip closure, the piece that fits on the end of the bag and looks like a hair barrette. That mess happened to me one time for I quickly learned the clip only kept the bags closed when I used it!

I slowly adapted to lying on my side, the side without Lucy. *Hmmmm. I have a colostomy. I have to poop in a bag, through my abdomen.*

Because I felt like crap in the hospital—on morphine, and not eating well or sleeping much—I didn't pay close attention to the directions from the colostomy nurse. Great time to teach me how to do something new, especially something I have to do several times a day every day! I resisted learning how to cut the hole in the flat piece of plastic to match my stoma, or how to apply what looked like toothpaste around the hole as glue. I would rather have done anything else than learn how to tape the appliance to my skin and then snap the bag into place.

The responsibility proved too much and too soon. I wanted to rest and poop like a normal person. I thought I'd get the hang of it eventually. Now I will never take pooping for granted again!

> *SPIRITUAL TOOL*
> *Show Me How to Laugh at THIS!*
>
> *Sweet Spirit, my prayer today is to laugh, or at least to smile.*
>
> *Show me how.*
>
> *I am gently led to laugh at my new "friend" Lucy when she expands the bag and needs "burping." When she smells to high heaven and needs deodorant, I will try to laugh, or at least smile. When she's full of shit and I get to empty her yet again, I will try to laugh, or at least smile.*
>
> *Sweet Spirit, Show me how to laugh at this!"*

Dad had called from the road on his way home to joke. Could he introduce me now as his daughter with two assholes? We both laughed quite a lot! Dad confessed to my husband that his biggest fear was wearing a bag, getting a colostomy. But seeing me with one and watching how matter-of-factly I dealt with it, he no longer feared it for himself. I'm glad he saw me handling it well. I didn't feel that I was doing it well at all. Hey! Healing was happening already.

While I tried to keep my humorous outlook, I learned right away that laughter was out of the question. Full belly laughter hurt. Also, I required that Phil watch the news on his computer away from me. I didn't want to see or hear it. I asked him to play only comical movies on television, thinking about the connection Norman Cousins made between humor and healing, I had nothing to gain but fun and nothing to lose but fear. Phil naturally obliged me.

We quickly fell into a routine. Sleep took up most of my time and I relished every moment of it. I dreamed wonderful morphine-induced dreams of being healthy, back to my earlier long, flowing, shiny hair. When I woke up, I rested in the fully reclined chair. I scanned my thinning frame, foreign to me now. *Were those really my ankles? What happened to my butt? Where did those bones in my chest come from? And get a load of that scar!*

Life can be wildly tragic at times, and I've had my share. But whatever happens to you, you have to keep a slightly comic attitude. In the final analysis, you have got not to forget to laugh.

—Katherine Hepburn

Besides sleeping, I spent time on Facebook. I posted something almost every day about my progress. Sometimes I vented, but mostly I posted gratitude for being alive. I visited other Facebook pages to get inspiration and humor. I noticed the growing number of people liking, sharing, and commenting on my posts. Some old friends from the distant past resurfaced. Many friends from my travels, and more people whom I had never met, connected with me now because of cAnswer.

Still, I wished for enough energy to do something—anything. I considered assembling my stained-glass supplies to produce something magical, or rediscovering Grandmama's kiln and copper enameling tools, or learning how to create watercolor paintings. All required too much energy. Instead, I created pictures on my MacBook and posted them on Facebook. That welcome outlet allowed me to *do* something.

I understood that in healing I *was* doing something. But I craved more activity. I missed my walks. At this point, I couldn't make it all the way down our deck without stopping to rest. I looked around the house and noticed many things I could attend to, but I didn't feel up to it. Phil waited on me hand and foot—offering a glass of water, moving my pillows, fixing my meals. I felt worthless. I had never relied on someone else for everything. Burden or not, I needed time to rest and heal. In that way Phil, and my family blessed me.

Eventually, I will see the Divine order of it all.
Until then, I will laugh at the noise,
breathe through the pain,
sing when I can
and trust that
Everything Happens for A Reason.

BARBARA JEAN: I have been thinking a lot about you and perhaps your whole life so far has been in preparation for this cAnswer.

Barbara's post nailed how I felt. Everything in my life had led me to this experience. Every ounce of emotional release I had purged had cleared the way for light and love and pure healing to come in its place.

Meet Mary Ann

Mary Ann and my dad married each other over 35 years ago. She makes up part of my extended family, the family that surrounded my bed in my hospital room: my mom, my dad, my stepmom, my sister, and my husband. We spend prolonged time together and often travel as a group. For example, we've sailed together on three cruises and vacationed in Playa del Carmen.

The visible love of this extended family amazed everyone at the hospital. I enjoyed watching the nurses and doctors do double takes when I introduced everyone. "This is my mom. This is my dad and this is my stepmom."

Mary Ann drove up from Florida the day after my surgery. She brought many gifts with her, including an old–fashioned Scarlett O'Hara style hand fan that I continue to use every day. Her presence and love added greatly to the peace exuded by the entire family. Thank you, Mary Ann, for all you do and everything you are. You are so special.

My sister introduced Mary Ann to my dad at a Unitarian Church festival. They married October 11, 1975. Kristen and I happily sang in their wedding. Mom and Dad had divorced the previous

year, and had separated a year or so earlier. The combination of seeing my daddy happy, while at the same time knowing my parents would never reunite, felt bittersweet. At age fourteen, all I could see was the woman who took my daddy away from me. Gently and slowly, Mary Ann loved her way into my heart. She was the only one who ever took my side when Kristen and I fought. Mary Ann, as a fellow older sister, understood how *pesky* a little sister can be. One time she rescued me when I didn't understand Dad's instructions for playing euchre. I ended up crying in frustration. The next day and in a slow patient way, Mary Ann taught me how to play euchre. I knew then why Dad loved her. Now she has become family in my heart. I appreciate her presence in our lives and her great care of my dad.

This is who I thought I was. I wonder who I will become?

I can practice grieving and letting go of her.

Okay, I finally did it. I lopped it all off!
I did not see as drastic a change as I thought.
It merely looked like me with
my hair tied back in a ponytail, except
I had no ponytail. Oh, well. In a couple of weeks,
I'll shave off what is left, before it starts
falling out with chemo.

I am NOT my Hair!
I am NOT my Hair!
I am NOT my Hair!

"I love you. I love you. I love you." I tried to say this to that stranger in the mirror whenever our eyes met. "I'm sorry you have to go through this. But go through this we will!" Sweet Spirit, show me how.

May 9, 2012 FB Post

Good Morning Facebook friends! I hope you enjoy this post. I did it myself with one of my photographs! What fun! I want to create many more of these and call the series "Lighten Up with Lauren" Hmmm, I like it!

The tide rolls in. The tide rolls out. Only our perception remains.

Whether we ride with the waves or try to stop the flow–

The only constant in life is change.

"Grief is a side effect, a symptom of real love. Because to truly love means we will experience loss. But the brave human heart knows love is worth it."

—Shannon Kaiser

May 11, 2012 FB Post

My task of the day was to begin filling out forms for Social Security Disability. Online, it wasn't too bad. When the questions asked me what work I did before, I thought, "Where do I begin?" I kept my explanation as brief as I could. When asked if I had to stoop, lift, crawl, sit, stand, kneel, or reach, there were multiple choices for how many hours of each of these that I did:

Up to 8 hours sitting—driving
4 hours standing—workshops 4–6 per week
3 hours stooping, lifting, etc.—setting up and tearing down each week
Then came booking and promo, as well as creating CDs and DVDs, and duplicating them myself as needed. There also was writing articles, creating fliers, posting events, etc.

As I typed, I wept. Twelve and a half years of this life would now be over, by my choice, I guess. The truth is I would not have slowed down to reassess my business, let alone stop. I knew it was time to do it all differently, whatever that meant. Knowing the Truth however, did not remove the grief I feel when anything "dies" and in every major Life–Change, there is a death of sorts. Old ideas, old ways of doing or being, old patterns die away when change occurs.

After a marvelous cruise was over ten years ago, my mom pointed out that I had been weeping and mourning the endings of everything all my life. When I asked her what she was referring to, she reminded me that when I was four years old, I had hauled the big easy chair in front of the Christmas tree and then fell asleep to it's red twinkling lights.

When mom and dad disposed of the tree, I cried and cried. She said that I love so deeply that I grieve any loss. Whatever it is…even with changes for the better! Then she told me how grateful she was that I did that. She reminded me how healthy it is that I love so much, so deeply, that when something passes, grief naturally comes next. Wow! I guess she's right! God bless the grief! I get to love that, too! It's all healing, isn't it?

SARAH: So glad Julie and I could be part of your seminars and your life. You can still sing and play bowls though, right?? Can't imagine life without your music (and your long hair!!) Rest and do what you need to heal and maybe God will give you more to do to reach the hearts of all the people you touch! Love you soooooo much. It was great to see you at the Christmas concert at Unity of Charleston.

MARIA: Don't doubt for one minute that though the expression of your gift may morph from time to time…YOU are the gift. Spirit will always use you, as long as you are open.

CAROL: You have blessed me so much with your ministry and your positive attitude. This does not have to be the end of your ministry. Whatever capacity you choose to continue in, I know that your smiling face and your giving heart will continue to bless many, as it has in the past. I am continuing to hold you in love and light. Bless you, my sister!

KALAR: Dear and sweet soul sister, I love you sharing your depths. Such a great gift in this world, where so many want to skim the surface. The only way to move from 3D is to move to the depth and width of the higher dimensions, and learning to navigate the emotional body is the only way.

JULIA: THANK YOU so much FOR SHARING THIS as I, also, grieve Endings and I Love Deeply. I see/hear you in myself, my dear & beautiful friend. Did I tell you that in my deep Epsom bath soaks that I always listen to your Metamorphosis CD? The blend of your voice, instruments, and birds is great!

This is the CD that Julia mentioned. I will be using it for my own healing meditations. It helps me sleep and will help me stay relaxed and at peace during my treatments

Metamorphosis

Harmonic Meditations with Quartz Crystal Singing Bowls and my Voice. From one track to the next our vibration is raised, note by note, bowl by bowl, chakra by chakra. Every other track or so introduces a different Freenote Wing.

Accompanied only by the birds and the wind chimes on our back porch, all tracks are performed and recorded live. Enjoy this meditative adventure.

I wanted to publicly address the question that came from a friend. I was sure this question had been on a lot of minds. I think she brought it out into the open.

DIANA: I don't understand how one so powerful as yourself is having to go through this all. I totally believed in sound healing and vibrational healing power. Now I do not understand anymore

LAUREN (my response): I know what you mean. Kind of shook me to the core too. What I am coming to understand is, all the healing I do for myself and others, all the Spiritual Understanding I have gained, all the toxic feelings I have released, all my sound healing work, everything I have ever learned and experienced has led to this point. Even a year ago, I wouldn't have been as strong as I am now to deal with this offering. I do still believe in my work and in the healing works of others and I am embracing modern medicine all at the same time. The network I have created through my work has allowed my family and friends to help me in wonderful, prayer–filled ways.

In late March when I asked "Why me?" I heard "Why not you? Who is more equipped for a journey of this kind of healing? You get to change the way cAnswer looks and feels for multitudes of people."

Personally, I have been doing this "on the road" for 12 1/2 years now and it was time to reach more people than I alone can. It has been time to work smarter, not harder. It has been time to change the way I share my passion. Up until now, I only reached the people in my audiences. There is so much more I can do to spread the word about vibrational healing! Slowing down was not possible or I would have. It took cAnswer to force me to stop completely, reassess everything and begin to use what I have more effectively.

I look forward not only to healing, but to using this sabbatical well. This allows me to stay put for awhile and finish my book. And then…begin again. It's all good. Truly! We are one and as I heal, I bring everyone along with me! So hang on and enjoy the ride!

CHARLAYNE: Yes. And yes again.You are not alone! Even in the darkest moments of grief, pain and transformation, you are not alone. Many of us, me included, keep you in our daily prayers.

DALE: Bhagavan Sri Ramana Maharashi was probably the most famous Indian sage of the twentieth century. He was renowned for his saintly life, for the fullness of his self–realization, and for the feelings of deep peace that visitors experienced in his presence. So many people came to see him at the holy hill of Arunchala, where he spent his adult life, that an ashram had to be built around him. He answered questions for hours every day, but never considered himself to be anyone's guru. He died of cancer in 1950, at the age of 70. To devotees who begged him to cure himself for the sake of his followers, Sri Ramana is said to have replied, "Why are you so attached to this body? Let it go." and, "Where can I go? I am here." Lauren, you are beautiful and I love you! I have great admiration for you, because you always find a blessing in every situation. I've never once heard you complain or find fault with anyone—and we even roomed together in Mexico!! LOL!

MARIA: For me, healing is an attitude—one of acceptance, thanksgiving and release. Though this human body knows pain and illness, it does not define me. It's merely "one of those things." What does define me is the knowledge and faith that at my core, I am healed and I refuse misery, grasping instead to the love that surrounds me. We love you, Lauren!

JONNIE BETH: cANSWER is your teacher and guide. I learned this when it happened to me. Each survivor has their own unique path. I was told that the Big C was my teacher. And it taught me a lot. That there is only One Mind and all those prayers from people I didn't know came to my aid. It was a wonderful experience, but I don't want another one like that. One has to trust their Higher Self for guidance and sooner or later the answer becomes clear. I'm glad you are sharing this with those who love you. Happy recovering. You have a lifetime of learning ahead of you, Lauren.

JOHN M: There is no better way to strengthen your soul than to challenge your Faith. Through this, you will know inner peace and happiness.

LYNNEA: Lauren, the mother bear in me has risen. The goddess healer that you are is no less because you are learning about the journey of cancer. There is a difference between healing and cure. A healing is in consciousness, and can take place at any minute. Healing is the ability to respond to a request for learning, growing, diving deeply into consciousness and being still enough to allow the stillness to inform the one seeking. It is a personal journey. Healing is an art form of listening and speaking and meditating in the Gap. The Gap is holy potentiality, the Creative Medium of Spirit, where the spiritual laws and principles of the universe are waiting in potential to act upon what is evolving, intentionally, passionately, and consciously. I am joining you in prayer, for the highest and best outcomes. Blessed Be. And so it is!

DEANE: The person asked the question that clarified that we go through experiences, including our lives, not just for personal growth, but to help the collective, or greater Oneness. (good question) The sacred feminine, collectively, is healing great wounds built up through eons of time. Some very brave women heal this imprinted pain in dramatic ways. I honor you, Lauren, for your courage. As you said, "Why not me?" Your teaching and beautiful gift from the depths of your soul keeps on giving. I still wish that you would not suffer and that you were back on-stage dancing and singing your joy now, especially on Mother's Day, making all the moms forget any pain they suffer.You are loved.

May 13, 2012 FB Post

What a glorious day! At noon my dad and I "facetimed" so he could read more from the "The Wonderful Adventure of Nils." After a few chapters, we took a break and then he read another few chapters. It was as if he was right in my living room. I *love* the technology that allowed this to be a reality! I *love* my Daddy, who taught me all I know about this technology. But reading to me, with his wonderful, theatrical voice, a book that he read to me when I was five…"precious" is the only word that comes close to describing these events!

May 13, 2012 HAPPY MOTHER'S DAY! FB Post

Today, I get to celebrate my two mothers, my biological mom and my stepmom. Both have influenced me and continue to inspire me by loving me so deeply. I am so blessed to have these two fabulous women in my life! Happy Mother's Day, Sandra and Mary Ann! I love you both so much!

KATY: Amazingly beautiful singer/songwriter Lauren Lane Powell's theme song! Thanks, Lauren, my kids and I LOVE it!! I have played it for them every night before bed for the last few days on my Ipad when they ask for a "talking picture." So inspirational and touching...never fails to bring a tear to my eye! P.S. I met you at Unity Grand Rapids, MI and your sister sang at my wedding!! :)

Some May Tell You! (Not to Sing)

(c)1992 Long Paws Productions

by Lauren Lane Powell

Not so long ago, when I was very young,
My mama used to kneel beside my cradle.
Tho I was just a babe, she whispered this to me.
She knew I'd understand when I was able.
She said, "Lauren, you're a gem. You can do anything!
The whole wide world is your parade. All you
gotta do is dream. Let the others do the scheming.
Come what may.

Chorus: Some May Tell You not to sing.
Some May Tell You not to laugh out loud.
Some May Tell You not to pray to your God!
Don't you listen to a word they say.
Some May Tell You not to dance.
Some May Tell You not to wave your arms.
They'll try to tell you not to use all your charms.
That's a game some people play."

Not so long ago, when I was 17,
My mama let me cry upon her shoulder.
Tho I was still naive, she taught me to believe.
She knew I'd understand when I got older.
She said, "Lauren, you're a jewel. People can be so cruel.
Don't let them rain on your parade. Hold on
Tightly to your dreams. Keep your light forever beaming,
Through the gray."

Chorus: Some May Tell You not to sing.
Some May Tell You not to laugh out loud.
Some May Tell You not to pray to your God!
Don't you listen to a word they say.
Some May Tell You not to dance.
Some May Tell You not to wave your arms.
They'll try to tell you not to use all your charms.
That's a game some people play."

Not so long ago—it feels like yesterday—
Someone tried to tell me, but I heard myself say:
Don't you tell me not to sing.
Don't you tell me not to laugh out loud.
Don't you tell me not to pray to my God!
I can't hear a single word you say.
Don't you tell me not to dance. I gotta dance.
Don't you tell me not to wave my arms.
Don't you tell me not to use all my charms.
It's my game, I'll play my way.
Don't you tell me not to use all my charms.
It's my game, I'll play my way.
 It's my game, I'll play my way. It's my game,
I'll play it my way!

This beautiful poem, *Harmonies of Love,* was posted on my timeline the day I sent out my irregularly scheduled newsletter. It was the first time in my life I had openly asked for financial assistance. What a scary place to be.

Pat, her husband Charles, and I have connected on my visits to Texas. They supported me in several ways: by purchasing crystal bowls from me and, hosting me in their lovely home on my trips to their town. In addition they provided their home as a location for concerts and singing bowl demos. When Charles upgraded his GPS, he gifted me with his older unit. I named the GPS "Charleen," a female counterpart to Charles, and have loved her guidance in my van for the past four years. Pat and Charles also (the first of many) sent me a donation to help with medical bills.

Harmonies of Love

by Pat Coughlin Mawson

Harmonies of Love
Could we come together
in Energy and Light
And if we gave from our Hearts
whatever seemed just right

With more than 1900 friends
just imagine what might flow
To show the world what happens
when one seed begins to grow

It's not about the money
it's giving from our hearts
In order to say "Thank you"
to each note she did impart

She sings us to forgiveness
she brings her energy
She smiled until we opened up
so we could clearly see

The beauty of our stories
and the joy within our souls
Let's shower her with gifts today
and sing her truly whole

With Harmonies of Love

May 15, 2012 FB Post

HOW DO YOU KNOW ME?

For less than a month, I've been posting on Facebook about my journey thru cAnswer. It's incredible how much support I've received from so many people.

The comments I read around my posts are heart–felt, prayerful and filled with love.

I want to put into this book as many as I can.

So I ask you two questions:

1. HOW DO YOU KNOW ME?

2. HOW HAS MY JOURNEY TOUCHED YOU?

NANCI SANDER: I knew about you through Francesca Bowling (my niece), but I think we actually met when I asked you to sing for a Unity service, when Unity was located on Burke Street in South Bend! At your suggestion, I met you and your mom in a practice room at IUSB. We rehearsed (get this) "I Am A Promise, I Am A Possibility"! In light of what you have, and are, accomplishing, perhaps through that song you were planting the seeds that are coming to fruition even as I write this note.

Nanci has been instrumental (pun intended) in much of my music making. As an accomplished, professional pianist, Nanci has played on almost every CD I've produced. Her expertise at my senior recital in 1993 was her largest gift to me, in addition to her long–lasting friendship. I performed my own music and Nanci read the musical score that I wrote by hand. This was before computer–assisted music notation, so when I say I wrote it by hand, I mean every single little 16th note, rest, fermata, etc. for a five–movement song cycle. Not an easy read but Nanci played every note perfectly!

May 16, 2012 FB Post

Today, real live Angels visited me. I didn't feel like receiving anyone, as I was tired, cranky, and in pain. The first set of Angels, Mary and Ernie, drove all the way from Lexington, KY, just to see me! Mary McElroy Perry rubbed my feet. Ernie Perry held my hand. They brought food from Trader Joe's, a bouquet of sunflowers, and so much more! They prayed with, and for me. I was so grateful!

Then Pamela Chappell and Pete Wehle from Douglas, Michigan stopped by on their way to Virginia. We're not exactly on their way! Pam gifted me with one of her wonderful meditation CDs, featuring her original music., and a miniature Zen Relaxation Garden. They, too, prayed with, and for me! I am so blessed, so grateful, so full of everything that is healing, peace ,and love! Thank you, my visiting Angels, for loving me so much.

I almost forgot, I had a visit from a fifth Angel —my visiting nurse and new Facebook friend, Jennifer! So great to see you today. Thank you for all you do. You rock! What a blessing you are!

I Love Lucy

During this posted visit I experienced severe discomfort and pain caused by my colostomy. I was newly learning how to live with and take care of a colostomy, something very unnatural. The stuff the bowels still held annoyed me the most. The remaining intestine, below the stitching and not removed, was clogged with waste. Suppositories didn't help and I couldn't take anything internally because my plumbing had been disconnected. So how was I supposed to get this rock out of me?

When Mary and Ernie visited me, Mary suggested that my visiting nurse may be able to help.

"How"?

"She could remove the blockage manually."

I tried fiercely to keep the images from forming in my head. But that afternoon, the images mataerialized when my brave new friend, my visiting nurse, my angel–of–the–hour, reached up inside me to grab the mass. I screamed bloody murder. My poor husband thought for sure I was dying.

Jennifer said no suppository would soften that baseball–sized mass with the hard consistancy of wood. OMG! I never thought what Jenny did for me was possible. Soon I experienced relief, sweet relief.

> **May 19, 2012 FB Post**
>
> Stretching, walking, moving. Doing a little more every day. It feels like I'm relearning how to live in someone else's body. Stronger yes, but thinner than I've ever been. I eat five small meals a day and I'm eating only the right things to heal...none of which adds weight! I guess it's more important to be healthy and skinny than less heathy and heavier. I do feel good and I am so grateful!! My only comfort challenge is sitting on my bony butt! More movement! I sleep well. Body is functioning divinely. I am peaceful and restful! Thank you for your continued support and prayers!

NATURE

ALWAYS

PROVIDES

PERFECT

BALANCE.

I LEARN

SO MUCH

FROM HER.

Photo and text
by Lauren from her
Lighten Up with Lauren series

May 19, 2012 FB Post

cAnswer feels like college, so much is new, so much information filling up my head!

COLLIN: Dearest Lauren Lane Powell, I am introducing you to Erica. She is a friend in Seattle, currently and courageously answering Life's Call through the experiece of cAnswer. My hope is for the beauty, courage and humility you both demonstrate to be synergized and shared even more fully in, as and through you. May you be a blessing this day.

LAUREN: Thank you, and many Blessings to Erica!

ERICA: I believe Lauren and I found each other through Lynnea a few weeks ago. Hi again, Lauren!

Collin's first introduction grew into many more connections. When friends read about my active participation journeying with cAnswer, they referred a friend to my posts. The healing network expanded from there!

I found a box of IU stuff.

This drawing is from 1989.

I remember taking 17–21 credit hours

every semester. What was I thinking?

I did love it, but this is what it felt like trying

to eat, swallow, digest, and memorize so much

new information!

It's a wonder I stayed as sane as I did!

Six years for a BA in Music Education. Wouldn't want

to do it again! But I'm glad I did it all.

I use my education every day.

Many Blessings!

Photo and text
by Lauren from her
Lighten Up with Lauren series

May 20, 2012 FB Post

Just finished with another three plus chapters of the *Wonderful Adventures of Nils*, read to me by my dad. So blessed to have the technology to see his precious face and hear his theatrical voice. Feelings of love pour through him as he reads.

I am so blessed! Thank you Daddy, again and again and again!

My Father's Voice

I'm sure I fell in love with my father's voice the moment I heard it from within the womb. His round, whole, colorful tones allowed mellifluous and dramatic speech. He nurtured and cultivated that voice into a radio show as a teenager and as an adult. He recorded entertaining jazz shows

in our basement. The title of his show, *Larry Powell's House of Sound* was music that carried me into adulthood. And now, as I healed from ovarian cAnswer, my dad and his magnificent voice, round and rich, dramatic and passionate, and filled with love, were present to soothe me. He read the brilliantly epic story, *Wonderful Adventures of Nils*, in a way that moved me gently into the enchanted lands of Sweden and held me spellbound until rest time. My father's voice, a symphony of healing sounds, transported me into a different world and away from the cAnswer.

Harmony and rhythm accompanied his profound performance that I willingly received for two mornings in a row. How wonderful it was to connect in this way so often! I was and am so blessed.

Chapter Five
I Really Love Lucy

Being hospitalized twice in one month, recuperating, and awaiting chemotherapy, provided opportunities for me to experience kindness, in both giving and receiving. I tried to smile in the midst of pain and fear and felt better instantly. When others smiled, I felt lighter energy surrounding me. Every smile on every nurse's face transformed my experience in an otherwise scary place. The housekeepers and the food-workers smiled. All the doctors smiled. All those smiles infected me in a good way that felt wonderful. I noticed them right away, being a conscious smiler myself.

Were they genuine? What can be ungenuine about a smile? When I faked it, I felt better. The forced smile turned real, warm, and fuzzy. So why not smile? On the rare occasion when someone did not smile, I simply gave them mine. I found that smiling lightened my pain. Smiling made my injections hurt less. Weird, and wonderful to know and practice. How easy! How fun! How healing!

I believe that attitude changes things. When I stay angry, hurt, sad, in judgment, or fearful, everything and everyone around me mirrors those feelings. When I stay in peace, act lovingly, and smile, the energy around me changes. Then, when others mirror me, that same positive healing energy comes back to me.

> *Too often we underestimate the power of a touch, a smile, a kind word, a listening ear, an honest compliment, or the smallest act of caring, all of which have the potential to turn a life around.*
>
> *— Leo Buscaglia*

And yet, knowing that Attitude is everything and is always a choice, sometimes I had to say WTF! I had to admit I was afraid.

At those times, I experienced the intensity of feelings, in order to let them go. Fear had to be felt before it could be released. I had heard chemotherapy was horrible and scary. What's *not* to fear? There must be a better way. No? You mean chemo was the best choice? What guarantee would I have that it would kill the rest of the cAnswer and not me? How could I stay positive about this? Then I remembered—feel the fear *then* let it go. I guess I needed more practice!

That's when I would scream and cry out loud, until I got it all out of my system. Sometimes I called a friend. I sobbed into the phone, "I know the truth, that this is an illusion and that I create my own reality and nothing happens that is not for my highest good, but still…WTF!?" Then we'd laugh together.

SPIRITUAL TOOL

Attitude is Everything!

In any situation, I can choose to be frightened about the disease, procedures, medications, pain, etc. or I can choose to find the magic in each moment. As I look for that magic, the blessings begin to reveal themselves like little rewards from the angels. As I practice maintaining a sense of calming peace, I receive more of it. Yes! Attitude is Everything!

OLIVIA: I believe God wants you to know…That is not a sign of spiritual weakness, but of spiritual strength. When we fall ill, there are some who say, "Why did you create that for yourself?" They might convince you to see it as a sign of spiritual weakness or failure. It is not. It is a sign of spiritual strength. All challenges are a sign of spiritual strength and of the readiness of the soul to move on, to evolve even further. Love from your friend.

Sharing my journey on Facebook was a form of journaling. I exposed inner feelings to examine and explore. Putting my fears on paper allowed greater self–transparency. The more I could see through myself, the more I could see the truth of who I am in any situation, let alone in a healing crisis. How peaceful could I stay when fear reared its ugly head? How would I embrace it, love it, and then transmute it as I've been guided to do? How indeed!

First I had to realize that cAnswer is *not* a death sentence. Next, I needed to understand that I had done nothing wrong to create this. Don't we all want to blame someone else or ourselves for the negatives, or the *perceived* negatives in our lives? Then I had to remember that everything happens for a reason. God is in charge and all is well, no matter what the appearances.

I Really Love Lucy

Writing became meditation and a sanctuary. I could pour out my heart and soul and renew myself by the words on the page. Emptying myself proved comforting and opened a clear path.

The difference between journaling privately and writing on the more public Facebook was receiving comments from my "followers." The inspiring, loving, calming, prayerful, and healing comments provided me with the support I needed to stay focused on the best that life has to offer, in spite of cAnswer. Although my family team strenthened me already, I drew courage from the love and the network of sustaining energy showered upon me from others.

May 23, 2012 FB Post

I have managed to stay focused and happy and able to maintain my peace, all of which I know helps me heal. Today, I find myself in a blue funk that I just need to be with until it passes. I get to grieve some more? I get to release more tears. I get to feel more fear. All of this allows me to be human. I guess I get to embrace it all! I got a call from my surgeon this morning. Time to talk about chemo. I'll call it "primo chemo" or my "illumination treatments" or something like that—I haven't decided yet. Tuesday at 1 PM is the consultation. The following week starts the process. I know my biggest fear is simply being in the unknown. I acknowledge, I embrace, and I ask for more assistance. Can you be brave for me when I find I have no courage? Temporarily—I know, but peace is where I desire to stay. Thank you all for your continued prayers and support.

KATHY: Lauren, we know that our bodies about the outer ? of who we really are. That wonder-filled light of God is not only at the core of your being, but IS the core of your being. I am seeing that light filling every cell in your body that has been temporarily dis-eased and bringing it into perfection. Sending love and hugs.

KAY: Dear Lauren, from your elegant writing I can know exactly where you are in this moment. Please know that I am with you as you are being with your "not so fun" but real emotions. Namaste.

PAT: My son Sean has been on chemo three times, and his heart is open, his mind is clear, and his appreciation of ALL has been activated—a metamorphosis! Love heals all, and we share the tears, too. It's a part of the journey. I will pray you up!

JO: We will play singing bowls long distance for you this weekend!

JULIA: Ah, my dear Lauren, you inspire by being honest. I don't have cAnswer, yet some uncertainty terrifies me, versus it being a terrific moment to trust myself and the process, to know that which I know, and to Give Over—Surrender—that about which I am continuing to have a question or two. Much love and continued prayers and Reiki. You, my dear one, are amazing.

JANE: Remember that we are with you always, each in our own individualized expression of Spirit. You are never alone. Always held in love.

MARCIE: Since God is perfect and I have been told I am perfect and we are all one…You get to be perfect, too! Call on the angels. They are here for us.

MELODY: I was thinking about you today. I know a lot of people that have been to chemo. There is a light on the other side. Make yourself as strong as possible as you go through it. Love you very much.

POOKIE LEE: Even though we have never met, I feel as though we have. Sending love and light for your sacred journey and divine transformation. Thank you for your openness to share your personal story. I know it has blessed many. Namaste'

MARYANN: When you are feeling fearful, tense, depressed, worried or stuck, just remember you are a survivor. You are so much stronger and so much more capable than you feel in this moment. If you don't believe me, just look at all you've already dealt with and remind yourself—you're still here! Allow yourself to hope and then trust that things will get better. ♥

JOHNNIE BETH: That must've been one hell of a purge! See, you don't need hormones for that to happen!

FROM GRIEF TO GRATITUDE.
LESS THAN A DAY!
JOURNEY FROM HEAD TO
HEART TO FINALLY, GUT.

FIRST, HEAD
EXPRESSION, EMBRACING
AND OWNING ALL MY
EMOTIONS.

NEXT, HEART
FEELING THE FEELINGS
FULLY ALLOWING THEM
TO MOVE THROUGH ME

FINALLY, GUT
KNOWING THE TRUTH
THAT EVERYTHING IS IN
DIVINE ORDER.

IN DEEP GRATITUDE FOR
THE GIFTS THAT EVERY
MOMENT HAS TO OFFER
EXPECIALLY MY FRIENDS.

Photo and text
by Lauren from her
Lighten Up with Lauren series

I just experienced a day–long series of releases. Just when I thought I have dried up, my tears would not stop. So I just let them flow without judgment. Not much fun either. But today I feel relief, like yesterday was crucial to bring me to today…does this make sense?

May 28, 2012 FB Post

We never know how we will respond to challenges until we are faced with them. My dad was at the hospital every single day. His cousin, Jon, lived in Indianapolis, so it was easy for him to spend the nights there. Jon's wife, Nit, always sent a CARE package filled with food with him. Such thoughtful people!

Phil was there every day as well, but he stayed in a hotel room. Often there was nothing to do but sit with each other. It must have been boring for them at times, but I was so grateful for their presence!

May 28, 2012 FB Post

| *Captain Laurence I. Powell* | *SP4 Philip M. Long* |

My two favorite men, both veterans. Father left to serve in the Air Force betwwen 1957 and 1959—1959 to 1962 in the reserves. Phil served n the army in Veitnam 1971—1972. I publicly honor and thank them for their service and surviving it. I love you both so much.

May 30, 2012 FB Post

So much for being proactive! I learned yesterday that the Primo Chemo I have chosen, every week instead of every three weeks, may *not* make my hair fall out after all, now that it is as short as it's ever been in my life! I am grateful it grows so fast. Fate sure has a sense of humor, doesn't she!?

JIM: Lauren, your husband is married to a wonderful woman. You are right. GOD does have a great sense of humor. That's why she is God! YOU ARE TRULY BELOVED.

JOANNE: LOL. I love her sense of humor! And I know you are beautiful within and without, no matter what the length of your hair.

LINDSAY: Oh Lauren! I don't know whether to laugh or cry. Maybe I'll do both!

"Healing does not mean going back to the way things were before, but rather allowing what is now to move us closer to God."

—Ram Dass

May 30, 2012 FB Post

CAT scan, EKG, port put into my chest and whatever else needs to be done to start the Illumination Treatments next week. Nice drive to Indy from Bloomington. I am so grateful that my husband actually enjoys the trip! One step at a time, I am healing!

ERICA: So grateful for the port—and I work with someone who had her port installed by the guy who invented them!

LINDSAY: On the port—Kudos to you for being so unbelievably positive and so creative and uplifting with your vocabulary. "Illumination Treatments!" You are an amazing gift to us all.

The port, the size and shape of a Mentos candy, lay just underneath the skin below my right clavicle. It required flushing with saline and another solution to keep it open and free–flowing. I would need to keep it for two years. In the meantime it bestowed a Frankenstein quality upon me.

The port sure as heck beat sticking me over and over again trying to find a vein. My poor arms stayed black and blue forever after each time I was dismissed from the hospital. I welcomed the port. It gives new meaning to "Any port in a storm."

June 2, 2012 FB Post

It's finally June. I've been waiting for May to finish already. Too much stuff. I let go of May, 2012 and all it offered. Now I embrace June and the green of summer. Each day gets me closer to chemo and there's so much to do!

Applying for Medicaid—again. I don't feel good at all. How do healthy people do this? Filling out all these forms and finding our records, scanning and printing, etc. is exhausting. I am worn out when I even think of filling out another form or going online again to find this document and send that one. I am so looking forward to a break. My best friend from high school is driving to Indiana from Colorado in a couple of days. I am thrilled to be spending time with Monica! What a friend. I hope I will feel well enough to do something with her!

I would like to walk around downtown, then explore the campus. That didn't used to be a big deal. Right now, I wouldn't last five minutes. I am really trying to love Lucy, my beloved colostomy, but she hurts constantly and it's getting worse. I think something is wrong with her. I don't think I should be in this much pain. Then again, what is a colostomy supposed to feel like?

If a friend came to visit, they would have to accept everything, myself included, in its natural state as I remained in bed most of the time. When I wasn't in bed, I stretched out on the couch. I managed to sit outside on cooler evenings, but record high temperatures in the high nineties for weeks at a time that summer made stepping outside after 5 AM oppressive.

I Really Love Lucy

Our air conditioning worked well in spite of power outages all over the rest of the region. Phil kept me cool and fed with what I could eat. Lucy hurt more than ever. Giving her a name when she was first installed helped ease my trauma of wearing a bag. I continued to personify her as the pain increased. However, severe pain woke me up the morning of the 4th. I called my oncology nurse who directed me to the ER in Indy. Holy Shift! I was in no position to argue. I hugged my pillow, placed both feet on the dashboard, and toned to my tummy, trying anything to ease the pain.

My icy cold and sterile room in the ER felt like an alien abduction. I laid in stark white and silver metal surroundings. Then the only doctor I had to really work at to find any good in at all, came in. I thought, *"He is a great surgeon,"* trying to comfort myself. I concluded that his social skills were equal to that of a unschooled ten year old. I remembered him from a few days prior to my dismissal, after the emergency surgery resulting in Lucy. This doctor stopped at my room on rounds. At that time, I was swollen from the waist down with my legs so enlarged I couldn't see my feet. When I stood up, fluid would rush to the floor from all parts of my body. I asked this doctor why the lips of my vagina felt so heavy and enlarged. I was worried about more cAnswer showing up in other places. He blushed and responded, "Too much information," and never answered my question. Now I had him as my ER doctor.

He pulled his gloves on and looked at my stoma after I removed the bag, the appliance, and the adhesive. As I reclined I exposed Lucy in all her glory. To me, she looked different than just a few weeks ago, redder on one side. As he looked at her, bewildered, he stuck his fat pinky finger deep into Lucy and made her bleed. I screamed in pain so he removed his finger and stopped me up with gauze. OMG! I asked him when he thought it would stop bleeding, as the gauze turned crimson. He snapped back at me,"Everything will stop bleeding sometime." And again, never answered my question. The pain felt worse than it had at home. I received another pain pill and he sent me home.

SPIRITUAL TOOL
Willingness

I don't have to know how to do anything. I only need to be willing to change, whether it's changing my diet, breaking a bad habit, treating myself better, or writing a book. My willingness stirs up the energies of potential.

June 5, 2012 FB Post

Big Spiritual Question for all of my angel friends. How can I stay prayerful, peaceful, full of gratitude, and positive when in physical pain? Emotional pain seems to be easier to let go of, for me anyway. But when the body hurts consistently, how do I *not* dwell on that? I know this, too, shall pass, but I'm so tired of hurting! This is coming from one of the most positive people I know… me! I need your help!

KALAR: Dear and sweet Lauren, I send you light to help ease you through this. I know it is one of the greatest spiritual challenges. Myself, I have gotten migraines for a long, long time. Thank goodness they have eased with the change of life. But once when I was in such pain and struggle, a being of light appeared to me, and taught me a technique. I was instructed to realize that the pain was a pattern of constriction and contraction in the physical (of course it could be template in karma and other bodies) but that somewhere, there is pure light, so I was guided to visualize that at the core of the pain was a template of light. It didn't matter, if I could only visualize a thin sheath of light at the core, only a neutrino wide, but to see it, and that would give some stability within so that the pattern does not consume your energy like a black hole. I hope this may help you. I do believe that the headaches I have had were a type of karma and the pain that has been generated in them was a tool to work through negative karma. It doesn't make it easy when you are in the vice grip of karma.

JAMIE: Think of how much love and joy you give to others, have given through the years and that every step you have taken and continue to journey is a gift not only to those whom you encounter, but to yourself as well. Many have found their "voice" through your love and light and it is there now, supporting you as you RISE HIGHER. Keep on Keepin' on, Lauren.

JOHNNIE BETH: Keep breathing into the pain and exhaling thru it. I'm sorry to hear that you are having pain. I'll be loving you thru this. Make it your friend—one that you won't miss when it is gone.

AMIE: For me, I go into the pain and listen for what it is trying to bring to my attention. The longer it takes for me to stop and listen, the longer the pain remains. Remember, the body holds all the cellular memory of not just our life experiences but also those of our whole genetic light–line. I truly believe we are the ones here at this time to bring much of that unconscious information to awareness. Pain sucks, but it has a purpose. Much love to you, dear one!!

ALICIA: Wherever the pain is within my body, I focus on sending light to it, seeing that space filled with light and releasing the pain, dis–ease and discomfort. I try to remember that the moment is temporary and there will be a time when I am no longer in pain and focus on the moments when I wasn't in pain. Try to see the pain as a blessing of your body healing, mending itself and correcting the cells and any damage that has occurred. Pain is not always negative, but is a way to bring about positive change, blessings and growth. Remember that the angels hold you in their wings. Take comfort and rest in their wings of peace, healing, love and grace. I call upon all of the angels, your guardians and guides to surround you in a healing crystal, shining brilliant love, light and physical comfort into your body, releasing all pain and discomfort, allowing your physical body to heal with ease—pain–free and stress–free.

JOANNE: Rather than resisting the pain, embrace it. Let yourself feel what is there to feel and as best you can, let go of the "idea" that it needs to be different. Perhaps the peace can then arise in your mind, in spite of the pain. Meanwhile, I see God's holy, healing light moving through every cell and atom of your body.

MARY: Focus on the area of pain. Visualize all its aspects: color, size, texture, etc. Feel all the aspects. Breathe deep into the area and say "Thank you". A few more breaths. Then return to the area. And keep repeating. Often the area will get smaller and smaller.

CC: The Buddhists counsel us to look at the pain and realize that it is not continuous. Like everything else, it comes and goes, and comes and goes. Somehow, for me, that makes it easier to take. It is also good practice to lengthen the gaps between it "coming' and stretch out the "going" part. Hugs to you!

ROB: Having dealt with chronic pain for 7 years now, I have found that one of the best approaches to "surviving" is to choose to do something you really love— put all your energy into it—and all your focus (that you can muster)—and the pain will become secondary, at least as long as you stay focused. For me, it is doing artwork, i imagine for you playing music and singing would be the key. maybe cooking, or as odd as it sounds, exercising can be a release. You just need to have faith that you can still do what you love even with the pain, and the pain will become more tolerable.

DONNA: Visualize the pain as dark and black as you can. Then focus on that tiny green dot that has always been at the center. As you focus on the dot, see that it is aglow and that it is getting bigger and brighter. It will take over the space inhabited by the darkness as the healing light drives out the dark pain.

ERICA: Ditto to much of what people have mentioned above, AND, although not a medications type person—pain is very draining and I am willing to use medication to give myself space for healing—I'd rather use my energy for healing than for "dealing" with pain.

ROSANNE: Hi Lauren, I have had pain before, but I've had one other thing I've had to deal with physically for the past 13 years nonstop 24/7 and it's called Mal De Debarqument syndrome. It is like you are on a boat on tidal waves and have g–force feelings in your head constantly, amongst other feelings. Let me just say, have you ever gotten off a boat or plane and still felt the movement? Well, it's the same but about 10,000 x worse. There is no cure. I have tried everything, but the only thing that has me going daily is my thought process and how I give it to God and keep going on. What I try to do is focus on other things than the symptoms . It's hard and it wants to distract me, but I keep on ignoring feelings (and this is hard for sensitive people like us, who are used to listening to our bodies long before others would because we are so aware). Try to focus on other things. With pain, I know it must be harder. I am sending you healing energy and prayer. I know I've never met you, but I feel connected to you, and you are in my thoughts and prayers. Also try to focus all of the pain and all the energy of it flying out the bottom of your feet or wherever it can escape and going into the ground or to God to neutralize it. And God's pure light and healing and love are flowing in the places it left. Sending love.

DEANNE: Sometimes you just have to surrender to the pain and move through it. Cry, yell profanities if you want, kick pillows—just be with it and then let it go. Don't deny or resist it—get past it and let all the love people send you help you release the toxins, the pain and all the challenges you face.

SHAN: Lauren, get some paints—acrylic or finger paint— and paint everything you see. The colors will fill the space up in you with something new and heal the different aspects of your body! Love and Hugs, you magnificent being. We sent you peaceful healing energy!

MARIA: That IS the question, huh? I can only speak for myself and I am not wise enough to give you advice. I'm happy to share what pain has taught me and if anything fits, that's great! Often times, I don't remain calm, centered, peaceful and in a state of bliss. My physical–ness will rail against the pain, complete with tears, gnashing of teeth and the occasional "why me???" But the spiritual me knows without a doubt that this is a temporary situation. I am loved and held in the arms of God and I know that both the physical and spiritual sides can coexist at the same time. It does not mean that I am less centered or balanced than at any other time. It's just that I am a spiritual being having a human experience. Pain is a lesson and you will learn what you need to learn from it. In the meanwhile, be gentle with yourself, try to go with the flow in the moment. Take pain meds, sleep, cry, find a good friend to hold you and let you be little when you need it. Eat your favorite foods, if animals are important in your life enjoy them in large doses. I use some CDs with guided imagery when it gets really bad and I misplace the map to my happy place. With much emphasis on remaining positive, I want to be a voice that says, "Lauren, honey, you are going through a really tough thing right now. You have permission to be sad and pissed off. I give you 10 minutes a day to hold a pity party. (But only 10 minutes)." Healing is as individual as dis–ease. Give your body and mind what it is asking for. This from someone with no answers. Hope something in there rings for you. Blessings!

CHERYL: Healing touch on yourself or get someone there to pain drain clearing and ultrasound. Another good choice is to use heart math breathing and visualize the pain leaving your body thru your positive emotions. I have a coach who could help you. Let me know.

LORI: I speak from experience. Choose other things to dwell on that keep you busy and bring you emotional and spiritual joy. Know deep in your soul that this, too, shall pass. Focus on knowing that physical comfort and wellbeing is your birthright to experience.

KRISTEN: I remember something Daddy once told me—it was something like, when I stub my toe and that toe is in pain, I give my attention to the 9 that feel fine. He mentioned that, while in the shower, he goes through an inventory, giving attention and gratitude to that which is working well. Thank You God! type of thing.

ELLEN: Lauren, I talk to the pain & ask "What do I need to know, do or be to be free of this pain or whatever the current situation is?" While I wait for my answer, I walk through each moment with the knowledge that my body has the answer & I will receive my answer.

MARY ANN: Could you listen to books on tape from the library to avert your mind from your discomfort? Maybe there are Eckert Tolle sets available. So sorry that you are hurting and pray your trip back to Simon Center sets all this right and comfortable.

BETSY: Hi ya, honey! Wow, you are sooooooo brave. I wish I could tell you about how to handle constant pain. I have found some ways with my RA—yoga, massage, chiropractor and supplements. Perhaps just move into it—just be really tired of hurting—when the other side appears, there is sweet relief. I am singing sweet songs for you, like you have for me!

JOHN: I will think of you multiple times a day and see you released from pain. As others do this, this energy will be increased and pain will not be.

BARBARA: Insight Meditation has been a powerful practice in my life. In the teachings of Buddha, we suffer when we crave something that we don't have or resist something that we do have, such as pain. Through insight meditation, you can focus on the pain by observing it and "being" with it. As you cease to resist it, the suffering will lessen. At first, when you focus on the pain in your meditation, it may increase for awhile during the meditation until you shift into that state of "being" with it. Then it will significantly lessen. It takes practice but it really does work! Hugs and Blessings.

CHARLES: Lauren, what I have done with physical pain is to step outside of it or to place it outside of me. It is a good use of a disassociation technique. It has assisted me in getting through a number of physically painful incidents over the years. You are NOT denying it's there, you admit it is there, and then move through it and past it.

SHELLY: Stephen Levine said resistance just increases the pain. His books are great on the topic of pain management. He says you have to love the pain. I wouldn't have any idea HOW to do that, but I would check him out.

I Really Love Lucy

Ordinarily, I would not have shown so many comments, but I want to share the overwhelming love and compassion that came through the Internet when I asked for help. So many wonderful ideas and techniques around controlling and releasing pain from angels who know the truth, that pain of any kind is our teacher and our gift, helped me so much.

My best friend from high school came for a visit but I worried about what kind of hostess I would be? I thought I'd feel better by now. I didn't know why I was feeling worse, sicker, and weaker. The pain in Lucy increased every day,

As crappy as I felt, I loved seeing Monica. She drove from her home in Colorado Springs to our home in Bloomington. Though I stayed immobile, we shared stories that caught us up to date about who, where, and why. We celebrated how we could fall right back into our friendship as if no time had passed or nothing had changed.

This time a lot about me had changed—my hair chopped, my face hollow and gaunt, my arms thin and frail, and my posture slumped. I had become a pale wisp of a being, not female, not male, barely human in my own eyes. I stood as a dark, deadly caricature of myself. I professed out loud and often "I am healing! I am healing!" but you sure wouldn't have known it to look at me!

Monica and I talked about everything growing up. When I was twelve, she acted was my confidant as my mom and dad split up. Well…she and my Siamese cat. I poured out my soul to her then, and I poured it out now.

"What if I die?"

While she held no answers, she put her arms around me and we wept together. From teenagers to adults, now growing into our Crone years, the familiar feelings of fear and helplessness took on new tones. As a teenager, I thought everything was about me and every drama rocked my world! Now, I know everything is about me and every drama takes me to a deeper place of healing. cAnswer feels light, airy, warm, and fuzzy compared to the trauma/drama of high school.

My mom reminded me early in my cAnswer journey that God would never give us more than we can handle. She said He knew that she couldn't handle my dying, therefore, I wasn't gonna die. That made perfect sense to me and I decided to stand by it! Monica liked the logic.

So the cAnswer departed with the hysterectomy and I'm looking forward to chemo. I have a colostomy and the stoma itself hurts. I'm receiving many helpful hints about pain and healing. Right now, I am grateful for morphine.

Monica's visit felt like days of unending naps and nurturing. The pain grew more severe. Pain pills no longer helped. Pretty sure by now that Lucy was experiencing trouble, I made another appointment at IU Med in Indianapolis. I could stay with Monica's parents who retired to Indy years ago. The night before my appointment, Monica drove to her parents' home in Indianapolis with me curled up in the reclined front seat, surrounded again by pillows. We stayed the night with two of my favorite people from my past.

That night, I endured heavy and gross output from Lucy. The skin around her chafed and bled from the appliance adhesive, and the stoma disappeared back into my body. In contrast, comfort surrounded me. The bed I was trying to sleep upon was comfy, plush, and supportive. Handmade needlework pillows propped me up along with the pillows I brought with me. I could feel the family's love for the books, trinkets and crafts that lined the top of the bookshelves. It gave them a life and an energy of their own. I thought about how much and how long this family has loved me.

Lucy's pain wouldn't let me sleep so I breathed as deeply as I could and used my imagination to shift my reality. This became my meditation. Lying in the dark I remembered my sister Kristen, Monica's sister Ann, Monica, and me all as friends in grade school. They went by Kristie and Annie then, and I was called Laurie. Never having been around a big family, I marveled at the noise level when I joined them for dinner. With two adults, seven kids, and me, the commotion was like a zoo! But what I perceived as complete chaos, seemed utterly normal to them!

With eyes wide open in the dark, I begin to shine my light upon what is real. Love and friendship are real. My gratitude is real. This time, this place, this pain are real. And all of it is real precious.

In contrast, I appreciated the self–contained unit of Mom, Dad, Kristie, and myself—a small, intimate nuclear family—all the more. Then that family fell apart.

Monica lived through the divorce with me. She and I survived high school together and also Mom's abusive boyfriend following the divorce. Now Monica shares my cAnswer Dance. Who else would I ask to be with me now? What magic of the Universe aligned the stars so perfectly to bring her here to me at this particular time? My blessings continued to flow.

The next morning we drove the short distance to the cAnswer center. The doctor I saw didn't know what was happening to me. When I told her it felt as if Lucy was receding into me, she admitted me to the hospital. I settled into what was too quickly becoming routine. Phil, Mom, Dad, and Mary Ann were not far behind. The joke about putting a zipper in my tummy no longer seemed funny. I was so thin and my skin so tight that I wondered how they were ever going to close me up? I thought, *"Here we grow again! I surrender! Help me heal! I am willing to do what's mine to do."*

"We must embrace pain and burn it as fuel for our journey."

—Kenji Miyazawa

When I learned about "willingness" my life shifted. In my Spiritual education, a new idea comes in threes when I'm ready to learn something new. For example, the minister at a church I attended in Charleston, SC spoke about "willingness" as the first step in creating change. The very next day Kristen shared a lesson from *A Course in Miracles*: "Show me a different way to see this," to which she added, "I am willing to see this differently." Then I read a book by Catherine Ponder. Her use of affirmations shifts a belief system from one of lack to one of plenty. So many of us simply learned how to be poor. I was a pro! As I reworked an affirmation of hers to fit my need that week, I spoke out loud. "I am willing to do what needs to be done by me to allow prosperity to flow into my life." I heard that word again. "Willingness!"

Being willing to undergo yet another surgery was the next step in my healing process. With Lucy not well, I prayed, "Sweet Spirit, if it is the right and perfect thing to do, I am willing to go into surgery tomorrow. I know Your Spirit within me will keep me strong and help me heal. I am willing to do what needs to be done by me to make this a positive situation. I am willing.

"Start by doing what's necessary; then do what's possible; and suddenly, you are doing the impossible."

—St. Francis of Assisi

June 6, 2012 FB Post

Third time is a charm! First of all, thank you all so much for prayers and techniques around pain release. What hurts is not the cancer or anything having to do with it really. It is in the stoma, the intestine sticking out that the colostomy comes from. Pain is not normal. Neither is the stoma receding! So today I was readmitted for a 3rd surgery. "Repositioning" of the stoma, making sure that the leak is not leaking into body. My initial incision is weird too. They will use that to make sure my belly is clear.

Big picture. I am no longer worried about chemo. Talk about a counter irritant!

While I'm here again, after I'm all fixed up, *then* I'll begin chemo! I am done with pain and *know* that this surgery will only help. Thank you again for all of your prayers!

BARABARA: Dearest Lauren, Have you thought of getting help through Healing Touch? I will also hold you in my prayers for release of pain and for healing.

MARIA: Seeing you surround with love and healing. Love to your stoma and we will surround her with cool, moist, clean and healthy good stuff.

ANN: So many loving prayers for your complete healing. So much concern from us over your physical pain. I feel sure, as I believe you do, that the upcoming surgery will make possible your body healing just as your soul accepts spiritual healing.

ALLISA: Lauren, You are sooooo very Brave. Light, Love, Peace, Healing. GOD loves you and so do we!

MARY ANN: This must be the time and place for all to be rectified. You have paid your dues one thousand times over. Peace and Comfort are my prayers for you.

SARAH: I really don/t want to be negative in my messages but could you get a different doctor???? These complications are not the norm. On the other hand, you are blessing all of us by sharing your story and life.

YVONNE: Lauren there is an easier way to teach doctors and nurses about love, light, healing vibrational energy. Give them a free ticket to one of your classes. :o) Way better than you continuing to go back to hospital to teach them. lol ~<3~ I'm keeping you in prayer sweet one, knowing the Universe has got your back. Keep on smiling, healing, learning, growing...

CHERYL: Good Morning! My heart is filled with the awareness of the enormous love and the concert of angels that God has surrounded Lauren and each of her family with in the midst of this earthly experience. Lauren has blessed so many lives and brought the joy and healing love of prayer, musical harmonious vibrations, laughter, passion, and accountability into the experience of everyone around her. May Lauren experience a complete healing of the physical as her spirit is singing and dancing in the arms of God right now! Love and Appreciation, as always.

PAIN *vs* PEACE

MONICA: I am watching so many of my friends battling cancer (cAnswer for Lauren Lane Powell) and other unsolicited illnesses. It has made me aware how often I have disrespected my own body. How very blessed I am to have been gifted with a healthy body to house my spirit. How can we continue to pollute and destroy what was given with love? These bodies are the answer to prayers of others. We can not serve if we are not healthy.

SHARRON: Joining hearts with your friends and family & continuing to hold you in prayer and in the light. By the power of every moment of your goodness
May your heart's wishes be soon fulfilled, as completely shining as the bright full moon, as magically as by a wish–fulfilling gem.
May all dangers be averted and all disease be gone .
May no obstacle come across your way.
May you enjoy fulfillment and a long, joy–filled life.

Almost a week passed after the *third* surgery before I posted anything on Facebook. I was getting sick and tired of being sick and tired. At least the surgery relieved the tummy pain. But I needed fluids pulled off my lungs again and I was thinner than the last time. Although Lucy hurt less, she caused problems. I had to change the bags every hour or so.

My first Chemo/Dreamo treatment had been scheduled for June 12, 2012. I learned my oncologist wanted to have it administered in a drip through my port at night, after an hour or so of premeds, as I slept...or tried to sleep. I felt so betrayed. I thought I'd have a week or two to get stronger, gain weight, and feel better before I started Chemo/Dreamo.

I didn't know what to expect so my fear grew. At least my mom stayed with me. At least they now monitored me. At least my morphine pump might help me sleep. But I didn't want to sleep through it. I wanted to play an active role in taking treatment.

Mom wanted to participate in as much as she could with me. We knew better than to believe all the hype about chemo being poison—"It'll kill you before it can cure you." *No!* If I allowed this into my body, I would think about it differently. I had to believe it could heal me so we would bless it, appreciate it, and allow it.

I willed to release *everything* I had ever heard and/or believed about chemotherapy.

I had to be willing to release *everything*
I had ever heard and/or believed about chemo therapy.

I stayed in a space of peace with no television, conversation, or reading. I planned to listen to a playlist of meditation music I had previously created and recorded on my iPod to help me relax, A happy accident occurred when I discovered I had left my iPod containing my chemo meditation music at home, not anticipating I would need it on this trip. However, I had brought my MacBook with me and it contained *all* of my music. I played it over the speakers so Mom could hear it too.

At 10 PM, the nurses administered the premeds. The technicians hooked up tubes and wires to all manner of machines. They dispensed steroids, Benadryl, and extra fluids, with heparin in between to clear out the port. Each med took time entering my body. I learned later that if Benadryl is pumped in too fast for some people, restless leg symptoms can develop.

A guided meditation finished by the time the Taxol started to drip, then my own music played in alphabetical order starting with *Angel Flying*. Mom and I held hands through the first three songs. Neither of us would sing tonight. But we would receive the gifts of song already sung. I danced in my head with my long hair flowing behind me, I pictured myself in perfect health. Together we traveled between meditation and dream. Midnight found my first Chemo/Dreamo treatment complete. I had made it through safely and positively!

My new friend and chemo–mentor posted this when she danced with cAnswer:

AMI CAMI: I hope you all can feel that I'm very comfortable and at peace with this decision. Today when I was listening to "The Magic Mirror" I felt and saw how I will actively participate with the chemotherapy drugs as they enter my body. Realizing that nothing in this world is all good or all bad, there's a beauty and peace when the balance is recognized. I recognized that in life, death and decay must happen for new life to emerge...so, I am actively thanking all my cells and when the chemo enters, I will consciously embrace each cell that is destroyed with love and release it with gratitude knowing that the healthy ones will return, renewed. This is a deep, cellular clearing that I have been preparing for all my life. Thank you all for walking this journey with me. I am honored and blessed!

CHARLOTTE: Lauren, we met when you came to do a workshop at The Church of Today in Baton Rouge, LA about eight years ago. My husband and I volunteered to 'host' you and welcomed you into our home. Being a massage therapist, I gave you a massage to relax you after your travels and you gave me a voice lesson the next day. I also bought one of your CD s and a songbook and later taught some of your songs to the church congregation. I loved your workshop, the crystal bowls, and the Goddess dresses. I still have the dress I bought from you and still wear it and love it. Back then, you were a picture of health, vitality and confidence. You moved with grace and beauty and I felt very blessed to become acquainted with you. As time went by, we stayed connected by email and later by Face Book. When you announced your diagnosis, I was shocked and could hardly believe that such a nightmare could happen to a person like you. The outcome seemed grim, but I knew that if any person on earth could live through this and survive, it would be you. Healing is what your life was about, and now you were called upon to face the ultimate challenge and have a 'healing experience' of great significance. Instead of cowering in the shadows and withdrawing from the world, you reached out to your friends and family and all the people who love you. You shared your fears, your sorrows, your hope, your joy. You took us on the journey with you, and we all benefited. You were very brave to lay the facts out in every detail. When you showed photos of your colostomy, I thought that some people may find that disturbing. However, I had a massage client who has lived with one for many years, so it was nothing new to me. The good thing is that yours was temporary. To think of all this from a medical perspective, it is nothing short of a miracle that doctors can perform surgeries like that. However, the greater miracle is how you clung to the Divine healing energy and called it forth to flow through you and make you whole again. The flower which started to wilt has come back into full bloom. Now, you are spreading your sweet essence to all who will breathe it in. Day by day, you make the world a lovelier place!

Chapter Six
Loving What Is

June 13, 2012 FB Post by Larry Powell

Good News...for all of Lauren's Angels, Friends and Family (three names to describe the same wonderful group). Lauren and I spoke just now on the phone and she sounds like Lauren. She is healing from her third major operation where they inspected her abdominal cavity and discovered NO NEW CANCER. The infected incision and colostomy were repaired without incident. The last few days Lauren has been... recovering and preparing for the next phase of her cAnswer treatment. Her first chemo is over (last night at 10PM) and she has minimal side effects so far. No sickness etc.

They plan to keep her in the hospital however, for observation over the next weekend. On Monday I had to leave her bedside to take her sister, Kristen, back to South Bend where she left her car so we could drive to Indy together. Sandye will accompany Lauren and Phil to Bloomington when she is released. Thanks for your prayers.

DAYNA: Wow, Lauren. My little light shines upon you and your healing. I see you vigorous and beautiful, as you were when last we saw you in ABQ. May the love of all who know you lift you to the highest renewed strength possible.

There were many posts of gratitude and celebration! My third and final surgery was a success. I was affirming this was my final surgery for God's sake! I am grateful I can still smile.

The real man (or woman) smiles in trouble, gathers strength from distress and grows brave by reflection.

—Thomas Paine

June 15, 2012 FB Post

Third time *is* a charm! I feel stronger now than I did after the first surgery. I feel like everyone around me is extremely attentive and proactive. Even though I am still in IU Med Hospital I will not be released until everyone is satisfied with the healing taking place. AMEN! I love the staff—nurses, techs, doctors—all fabulous!

I am still receiving healing prayers from all of you and feel so blessed as I receive them at a deeper and deeper level everyday! Best of all, no new cAnswer cells were found and pain is minimal!!

One thing I do need to share—My first Illumination Treatment/chemo was Tuesday night. It was like a dream...really! Tuesday at 10 PM listening to a guided meditation then my Natural Affirmations CD. Mom was here throughout. Together we formed a new healthy memory. At midnight it was over and I just fell asleep. Four days now, with no side effects. Just *big* healing. Thank you for playing such a major roll in it all! I LOVE YOU!

Needless to say I have made friends with the process and embraced the treatments. Thank you everyone for your concern and your ideas on alternative healing. My meditation, diet, exercise, meds, and treatment are all working together—along with your continuous prayers to see me through to an amazingly healthy body, mind and Spirit. Thank you so much for holding me in the light, now with with this new facet of Illumination. I am so deeply blessed. I get to change the perception of chemo.

MARIA: I wonder if the staff would let you blow bubbles while you get your treatment? I keep bubbles in my car and when stuck in traffic I open the window and let 'em fly. I can't tell you the number of fellow stuck motorists have given me a thumbs up! Something pretty about bubbles! I learned that from you!

Bubbles! What a great idea to have in the hospital! I kept a bottle of bubbles at hand the entire time I traveled on the road. Highway in construction, or any stop and go traffic required bubbles! Blowing them out the window gave me such pleasure I felt giddy opening up the bottle. Relaxation came instantly when I took a deep breath to create dozens of colorful spheres. Then I would release that deep breath. I'd watch the faces of those around me soften and the tension in their eyebrows unfurl when they saw the bubbles. Once a car drove up beside me and the driver rolled down her window to ask, "What are you doing?"

I answered without thinking. "I'm changing the way traffic jams feel!"

"You know!? You're right!"

Another time a driver proclaimed, "You're having fun and we get to enjoy it!"

"You got it!"

But now I had a hard time sucking into the breathing tube. I wondered how I could blow bubbles. And I thought it wasn't a good thing to do in the hospital anyway.

Mom and I did not sleep well during the nights as every four hours nurses came into my room to check, poke, and prod me. When the dripping fluids settled to their last drops in the bag, a loud buzzer would beep. I found myself composing a melody from the nasty machine sounds. When my machines did not beep, I heard the incessant machines in the next room. Then red blinking and green glowing lights flashed brightly. I treasured the thick eye mask I brought with me. When I finally dozed off, the doctors woke me during their rounds. I slept more throughout the day as I could control my pain with the morphine pump and the morphine made me drowsy. I loved that pump.

I was certain our fuzzy children missed Phil so I told him to go home. Improving daily, I knew I would be released soon. Even with a full time house sitter (thank you John), Phil felt an uncomfortable absence away from home and all its activity, especially when he could only sit in my room all day. Ordinarily, he walks in our woods, chops and splits lumber, and builds and fixes things. Sitting still is not his forte, but he managed it with no complaints.

I greatly appreciated the nurse whose patience in showing me an improved way to work with Lucy, made my pending release less upsetting. She took her time with the demonstration, and made sure I was comfortable with going home. I walked slowly with no leg swelling this time.

Mom transported me to Bloomington. She and Phil set me up in my big chair, then unloaded the car. I felt so glad I wasn't as swollen as the last time, and was so happy to be home with our two dogs and six cats. The warm glow of lamplight versus the glaring fluorescence of the hospital felt welcoming. Lastly, I cherished the quiet.

Mom drove back to northern Indiana that evening, a four hour trip. She'd been away from her home long enough. God love her!

June 16, 2012 FB Post

Being overly prepared for chemo, I had my hair cut really short. I like it least this way and I cant wait to see it grow out. I feel strong and my fingernails are long and strong. It will be interesting to be the observer of my body throughout the coming weeks. My goal is to observe without judgement. I don't even know what that feels like…to observe without judgement…

I have had too much practice in judging. Looking back on it, I used to be very judgmental of everyone and everything around me and of course then, of myself. Everything was either good or bad, black or white. No room for gray. I treated my opinions as fact until proven otherwise. Growing out of, and away from, that pattern became essential for my happiness and peace of mind, because the more I judged anything, person or situation, I set myself up for being proven right! When I became aware of how judgmental I was and started to correct myself, lovingly, life around and within me shifted.

To judge is to be critical of. To discern feels more indifferent.

To judge is to be attached. To decide feels more informed.

To judge is to set standards. To be grateful feels empowering

June 16, 2012 FB Post, continued

Spending so much time with Dad in the hospital reminded me of one of those opportunities. While visiting him and stepmom in Florida many years ago, I wrote this in my journal-

Today is Non–Judgement Day!

Saturday evening, there was party with Dad's friends in a beautiful *big* home. In years past I would have dressed down for effect. I would have stayed to myself and observed. But this time I had a choice. Before the party I made a conscious decision not to judge…whatever that meant. I was so used to judging I didn't even know how not to.

Tonight I felt loved and blessed because I was loving and blessing everything I saw. Tonight I felt the Grace of our host's abundance. I was grateful to see what *can* be. Tonight I successfully put judgment to rest…a quiet, brief burial, no ceremony but there is grief. I think I will miss judgment.

It gave me an excuse *not* to fit in. Them against me.

It gave me an excuse to stay separate. Me against Them.

It gave me reasons to hate myself. Me against me!

Judgment gave me an excuse to hang onto *stuff! Yes!* Because of judgment, my money, as little as there was of it, meant so much to me, that everything I spent it on meant that much to me! Consequently, I have rooms full of stuff that means so much to me because of the money spent on them. Good stuff or not! Needed stuff or not! It was stuff that filled the void created by the fear of not–enough–ness. Not having enough meant not being enough.

I guess I've I've always had the fear of not having/being enough. So, having nice things felt good. Not having nice things felt bad. But I was judging those who had nice things horribly. Just like I felt judged for not having nice things, I judged those who did have nice things. How do I reconcile this rift?

Keep judgment at rest. I choose to release, not only old, unwanted ideas and things, but once loved, but now useless ideas and things. Now I am free to recognize that the fear of going without is the only thing I'm really releasing.

Tonight I put judgment to rest and will wake up to a new aware me—discerning, deciding, deliberately Divine!

CHARLOTTE: Lauren, You stayed at my house once when you were in Louisiana years ago. Although I haven't seen you since then, I have a wonderful memory of you and your beauty, both inside and out. A few weeks ago, I became aware of your health status and have been wanting to write you. Life is such a mystery….how the good and the bad can be so entwined. I'm glad to know that we are so much more than our bodies. As I'm writing this, I see you with that beautiful radiant smile and vibrant energy shining from your eyes. That's how I will always see you in my mind's eye, because that is the true spirit of Lauren.

Your work in this world was about healing, and now the healer is in need of healing. What better education can one get than to experience the need on such a deep level. From my own experience with pain and suffering, I've learned that fighting it never helps, but embracing it does. Never view an illness as an enemy; treat it as a friend and ask, "What lesson do you offer? What blessing will you gift me with?" If you look, you will find it. Wishing you a graceful recovery, and a life filled with love.

SPIRITUAL TOOL

Non-Judgment

When I judge, I am my accuser, my prosecutor, my judge and jury, and I am my redeemer. I am passing judgment on judgment. I find judgment guilty! Guilty of separation.

When I judge, it's me against them. When I judge, it's right or wrong, better or worse, higher or lower, and more or less. When I judge, I worry that people are, or will be, judging me.

What a great confirmation of my affirmation! Embracing and blessing everything in my life is that very Holy Shift from Judgment to Gratitude!

Stay in Gratitude

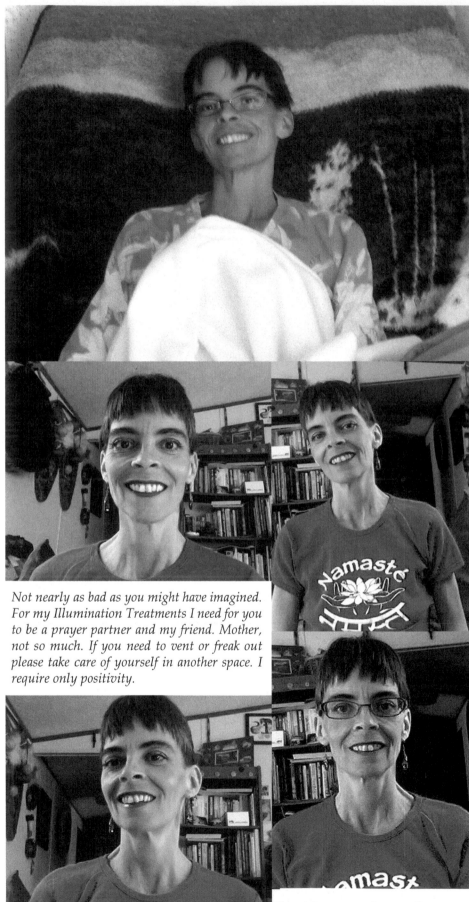

Not nearly as bad as you might have imagined. For my Illumination Treatments I need for you to be a prayer partner and my friend. Mother, not so much. If you need to vent or freak out please take care of yourself in another space. I require only positivity.

I am stronger and more vibrant every day. Thank you for knowing that.

Mom called me daily and often offered to stay with me. I told her it wasn't necessary as there was not much I needed at that time. Because she worried, I sent her recent photos. I wanted to show her how well I was doing and how good I looked. But with those scrawny arms, sloped shoulders, and weight of almost 93 pounds, I didn't look healthy to myself.

I wanted to protect Mom from my scary appearance. I feared she would break down into tears when she saw me, thinking I was dying. I wanted to comfort her, to let her know I was going to be fine. But looking at my own images made me tearful. I could only imagine their effect on my mom. I did not send this photo to Mom after all; nor did I post these on Facebook. I couldn't let her see me in this condition. Later, I lost more weight.

Phil took this picture a few days after I created the collage for Mom. The doggy and all of that healthy, green growing nature juxtaposed with a withered, weathered body seemed ironic. The smile on this stick figure is almost amusing now. Growing up with a photographer father, I learned how never to take a bad picture by always smiling. The smile changes everything... even at 91 pounds.

When the scale showed 89 pounds, I thought about my healthy body from a few short months ago. But wait! My body was *not* healthy then. It was sick with cAnswer. This skinny body does not have cAnswer. After three surgeries and maintaining an alkaline diet when I could eat, I looked like I imagined I would look while taking chemo treatments, not before they began.

I knew, if I was going to heal, I had to love this emaciated, hollow, bony shell of a body and feed it well. In order to do that, I looked at that body as if it were not mine. If I viewed it as a wounded animal, a scrawny cat perhaps, I might be able to love it. But all I felt was pity and bewilderment. How could my wonderful body have transformed so dramatically, so quickly? My bones protruded through my chest showing a ribcage I had never clearly seen. When I described how thin I was and how little I weighed to my sister, she said, "Take a picture now!"

I rebelled. Why would I want to capture this hideous image on film?

"Because when you heal, you'll want to see how far you've come and this is your lowest point!" She said that with so much conviciton that I believed her!

In April, when I was first diagnosed, I took the bull by the horns and researched the best healing diet for cAnswer. I released all sugar, coffee, dairy (except cottage cheese), meats, breads/pasta/rice, and most fruits. Anything and everything that will turn into sugar. Sugar feeds cAnswer.

My most painful photo. I shuddered when I looked at myself in the mirror. Horrified, I watched the numbers on the scale drop.

June 19, 2012 FB Post

Not withstanding a little fatigue, all is going well. My appetite is slowly coming back; pain is minimal; sleep is good, and I am grateful! I am on my way today for Illumination Treatment #2. Only an hour, low–dose, once a week. I get the best care on the planet and yes, I get to eat my words of distrust for the medical profession daily....

And with *no* health insurance! We may not even be eligible for medicaid and yet, I am being cared for by the best. I choose now to "Just trust!"

The funny thing is we, I mean Phil, has too many assets. He had worked all of his life in manufacturing plants to provide a decent 401K to retire on, in addition to Social Security. He invested wisely in a few stocks that actually sent him small dividend checks. All of this to live a retired life without much struggle and leave some money to his son and I when he dies. I guess we all just assume that the older one goes first. The things we take for granted!

What I've gained from my experience with the health care providers have given me more than hope. It's given me a chance to heal beyond survival. *I will thrive.*

So we wait and wonder and seek other avenues of help. If not medicaid, then what? It looks like our med bill may reach a quarter of a million. *Yikes!* And yet, I am grateful for the healthcare I have received. *So* grateful! I know *GOD* will provide the rest!

TED: A short while back all before WWII all communities had what they called the community chest (this was not a Parker Bros. invention). This fund which was made up from donations only paid for major medical care for those in the community who could not afford it. My dads mother and father had to use this when she was diagnosed with breast cancer in 1940 and during her 3 year ordeal they covered everything.

KALAR: You are an instrument to witness. With trust, care and faith you understand and give voice to the great medical debacle in this country. Money and healthcare should not equal. Health and care should be.

SHELLY: God I am so overwhelmed by the indomitable Spirit that lives, breaths and has it's Being within Lauren, her beautiful heart, her winsome smile and her powerful Mind! I love her much. Please guide me in my plans to travel to her at the perfect right time. Ring the bell!

JANE: Medical healers are gifts from our Source of Being. I learned that when going through my own cAnswer journey. The angels really are circling.

DOE: Lauren I think about you so much and send you prayers and healing sound. I'll be in Ohio Fri. doing a Crystal Bowl Meditation. We will put your name in our healing circle. Keep checking on possible sources for financial help. I was put in Medicaid to cover my breast cancer but I didn't own a house or anything else for that matter. I was surprised though at the help from the hospital and the cancer society. Much love and respect coming your way sweetie.

DONNA: YES! More evidence of the Consciousness Shift that is happening right before (and just behind) our very eyes. All IS well! We are ONE! God is Good! Amen

JOANNE: Thanks for sharing SO much with us Lauren xoxo

I sought out websites regarding Alkaline vs. Acidic foods. I understood that cAnswer cells cannot live in an Alkaline body. I didn't eat much in the hospital as I was so anti–sugar. An Ensure or a Boost shake came with every meal. The first ingredient was sugar. Sugar feeds cAnswer cells. Hello!? The menu featured items full of carbs. The typical hospital foods of dried–up chicken breast, meatloaf, or fish–sticks befitting of a grade school cafeteria made up the protein offerings. I survived on soup loaded with sodium. Oh well. What the hell!?

In June, I needed strength which meant I needed weight. As my appetite increased I gave myself permission to eat anything to add the weight. How bizarre!

The first week, when I arrived home, I started keeping an energy journal. I looked for patterns or relationships between the treatments and the way I was feeling.

All week I walked more often, with baby steps, and ate better. The hospital stay had seemed to last forever. Now I felt at home on our deck. Monday marked the sixth day away from Chemo/Dreamo treatment #1. I slept most of the day due to fatigue and weakness.

The Chemo/Dreamo treatments were adminstered at Simon Cancer Center in Indianapolis. Phil made the ninety minute drive easier by accommodating my needs. I appreciated the lack of conversation and the lulling drone of the engine. I could be still and cry. The pain lessened but weakness and extreme weariness plagued me. At least the Center gave us a break on parking. Valet parking for patients costs $5.00. They charge everyone else $20. Phil assisted me in getting out of the car. The valet made sure we had everything we needed, then closed the car door behind me. Phil supported me with both hands as I waddled into the building and up to the registration desk.

Trea, a genuinely cheerful and openly loving survivor, greeted me. She found a wheelchair for me when she saw my distress. I eased into it, mindful of my wounded tummy. Then clutching a pillow I tried to sit up straight, grateful not to have to walk any farther. We rode the elevator to the second floor to the infusion center. The elevator doors opened to reveal a wide hallway with floor to ceiling windows on the right side. Doctors' offices lined the left side. A stained glass angel greeted us as it hung from the ceiling.

I entered the waiting room for infusion pods A and B. Plentiful magazines and an ongoing puzzle atop a large round coffee table provided distractions. I signed in with Courtney, and she fastened a medical band on my wrist to ensure that the right drugs went to the right patient. (I hold my more precious information deep within me.) When she asked if I wanted a private room with a bed, I melted. Really? I had only observed rows of reclining chairs, each paired with their own television, on my previous visits. The noise from all of them blended into an uncomfortable racket. When the words "private room with a bed" danced from her lips, I gleefully accepted knowing I would find some peace.

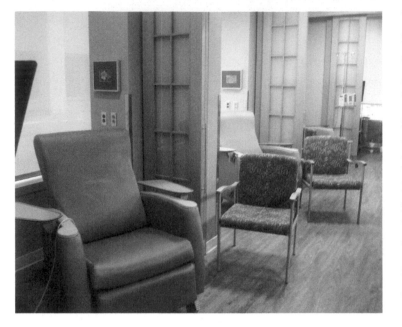

They drew blood through my port and sent it to the lab to see if my counts were good enough to continue with the treatment. The counts came back within acceptable limits. Because I felt the first treatment had been foisted upon me in the hospital I wanted this one to be more controlled for my needs. I remembered the advice given to me by friends and brought my comforts with me—a pretty fleece robe that I made years before, a cooler with fresh water, a peanut butter sandwich, and milk. I brought an iPod loaded with my music accompanied by earbuds. I hadn't been told that the treatment center had stocked refrigerated juice and ice cream for patients. I wasn't drinking the available coffee yet. I chose the free flowing crackers and peanut butter for my weekly mainstay. It wasn't necessary to bring my own blanket and pillow either. The Center provided everything I needed, including slippers. I welcomed their heated blankets. Quick enough, I learned to use the bathroom before they hooked me up. The machinery I dragged around with me created a hazard, but it didn't take me long to learn to navigate easily throughout the area. I then relaxed while the premeds slowly dripped into my port.

The chemo nurse fully supported my desire to *love* the drug before she administered it. I requested Chaplain Lorraine be paged and she arrived right before it was hooked up. Together, we held a little ceremony and blessed the chemotherapy bag, my body, and the expected healing work. Lorraine called God "The Master Physician" that day. We sang together. She provided me with *Healing Touch*, a form of energy healing. In my private room and lying on a bed, I could settle into a safe, warm, healing place where I thought only of love.

I remembered a point, after one of my three surgeries, when I felt helpless lying in bed and unable to do anything at all. I asked in meditation, "What can I do right now to help myself heal?" I heard the word "love." What does it look like to simply love? What does it feel like to be love? I decided to smile at everyone who came into the room and when I remembered, I would say in my mind "I love you so much. If you knew how much I was lovin' you right now, you would just pop."

SPIRITUAL TOOL

Loving What Is

I thought I understood the concept "love what is." I learned to love every part of my job, the lifting, the setting up/tearing down, the driving, the booking, the production. Now, I grieve its loss. I learned to cherish imperfections in situations that revealed syncronicities I might have missed. I'm getting better at seeing the blessings in ALL circumstances. But in loving "what is" right now, here in the hospital, with this big ole scar and swollen gut, unshaven legs, and unwashed short straggly hair my practice accelerates—hard work but it beats being miserable.

I have maintained this practice for years. I love people in the busy and noisy hustle–bustle of airports or restaurants. Sometimes the person of my focus turns and looks at me. Sometimes I see a sigh of peace and relief. If this practice did nothing for others, I would continue because it sure lifts me up. But I believe my sending love actually *does* something for others. I rarely have a negative experience, socially. Waitresses, toll booth operators, bank tellers, and bill collectors become more gentle when I shower them with love. Feeling helpless in the hospital gave me ample time to practice. When I couldn't do anything else, I would actively send out love. More than one person entered my room and noticed a difference in how the room felt. Love, that tangible force, works when I'm helpless.

When no one was around, I turned that love on myself—not as easy. Especially when a part of me believed my no–longer perfect body betrayed me. Especially since my habit was to love my body upon certain conditions.

Now I can Love what is. Holy Shift! What a concept! Especially in Chemo/Dreamo land. I love my cells and thank the healthy ones for dying for my health.

The first track of my musical meditation, Kristen's a cappella *Holy Spirit*, started at the same time as the drip. The music led me into deep surrender, through forgiveness, into release; then from love into rest and acceptance.

At five o'clock, as everyone else in the center finished their daily work, I was unhooked, checked out, and released. We began the process at noon. Wow! Phil wheeled me downstairs where we waited for the valet to retrieve the car. On the way home, the smooth, easy route we experienced during our mid–morning journey, had turned into a congested mess. It didn't bother me as I was still floating from my meditation and the Benadryl. I dozed most of the way home.

I woke up the next day at 9 AM and felt hungry. At last an appetite! I sustained higher energy than I had in a long time. With this energy surge, I attacked the bedroom and cleaned it like a white tornado. I reorganized all my clothing to prepare for where I would be in the next few months—keeping handy long sleeved tops and stretchy pants, and putting away blue jeans, tank tops, shorts, and skirts. I would wear nothing that bound me at the waist or revealed my skeletal arms.

The heat prevented me from wearing my turtlenecks to cover the port sticking out of my clavicle. I wanted to downplay my eerie, Frankenstein appearance, exaggerated by my short cropped hair. I reminded myself I was in no shape to be self–conscious. My job now was to practice loving what is. Practice, practice, practice. When I find it difficult to "love what is" friends like Carole help me.

REV. CAROL MULLINS: Lauren, FINALLY...today, I did not have to preach and remembered your request. I apologize for the delay. Here goes...I met you on Face Book. I was extremely touched as I observed your posts about your physical challenge and how you very courageously faced it and used spiritual principles to champion it. Your story and your photo–journal of it here on Face Book was so very delightful to observe. I sincerely believe that a good many people have received a great deal of courage to face their medical challenges from seeing how you were so lovingly successful. You applied spiritual principles and they worked for you. And for your courage and your willingness to share your story to help others, I greatly applaud you! May God continue to greatly bless you! Light & love.

Holy Spirit
by Kristen Hartnagel

Holy Spirit be my guide
Of myself I can do nothing
Seems it's always been my pride
Shutting out what You've been offering

Holy Spirit You decide
I don't know what anything means
I keep looking to the past
To define what couldn't last
When it's only now that's real

Holy Spirit You decide

Because I know You're always here
And when I listen with my heart,
And quiet my mind
And let go of my fear
What could I be afraid of
When I give my life to You
For I know what I'm made of
And You are eternal truth
Holy Spirit You decide
I don't even need to know
What the question is, or why
Holy Spirit You decide

Chapter Seven

Blessed Chemo/Dreamo

 June 18, 2012 Energy Journal

In my early adolescence, the movies I watched that addressed the horrors of cAnswer left deep impressions. The gut wrenching, tear jerkers *Brian's Song, Love Story,* and *Message from my Mother* depicted cAnswer's darkest side...always followed by death.

While the films did not portray chemo treatments, I learned that chemo may only prolong life...but at what cost? It results in weakness, tiredness, and sickness. It may not encourage any healing at all.

In the '80s, Randy H, Mom's boyfriend, went through chemo and radiation for pancreatic cAnswer. The radiation burned his skin, and they temporarily stopped the chemo while the burn healed. In that gap, the cAnswer spread. Back then I paid litttle attention to his chemotherapy as I lived in another world. I had fallen in love with an artist and moved thirty miles away from home to be with him. So when Mom was dealing with Randy, I was pretty much out of the picture. My sister lived near her at the time. She shared his journey to death with her. I am so sorry Mommy, I wasn't there for you.

The Get Well card she sent shares her full–of–fear feelings. Neither of us needs to allow fear a foothold now!

We've heard and read that chemo is poison and that it doesn't work—that it's all about the money, yet I choose to trust my doctors. My trust confuses me. Being a "sound healer," I should be able to take care of this all by myself, using my wisdom. How dare I attract this into my life! Ok, so I'm pissed off. I'm concerned and confused. Not always mind you, but I know the truth of who I am, so how dare I have those feelings at all? More embracing of my human–ness, don't you think? Holy Shift!

And my hair! I know I'll lose it all, but I feel I've come to grips with that already. I've been cutting it shorter and shorter. When it starts to fall out, I will have my head shaved all the way. I decided to be proactive. I do not want it to just fall out. Shaving it off feels empowering, like I'm in some kind of control.

June 21, 2012 Energy Journal

I see this all day outside our plate glass window. Our enormous Butterfly bush provides whatever butterflies like. It is visited by many different species! What a pleasure! What a healing space! My metamorphosis! What a blessing!

The heat prevents me from going outside, but the picture window provides plenty of nature viewing. Butterflies and hummingbirds dance all day not knowing they have an audience. I could breathe in the entire outdoors as long as the air–conditioning is running full tilt all the time, and I am propped up in my chair with pillows.

June 21, 2012 Energy Journal

As high energy as I was yesterday, today I am that low. I might sleep all day.

That ended the entry. I must've fallen asleep. I could handle fatigue for I found great comfort in sleep. I escaped in dreams of health, so I would sleep for days at a time. My prescribed nausea medications worked to keep me from being sick to my stomach.

While I could keep food down, and while I did have an appetite, another interesting challenge on Chemo/Dreamo had arisen. My mind thought "Mmmm, that will taste good!" Upon the first bite my taste buds betrayed me. Nothing tasted the way I remembered it tasting. I wondered how long this would last? I went through three different breakfasts that morning and made several attempts at lunch. Soup for dinner was something I could drink but could not taste.

Everything tasted like cardboard. Phil tried to poach eggs the way Mom made them, over crunched up saltine crackers with a little pat of butter, my comfort food when I was sick as a child. The combination of the salty crackers, butter, and hot runny egg yolk always made me feel better. This time, I barely choked down three bites.

"Life is a series of natural and spontaneous changes. Don't resist them; that only creates sorrow. Let reality be reality. Let things flow naturally forward in whatever way they like.

~ Lao Tzu

June 25, 2012 FB Post

Interesting new challenge! All my adult life I have struggled with my weight. My top weight was 150 lbs a few years ago. I know that's not much comparatively, but on my small frame, it may as well have read 200 lbs. I hated my body with the extra fat on it. I heard that's what happens when you get older, menopause etc...blah, blah, blah. On my 50th birthday last September, I did it! I reached my goal weight of 120 and was maintaining it well. I used prayer, meditation, and self love to ask my body what I needed next...exercise, what kind food etc. I excelled at this. Then in April I learned I got to heal from ovarian cAnswer. Three surgeries later (complications) and so far two rounds of Chemo/Dreamo (actually awesome) I am 91 lbs. I don't know myself. I have this skeletal quality. Beyond thin, my arms and legs are wrinkled. I know this is temporary, it's just bizarre trying to put weight on now after a lifetime of trying to lose it. What a lesson...many lessons in self love, diligence, seeing the big picture. Now I'm grateful my body is healthy, period! Even in front of the mirror where it is a struggle to see my skin–ness, I strive to love what is. Right now. But what a Holy Shift in the last 6 months!

Taking stock in what's really important.

VERNON: God bless you in your journey. You are an inspiration. Thanks for sharing.

BRENDA: And you had no idea that I needed your words here today, right now, to change a thought pattern with which I have been struggling regarding my body image. Thank you for being a blessed messenger!

JOHNNIE BETH:Your space suit is shrinking, I hope it fills up a little more than 91 lbs. I haven't weighed 91 lbs since I was in high school. Feed it, move it and groove with it. It is your space suit for this planet.

ANN:Our bodies are such temporary temples! Our society places so much emphasis on what they "should" look like... just like before, this is a "before" picture and soon you will have the "after" picture to compare and show what good things have resulted!

MONICA: I am so proud of you. We are beautiful in whatever body we have. I feel confident I got that across to my girls after a lifetime of my own low self esteem.

CYNDI: Dear Lauren, I am sending you so much love and light and smiles and bubbles! What a beautiful shining light you are! Thank you for being in my life! <3<3<3

SHELLY: Prescription—1 to 2 delicious milkshakes a day. Love you. Thanks for birthday wishes.

SANDRA: HOLY SHIFT! WE "ANGELS" LOVE YOU JUST THE WAY YOU ARE BE-ING..Holy Kisses

JOAN: Lauren darling… the answer is in your own words…"I used prayer, meditation and self love to ask my body what I needed next." You will know what taste and feels best for you..... because you already affirm that God is taking care of this as well. Other than that..... perhaps you could just follow me around and eat my stuff ;-}

JUDY: I once had a wonderful opportunity to visit with a man receiving chemo. His statement was this..'all my life I have been teased for being overweight...now that I am going thru this (chemo) I am thankful I had it to lose' . There was wisdom in his words & gratitude in his heart...I will never forget him. You never know what lives you touch in the smallest way and have the greatest impact. Blessings!

ROSS: Lauren your sharing moves me deeply. Thank you for your courage and wisdom. Love Love Love

MICKEY: Thank you, Lauren--for this perspective. We really need to be clear on our intentions--to know what deep messages we might be unaware of that we are nonetheless sending out for an answer. You're so right. Our health is more important than our size.

LYNN: Lauren, I can SO relate to the having to gain weight issue...I had lost way too much weight and needed to build my body up again for a 2nd surgery. I began drinking Isagenix, which is usually a weight–loss drink, drank in place of a meal with water as the mix, but I used whole milk and drank it along WITH my meal, and gained 6 pounds in less than 4 weeks. It is amazing... Builds lean muscle mass, loaded with good stuff. If you want more info, let me know! You are always in my thoughts and prayers ~ Love to you

DONNA: Oh; what a tangled web...Enjoy every moment of the new perspective that allows you to LOVE YOU from every angle!

   LAUREN (my reply): Thank you everyone! I am at my 3rd round of Chemo/Dreamo right now. The scales said 92.4 lbs! I gained a whole pound this week! Way to grow body! Lynn Kirk, I know Isagenix personally! I do the shake 2 times a day plus eat every other hour or so. Weird place to be huh...to need to gain weight!?

ELLYN- You inspire me!! I am a work in progress when it comes to accepting me and my. It can be difficult. Especially when you keep getting the message you don't fit. Thanks for the assist and I know it will get better for us both. Day by day and step by step.

BETTY: Sending warm blessings to you, Lauren. You are an inspiration to all of us! I'll look forward to seeing you again in Florida at your perfect weight. Come on down to visit us at Unity Community of Joy in Sun City Center. We love you.

SHADDIE: Thanks for sharing. It speaks volumes. I hear self acceptance and self love just as I am. We as humans are always trying to improve ourselves instead of loving ourselves just as we are.

RHONDA: I will spiritually send you all my extra calories--honestly, you are in my prayers. Love from one goddess to another. Namaste.

Then there is the magic that happens in the midst of all the shift!

June 25, 2012 FB Post

OMG! I just learned that my van will be paid off in ONE MORE PAYMENT!!! I thought I had another year to go! What a surprise! What a blessing! I had NO idea!!!

June 25, 2012 Energy Journal

The fifth and the sixth day after treatment #2, I slowly felt some energy come back to my body. Walking out on our deck to the end and back is all I can handle. It seems weird to get weak so quickly doing such insignificant things. Getting myself a glass of water is physically taxing.

The day before the next treatment I feel more energy and less pain. I am able to sit out on the deck for a few minutes at a time with big pillows for my bony butt. And just think, I believed my butt was too big once upon a teenage time.

When I visited a bookstore a few years ago "Why I Hate My Thighs" jumped out at me. Opening the book at random, I read a single paragraph: "When we are teased about our body and believe the criticism, our body can become that. Energy flows where attention goes."

They called me "thunder–thighs" and "dunderbutt" in Junior High. I believed their words and they became my truth. I grew literally into the nicknames. My butt and my thighs grew fat.

After high school I taught aerobics and worked my ass off, pun intended, in order to feel good about my body. Ironically, many of the same people who made fun of me in Junior High and High School are friends now because of Facebook and the cAnswer dance. How can I *not* forgive them? They probably don't remember teasing me. Forgiveness may or may not do anything for the other person, but it heals me in so many ways and on so many levels. When I forgive, I release my attachment to wanting to change the past.

SPIRITUAL TOOL

Forgiveness

Reflecting back upon my teenaged angst reveals another layer of the onion to peel. I have actively forgiven the guys in Junior High School, but in my condition now with no butt at all, it's time for more forgiveness. Today I forgive myself for believing the lies in the first place.

June 26, 2012 FB Post

I didn't realize the difficulty of self–acceptance. I was aware of the term "Self–Love," but when I looked in the mirror it was always so conditional. It wasn't until I broke down and felt my true feelings: hideous, out of control, out of shape (this was at 150 lbs) that I knew loving myself was conditional. I prayed to be shown what real love for my body feels like. I grieved. I loathed. I forgave *then* I loved. In 2 years, 25 pounds were gone because I learned to truly love me. After that, everything else fell into place.

Now I celebrate gaining a pound, I'm 92.4 lbs now. Whoo hoo! I see my skinny self and think hideous, out of control, out of shape. I get to learn again in a different way , on a different level, to love me and my body as it is. I get to love me to health.

Just like last week, I have a private room and bed for my 3rd treatment. All the chairs are filled. So busy! I am however grateful, continuously grateful to receive the highest level of care from everyone here in Indy at the IU Medical Center.

My husband is talking to a social worker who is taking our case for medicaid. It is indeed strange to contemplate that all this great service is provided for those of us with *no* health insurance, no visible means to pay. And yet...great care is provided. I am so blessed! I know the $$ will come from someplace. My husband could use your prayers of faith. He is starting to freak a bit with all the bills piling up.

We know the truth and we can hold him in the light of prosperity. Thank you my friends!

KALAR: Sending you love and prayers sweet pea, for an attitude of deep acceptance and understanding at this trauma of the body.

BARBARA JEAN: Lauren how about setting up a medical fund where family, friends, FB friends, the unity community, other spiritual contacts can contribute to help defray the medical costs? Or holding some local fundraisers for your medical costs? People can be really generous when given the opportunity to support the ones they love. I know I would send a contribution. :o)

LAUREN (my reply): Thank you Barbara! I do have opportunities to contribute scattered throughout face book and email. For what I have already received, I am grateful! I'm having people who chose to contribute to payment medical bills send checks to Lauren Powell, PO BOX 1 Stanford, In 47463
Or paypal my email address: singforyoursoul@aol.com

I have had a few Unity ministers send letters/emails to fellow minsters with whom I've served, about tithing to me monthly! What a cool thing! Thank you for holding me in the light!

MARIA: So glad you have a social worker to help you navigate the often deep waters of the Medicaid system! Continued prayers.

GIEO: You are a blazing light even in the midst of all these challenges!

ELLEN: Lauren, remember that God has a store house full of all things needed. All you need to do, is to ask & know that whatever you need can & will be supplied! Lots of love & light is sent as I hold you in the healing love of God, the Creator. You deserve good medical care & treatment as all of do. Don't accept less! Knowing your wholeness

June 26, 2012 Energy Journall

Chemo/Dreamo #3 in Indy. Feeling good and energized this morning. We have to depart home at 11:15 to arrive comfortably by 1:00. Then it's an all day event. When I check in at the Infusion Center I am asked if I have a port. I tell her yes. She then tells me where to wait, suite A or B. When my name is called, a nurse takes me into the bloodwork room. There she accesses and opens my port by pushing in a large but short needle type gizmo. Then she flushes it. Next she draws my blood to be tested. When my numbers come back they decide whether or not they can treat me that day. I go sit back out in the waiting room.

When my name is called again, Phil goes in with me. Today the chairs were all filled so we got a private room. I am so blessed! Zeddy offered me a warm blanket. Phil reads his book while I stretch out among a bunch of pillows.

They took out my staples that day, three weeks after the surgery. The doctor expressed surprise that I hadn't received proper instructions of care. Although my incision showed evidence of healing, it had formed a crust which I thought was normal. So the nurse cleaned me up, then crimped and popped out all eighteen staples. The numbers from the blood draw came back okay, so that day's chemo nurse, Kristen, started the premeds. I always ask for their name. And I love to make the nurses smile and laugh. I can only imagine how high the stress levels remain in a chemo ward.

I assumed the position for attachment of the hoses to my port that allow administration of the antibiotics and the anti–nausea medication. Chaplain Lorraine had been paged and already stood by my side to pray. I loved our brief but powerful visits. Again she offered me healing touch which I joyfully received.

The last of the premeds, the Benadryl, signaled the moment I started my music, *Holy Spirit,* and the next piece, *Every Need is Fulfilled.*

The drugs made me sleepy so I drifted in and out. When the chemo drug, Taxol, started to flow I was already deep into the meditation, and I floated for another hour.

Often I sobbed tears of joy, or tears of fear. I learned to stop judging them and let them flow. When they ended, I was left relaxed and relieved. My gratitude poured out.

Every Need is Fulfilled

by Lauren Lane Powell

Every Need is Fulfilled.
I am rich. I am wealthy.
Everything is provided for me.
I am rich. I am wealthy.

Every morning brings me more.
Too much bounty to ignore.

Every cell is renewed.
I am whole. I am healthy.
Every breath only strengthens my soul.
I am whole. I am healthy.

Every evening takes me home.
Now I'll never be alone.

Every truth is revealed.
I am wise. I am worthy.
Every question is answered in time.
I am wise. I am worthy.

Every dawning brings new light.
Understanding comes with night.

Every thought is a prayer.
I am here. I am happy.
Every day is divinely inspired.
I am here. I am happy.

In the stillness I find peace.
Love and light will never cease.

Every Need is Fulfilled...is fulfilled.

I couldn't yet walk the length of the hospital so Phil wheeled me up and back down again in a wheelchair. We experimented with different routes traveling home, but by the time we got back to Bloomington, it would be close to 7:00 if we didn't stop for dinner. This night, we stopped at Walmart for some groceries, not usually a big deal; but it was the first outing I'd had in forever. I leaned on the cart and moved slowly. This small effort exhausted me, but I found it interesting to watch myself move in such a tentative and calculated way. I would fall over if I didn't brace myself with something. I couldn't help carry the groceries. And with sweet Lucy, I couldn't go the bathroom like normal. *Nothing* was normal.

I filled the week in between treatments with rest. Every day I struggled to walk around a bit. My energy levels rose and fell with no apparent pattern. I could do some data entry, a Facebook post, or work on a newsletter, but mental work wore me out too. When I walked halfway down the driveway, I experienced a big thrill. Otherwise, I contented myself with ambling down the deck and back.

I required less and less morphine to control pain, good news. I took a couple of pills during the day and one at bedtime to help me sleep. Dealing with Lucy woke me up at least twice every night, not pain.

I found loveliness and constancy in the sounds and the sights of nature all around me. When I couldn't count on anything else, I could count on the sun coming up and shining on our yard. I could count on the hummingbirds and butterflies feeding on the flowers. I could count on

**The sounds of nature are the sounds of Love.
All creatures are grateful.**

Blessed Chemo/Dreamo

June 29, 2012 FB Post

OK, I need some clarity. I've been pouring over medicaid forms. If my husband did not have a 20 + year old life insurance policy, if he didn't have a retirement 401K ....? *then* we would be eligible for medicaid/disability. How odd! We have worked all of our lives to do the right thing. Now we learn we have too much to receive help! The money they say we have we won't see until Phil dies. How bizarre is that!?

More trust. More faith! God will provide. God is my source! i just don't get it!

JOHNNIE BETH: Never lose your faith that it is in God's hands. NOW, leave it there. I have a feeling this is all for your husband's faith testing along w/ yours. NEVER GIVE UP!

LINDSEY: And then here is a bizarre possibility...you get a divorce and Phil's resources don't affect your eligibility!!!! Not sure if that is correct or not but would sure be a statement about family values wouldn't it????

SHIRLEY: Correct, friends of mine got a legal divorce and he became eligible. He needed it because he had a liver and kidney transplant and his lifetime limits were used up under his wife's health insurance policy. The only way he could get the ongoing meds he needs was for them to divorce. But their union is with each other and GOD not with each other and USA! Blessings to you Lauren you are surrounded with Love and Light!

TED: Too bad things like the community chest (they still exist in monopoly games) organizations went away. I think you'll just have to become a Pop-Star and then it will be pocket change! I have met people who have had to give up family homesteads.

LAUREN (my reply): You are all right. But sometimes I just need to vent. Thanks for the reminders! What is mine to do is to allow Phil to vent too and not take it personally and stay in my peaceful, prayerful state. I appreciate you allowing me the luxury of "piss–off–ed–ness!" Now please pray for Phil, my husband. Pray for his peace of mind and inner knowingness that All is well and God will provide.

LARRY (my dad): Concentrate on getting well, thank God for the excellent medical service you continue to receive. You are in charge of creating the rest of your life, not fixing our dysfunctional Medicare system. You have what it takes.

JOLLEN: Faith as a mustard seed...the lesson today by Lisa Greco. When it gets added to UCP website, one to listen to.

PAULA: It's expensive to be well. I live just a notch above what they call the "poverty line" and sometimes struggle pretty hard to meet the ends. I don't qualify for any benefits other than my SS disability. But God does provide. It's amazing the channels through which Spirit flows. And what a relief that is!

"Got no checkbooks, got no banks. Still I'd like to express my thanks – I've got the sun in the mornin' and the moon at night."

— *Irving Berlin*

July 2, 2012 FB Post

Here I am in Indy for my 4th round of Chemo/Dreamo—Illumintation treatments! Every forth treatment is a longer one with a second chemo drug introduced. I've got my Amy Camie CD this time among others to keep me in the healing zone!

Lots of good news today! My colostomy and the incision from the surgeries all look great! Dr Schilder was pleased with the weight gain and energy level and used the word "remission" for the first time! What a lovely word!

ALLAKARA: So good to hear from you! Last time I was in church Ed was saying things were not going so well, but sounds like the light and love has been spreading your way!

KALAR: Dear beloved, sending you love and courage and resilience. I know it is so hard, as I have held the hand for another dear friend through two months of chemo and radiation. Keep the faith.

JOHNNIE BETH: YES! YES! YES! I LOVE THAT WORD. I'VE BEEN REMISSED OVER 20 YEARS. REALLY OUT OF THE WOODS. The last X-ray I had for another reason said their were no tumors, just threw that in as part of the diagnosis. I know how excited you must feel! Congrats! Praise God! All IS well!

MADELINE: I see you surrounded by healing light, whole, healthy, full of Love and Life. Blessings Dear Heart.

CAROLE: Yes, remission is a fantastic word! Rich blessings of continued healing to you, Lauren! God's got your back!

STEVE: I like that word—re–mission. It's like gaining a whole new life purpose. Be well.

MICHELLE-Sending love and light your way, Lauren!

KIRA: R E–M I S S i O N...resume your mission!!!! Yay!!!

JOAN: You go girl.Seeing you in radiant health and love, surrounded with all things healing and love filled.

NANCY: What a blessing it is to recognize and see God in action. Have fun with life. Each day is a new beginning with God as your partner, how can one fail. Life is so good!

MARIANNE: Happy Days are here to stay! I love you girl!!!!!!!

PAULA: You are as you were created in love—perfect, whole, healthy and free. And you are loved!

DIANE: So many of us have been through the cancer healing experience. Yes, Remission is a wonderful word. We love it! Join the grateful club. We have amazing doctors that help facilitae our Spritual healing and growth. Blessings and Love

REMISSION

ABUNDANT GRATITUDE

The fourth round of Chemo/Dreamo left me in a state of excitement. The doctor who looked at my numbers told me all were good. She said, "You're headed for remission."

What a lovely word! Remission. I asked her to say it again.

The next morning I awoke in such a state of thankfulness that tears flowed from my eyes. Everything seemed to work in my favor. The centrally located cAnswer was removed, I've experienced wonderful medical care, and I have had the opportunity to live and heal with my best friend, my husband, on twenty–two acres of green rolling paradise. I breathed more deeply every day. In addition, my incision was healing and the swelling was vanishing. Now it looked like a wide, happy smiley face. My energy came and went, but when it went, I took a nap!

More gratitude poured out. I affirmed I was taking the time to heal and did not try to work. I believed I *could* take this time to heal. To all my angels, on this plane and beyond, lifting me up and holding me: You gave me strength when I needed it. You continue to see me well, in a better space than I sometimes see myself. Your vibration keeps pulling me back to Truth. Love Heals! I/we really *are* going to *love* this body to peace. What a gift! I bubbled over with blessings. Thank you again for staying in touch and for all your love and prayers! They form a large piece of my healing matrix!!

The marvelous numbers in my blood count caused the word *remission* to be spoken at this early stage in my healing. To remember when I was first diagnosed, in April, my CA–125 test read 2679. After the hysterectomy it dropped to just above 740. The test is repeated at every fourth treatment when I receive a double dose of chemo drugs. After only three Chemo/Dreamo treatments the infamous CA–125 was just over 400. *I love it.* I did my happy dance!

SPIRITUAL TOOL

Embracing Change

Embracing Change is a lot like Loving What Is, as it is happening. In order for me to love myself in the midst of "dis-ease" I need to see this as a once-in-a-lifetime event. Never before have I experienced all that I am experiencing right now and, I affirm, never will I experience this again.

For me to truly embrace change, I celebrate every passing instant as it happens. I celebrate every instant that has led me to this moment. For me to truly embrace change, I celebrate every dream of seeing tomorrow.

For me to truly embrace change, I bless impermanence.

July 4, 2012 FB Post

This is a recent picture of me walking outside. Don't do it often enough but I am attempting a little yoga now and then. I am up to 95 pounds today and growing stronger!

I made a comment to Phil about my hair being short. He made a valuable observation:

I will never have my long hair and cancer at the same time. "Maybe" he said "Lauren with short hair is the alter ego so the *real* Lauren doesn't have to identify with illness." What a smart man. makes sense to me!

Obviously I was not yet ready to make a current profile picture. I really *loved* the one with the long flowing hair and the elegant yet playful feather. My new do was cute. I was happy to have hair at all. But I missed my mane!

DIANE: Your honey is a smart one! thank you sweetie, for posting this! You are doing so much better. It is good to get a peak;) xox

LITTLE WHITE HAWK: Namaste ~ You are our Beautiful Goddess of Love You look Amazing The little dog looks like he is having fun as well....Looking forward to seeing you again Love and Miss You.

JIM: Lauren Your husband Phil has great wisdom you are looking much better and just remember you are beloved and trust God you will be fine keep those posItive vibes flowing. NAMAST'E

MONICA: Okay well I am just jealous because you look good with short hair. I want to cut mine but it just does not look right! You look so good!

MARIA: Wish I could "beam" you about 50 lbs! You are looking bee–u–ti–full!

LIZ: Short hair is super cute with those gorgeous cheekbones of yours!

CAROL: We are "bowling" for your perfect health here in Texas!

LARRY (dad): So glad to see you venturing out. A step at a time. God bless you Darling Daughter.

KALAR: I'm so happy you are out in nature. It will help heal you. As well as that dog loving on you.

OLIVIA: Nature and fresh air are such marvelous healers. Accept their gift as often as you can sweet Lauren. We love you!

MICHELLE: I love Phil's thinking!!!!

DOE: You look wonderful...Remember to sing for yourself and your healing as you have done for so many others. I sing for you often dear one.

JOHN: Dogs tail is up. You look great. WE played the bowl today at 5. It's a done deal. Sprits are with you. I can feel it. Let it go!

CATHY: Both Laurens look beautiful to me--really, you look very cute with that short hair!

ELIZABETH: You are an amazing lady. Thank you for sharing this journey with us. Peace, love, and wholeness on every level to you.

CHERYL: LOVE this precious visual of Lauren Goddess in her healing energies of nature and pets too!...and the loving wisdom of Phil...Divine!

GIEO: Glad to see you out and about. You have the most inspiring spirit!

KATHY: So many prayers are being sent out to you and for you, keep the faith, love the smile and take it from someone who has dealt with hair issues her entire life...hair is way over rated! Looking forward to you singing the devotion at Peace Cafe again soon.

JOAN: Such a BEAUTIFUL SPIRIT I see here! Thanks for Phil's wonderful comment. What a Sage.

DAN: Thank you for sharing this with us. Be assured of our love and prayers.

TRISH: What a gift you are to the world...know that you are loved by many...seeing you healed right here & now.

EMERY: Peace and love to you and Phil. Thank you for sharing, Lauren.

KATIE: Thanks for the wonderful picture. It's so great to go on FB and see postings from you!

ALISA: When I think of you Lauren I don't about you with your long hair I think about your BEAUTIFUL VOICE And GREAT SMILE...You are AWESOME just as you are...GOD LOVES

Since I couldn't do much else except sleep, time opened up for contemplation and meditation. When I thought of embracing change in the context of my life, I felt irritated and betrayed. But when I meditated on embracing change in the context of my life, everything shifted. As I breathed deeply, I asked, "What does it look like to embrace change? How does it feel?" As I relaxed more deeply I listened for an answer. It came...*gratitude.*

Be grateful for grace when I have it, period. I had learned that lesson years ago. Living a life of love and loss helped teach me to count my blessings while I could. Now, I felt grateful to be alive and that Chemo/Dreamo was working, *not* kicking my ass!

July 7, 2012 FB Post

Is it just me, or are there more of us feeling the "pull?" I know you know how I loved my life on the road by design. I was good at it and touched many people by being a Vocal Visionary. (My dad's words) The pull I feel is to do it differently, bigger somehow, reaching more people than I can on the road. I have no idea how to go about this, yet, but it will be October before I'm out working again. I have lots of time to listen.

Those of you who feel the pull and don't follow it's nudge, prayerfully, be aware. If we don't move on purpose, or in my case *stop* on purpose, Sweet Spirit within creates the Holiest of Shifts that force us to heed the call.

Twelve years doing what I did, loving it yes, But driving, unloading, setting up, doing the workshops, creating the product, on and on. Two years ago I did start making some changes but I wound up working more often and even harder! Who said creating a better life has to be such hard work? I'm ready to work smarted not harder.

Wednesday a friend told me a group in OKC were playing the bowls in my honor. She suggested I join them. Phil got the 17" A, I had the little F. It sounded sweet but after 10 minutes I had to just let Phil play. I couldn't stop weeping, sobbing. Big changes are happening and I grieve letting go of what no longer serves me and God. I ask "What next? Show me? I'm open."

In my case, right now I hear, "Rest, heal, just Be. It will come in due time." Meanwhile I cry. Yeah, this has been a weird week. Phil recognized that I have just about stopped all morphine. Plus double Chemo/Dreamo Monday and now I am losing my hair! I guess I can't escape all of the side effects.

So I just feel what I feel and remind myself that "this too shall pass" and stay connected with family and friends. I realized that I was trying to shield my mom, sister, dad, and stepmom. I wanted to have them and the world see me as consistently optimistic... After all, *that* is who I am! Not this blubbering depressive.

I do not need to shield my family. All of them are here for me. To cry on their shoulder I what I am supposed to do.

Mom's taking me to Chemo/Dreamo Monday, giving Phil a break. It's what she wants to do. Still feel weird about asking for and accepting help. What's up with that?

Thanks to my family and all of you I am feeling better. All we really have is each other. I am grateful. Let us all know that we are being pulled together to create more peace on our healing planet in whatever way we can.

ALLIANA: Thank you dear Lauren. Yes, one time it was my last swim on Baldwin Beach in Maui and I was taking in every single second of the feel of the water, the beach and direct communication came from a whale, "Just Breathe, Just Be..." only to my mind is it a challenge to embody the Truth of these words!!!

MARCY: I've learned the difference between Joy and Happiness myself, recently. Having inner Joy doesn't mean that we're Happy 24/7. We all have Pain and Sorrow and Learning experiences that are Hard... but those are the times that God seems to speak the loudest. I love you so much, Lauren.

JOHNNIE BETH: You maybe be pulling toward the Mayan Calendar prediction. Everyone is really getting anxious in our lives and with our lives. Just fasten your seat belt, I have a feeling it's going to be an exciting ride in the next few months.

ERICA: I know EXACTLY what you're talking about. I think that being my authentic self is my Purpose - this stuff absolutely sucks,and the anger and grief and fear are absolutely part of the Deal. I too, am usually pretty optimistic.

MICHELLE: You inspire me with your wisdom. Hugs and blessings surround you.Lauren.

DIANE: I am glad you're feeling better...I've been pulled from the beginning, and pulling back against it is twice as hard as going with it...just go with it, my friend and don't lose your faith in the Lord.

MONICA: I am letting go of something and grieving. The funny thing is I realized today that not letting go is hurting not only me but the one I should let go. Ouch.

SHERRIE: You sound like Chuck. He doesn't like others to see him less than totally positive and happy. It's totally okay to fall apart sometimes just as long as we don't stay in that place. I've found the need to cry a couple times a week and feel better when I do (I'm not normally one to cry). We also have had to get over asking for help. We are blessing others by allowing them to help. Sending blessings, love and healing thoughts your way!

MAMA RED: Ah sweetie...such wise words and that asking for help thing is/can be a toughie for sure. I know that pull and I know sometimes listening to it can be a challenge too (I've done that "OK, I'll get you to listening by STOPPING you thing and admire you for listening now.). Please ask, please receive. You're so darned amazing!

SUE: I know not what to say except that we continue to hold you in light and love and know that you are still as God created you...perfect and whole

ART: Lauren, when I was in this position, my calling was to begin writing books. It took getting the message several times before I actually acted upon it. Now I have three books published with more coming. And it just feels right, because it is God who sent me the message.

JOAN: Darling Lauren, I know how difficult it is for you to yield to tears and to ask for help.... but it is the Yin to the Yang of helping others. By "asking' you are allowing others to help you.... which helps them. It is all a lesson.

CHERYL: Thank you, thank you, thank you, Precious Lauren for your heart and soul sharing, and for the Gift of You! YES ... I am feeling the Holy Shift, the Pull as you can it, personally and collectively. The time is NOW, we awaken to the Truth of Holy Spirit and the availability of doing things differently and being BLESSED magnanimously as we open our consciousness to the LOVE and guidance that is eternal. EVEN, and ESPECIALLY, as we have our earthly, human emotions and breathtaking pains, we EMERGE into the TRUTH of our BEING. LOVE and APPRECIATE YOU ALWAYS, DEAR ONE

DOROTHEA: Yes, me too, I am feeling the pull. Reaching more people with music without stress could be producing CDs peacefully at home and then release them to the world.

SHARON: Dear Lauren remember the last Reiki Retreat? Receiving gifts accepting them? Whether it be compliments, material things, HELP with what your needs are at this present time. I learned so much from you at the retreats that have impacted my thoughts.

KRISTEN, my sister: Your sharing of the story of your journey means so much to all but being a part of it with you means so much to those allow the privilege

KATHY: Lauren you are wise beyond your years!! I truly think you have connected with the source of your being (GOD) and are being guided in ways you have yet to discover. LISTEN to that source without worry or guilt. REST the body and soul. LEAN on others as they are with you on this journey. IMMERSE yourself in that wonder–filled presence of God

JUDY: With ya girl...listen and you will know what to do. You taught me that!

MARIAH: Sometimes those of us in 'music service', especially in Unity, I think can sucumb to the pressure of feeling like we have to be 'on' all the time. Having been doing this for 13 years, I used to find I would be embarressed if I was at a service and didn't feel on top of everything. Then I started to find that if a minister's talk moved me to tears, I didn't have to pretend I was ok, but let the emotion take me deeper. those are the time when people were often moved. These days i am feeling incredably pulled, but not sure exactly why or how it will all look. I know totally what you are saying. And yes i feel it is supposed to be bigger, reach more people. I totally applaud your courage and faith as you go through this challenging process!!

BARBARA: Dearest Lauren, You are not a "blubbering depressive." You are doing some grieving and deep inner adjustment. The tears can be humbling but they are also healing. No need to judge or condemn your natural process. For me, every major adjustment takes some scary, painful letting go. The beauty of it all is that God knows and God shows the way. New doors of GOOD are opening to you and I see you going forth with all the strength and support you so richly deserve. For now and for as long as it takes, rest, bless, BE and know that you are in the arms of the BELOVED. Let the future unfold. It may surprise you and wouldn't that be fun?

ChapterEight
Holy Shift! I'm losing my Hair!

Spontaneously in January, before my diagnosis of cAnswer, and as an act of service, I cut my long hair to shoulder length and donated ten inches to Locks of Love, a charitable organization that makes wigs for cAnswer patients. In April, it had grown enough that I still had longish hair, just not *long* hair. Then, after diagnosis and mentally preparing for hair loss, I had it chopped into a shag–type style just before the first surgery in April. In June I had it bobbed three to four inches all the way around like Frankenstein. Taking gradual steps in reducing my hair length reduced the trauma of losing my mane of long, flowing locks all at once. But the first morning I woke up to see a furry pillow, I freaked out. In contrast, our cats left hair everywhere, including my pillow. I slept on that hair with great joy because it indicated a cat nearby that might curl up beside me. But rolling over to discover, in my periphery, a thick sheet of straight hair making a nest under my face proved shocking. I wailed in grief.

After the tears stopped flowing my face began to dry, leaving my wet lips tasting salty. The scene shifted when my heaving sobs dissolved into normal breathing. As I regained my composure, the air around me felt different, like the cleansed and refreshed air after a hard rain, as if the world has been rinsed clean. I really had to *feel* those emotions, so I could shift and experience true release.

SPIRITUAL TOOL
Grieving on Purpose

Mom says she is grateful that both my sister and I keep our tears close. We know releasing toxic energy contributes to a healthy body, and understand the damage created from stuffing our feelings and stifling the tears. I've been a crier all my life. I cry at the drop of a hat...

"Oh! That poor hat!"

July 12, 2012 FB Post

Thank you all for your peaceful thoughts, love and permission to be right where I was!

"This too shall pass" and it did!

This past Sunday mom came down. Monday she drove me to Chemo/Dreamo to give Phil a break. In that eventful treatment I had a mishap with Lucy, my colostomy bag. No more detail right now, but we spent 40 minutes in the bathroom waiting for a new bag to come from the farthest wing of the hospital!

Mom reminded me that she changed my diapers, then she started singing, "Today while the blossoms still cling to the vine." I joined her in harmony. We sang the entire song. Eventually I received what I needed. A very attentive chemo nurse and the ostomy nurse checked me out and assured me that I was not not their first blowout. The best news, after all of that, my numbers were good! Each week my white count is up a bit and my hemoglobin is a bit higher. Every sign points to healing fully!

I spent a relaxing and fun Tuesday at home with mom and Phil. A good day. Then yesterday for the first time, I ventured out of the house with mom...

This bit of background will paint a clearer picture of the magic that transpired that day. As I adjusted to Lucy I learned that she expanded due to gas that needed to be released. The ring around the appliance is built to be lifted off to burp her. This time I went to burp her and found out she was *not* full of gas. I had eaten handfuls of fresh blueberries the day before. Who knew? I didn't know I was supposed to carry extra colostomy supplies with me. That's why every poop bag company had sent me a cute little inconspicuous canvas bag the size and shape of a dop kit. (Toiletry bag for those of you younger than 50.) Live and learn.

You can paint your own picture of what happened next...or not. I had burped dirty blueberries! The pretty peach dress that Phil had bought me the week before, a light and breezy nothing that clung to my tender skin, streaked with dark smelly stains. Mom and I waddled into the chemo treatment bathroom and waited...and waited.

Mom washed the mess out of the dress while I stood there naked, crying. Thank God this happened at the hospital and nowhere else. At that moment however, I found no gratitude in my heart. Still thin, with a bony butt, it hurt to sit on the toilet. Tiredness and weakness prevented me from standing for long. And Lucy kept spewing into one container after another. It was like watching the "Alien" movie as this massive amount of crap spewed furiously from a hole in my gut. I was mortified, terrified, disgusted, and close to hysterical.

"Maybe one day we'll be able to look back on this and laugh," my mother offered.

I could find no humor in this now or in the foreseeable future.

"Honey, I changed your diapers!"

As if I didn't know that.

"But Mommy, I'm almost 51 years old!"

At that moment she started singing. The energy completely changed. Grace wrapped her arms around me and reminded me of the beauty in all things. I joined my voice with the voice of my mother angel, blending in familiar familial harmony that bathed the room with bliss. We had swaddled ourselves in sounds that offered serenity. When the ostomy nurse finally arrived with backup supplies a Holy Shift had happened, and all was well.

That day in the middle of a painfully disastrous moment by anybody's standards, my mom sang to me. She lifted the vibration and transformed the energy around the dreadful experience and its memory. I so love my mommy's voice and her willingness to use it to make me feel better. Thank you so much Mom. I love you.

July 12, 2012 FB Post

So yesterday, mom and I shopped for wigs! As we were leaving Phil noticed a bulge in mom's tire. After the bank and lunch in the air conditioned, pillow–lined car, we bought a new tire. 30 minutes tops. No biggie and now she's safe to return to South Bend.

The only place in Bloomington to buy a wig is the "Wigwam," a small privately owned shop near downtown. Charlotte, 82 yrs. young, spent an hour and a half with us. I tried on 10–12 wigs. I wound up buying two of them. As we wrapped things up, Charlotte said something about the owner of the Wigwam. We assumed it was she who owned it. She's worked there for many years but the owner's name is Claralee. Mom and I looked at each other in tears. That is *her* mother's name! No coincidence. We knew she was fully present, with us at that moment. What memories we created!

Blonde, brunette, long hair and short, we tried on all of them. As icky as I felt, this coming out gifted my mom and I. Since we couldn't get back to our old normal, we created a new normal.

My middle ached from all the surgery, Lucy stubbornly stayed active and boisterous, I felt I could sleep at any moment if I could just lie down, and my hair fell out in clumps. In spite of this, we celebrated every minute of our time out together.

> *"Ancient Egyptians believed that upon death they would be asked two questions and their answers would determine whether they could continue their journey in the afterlife. The first question was, 'Did you bring joy?' The second was, 'Did you find joy?'"*
>
> — *Leo Buscaglia*

My grandmorther, Claralee Schantz, had a reputation as a saint according to many family members and friends. In 1948, her husband, Earnest, died as the result of a brain tumor. Then in 1949, my mom, at age nine, and her brother, age fourteen, suffered from polio leaving my Uncle Larry in a wheelchair. When Claralee died at age forty–six from a second bout of cAnswer that showed up in her brain, my mom was only twenty–one. I could never imagine losing my mommy at such a young age.

Claralee lived with us for the last few months of her life. Mom cared for her and watched her die. Knowing what she knew about cAnswer from so many sources, Mom must've been terrified for me. I was determined to do it differently and survive. To give her hope would be a Holy Shift. I remained convinced cAnswer was *not* a death sentence for me, despite it taking so many others.

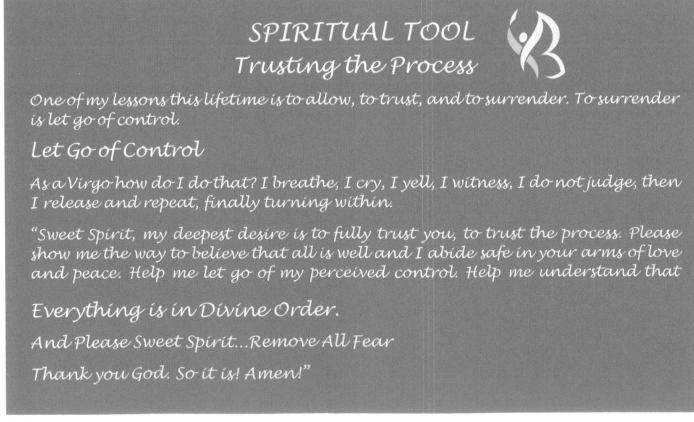

SPIRITUAL TOOL
Trusting the Process

One of my lessons this lifetime is to allow, to trust, and to surrender. To surrender is let go of control.

Let Go of Control

As a Virgo how do I do that? I breathe, I cry, I yell, I witness, I do not judge, then I release and repeat, finally turning within.

"Sweet Spirit, my deepest desire is to fully trust you, to trust the process. Please show me the way to believe that all is well and I abide safe in your arms of love and peace. Help me let go of my perceived control. Help me understand that

Everything is in Divine Order.

And Please Sweet Spirit...Remove All Fear

Thank you God. So it is! Amen!"

July 12, 2012 FB Post

Hey to my South Bend friends! I'll be in the Bend Thurs—Sun this coming week.

Mom and I will be at the Farmers Market Restaurant Friday, July 20th between 11:00 AM and 1:00 PM. We would love for you to come by and visit!

July 2012 Energy Journall

June 17th was a Tuesday and my highest energy day yet! I busied myself with organizing and cleaning all day. I felt awesome. I wanted to memorize how it felt to feel no fatigue and no tummy discomfort; and to be satisfied at the end of the day. I rested the next two days until it was time to go to South Bend—my first weekend away from home.

I'd been house–bound since April, only getting out with weekly hospital visits. At home I lived in Phil's anti–gravity chair. I hated it before I got sick, as it was so big it swallowed me up. Now I think it's perfect, with all the pillows and padding to cushion my bony bum.

Phil drove me to Kokomo, after finding an anti–gravity chair for me to use at my mom's. Mom met us there, the half–way point. As storms were forecasted, Phil had brought the dogs along with us. But he couldn't leave them in the car with the high heat, so he turned right around and went home. While Mom and I ate a bite at Ruby Tuesday's (we call it Tuby Ruesday's) the sky opened up. It poured for a long time. We left when the rain stopped. I didn't know I could sit at a restaurant that long ...upright. Remember I had been reclining for three months.

Mom pulled into her parking spot behind her apartment at 10:00 PM. By that time, I needed to go right to bed, but first I had to climb a full flight of stairs. I vowed never to take normal functioning for granted. I struggled up each step to the top, surprising myself with my strength. For the next couple of days I would need as much strength and energy as I could muster. Falling asleep, I prayed for a day like last Tuesday, pain free and highly energized. That is just what I experienced!

I love Farmers Market, the site of my meet and greet day on Friday. First my family and extended family met for breakfast—Mom, Dad, Mary Ann, her sister Sally, my nephews Ridge and Mattux. I was trying to put on weight so I ordered eggs Benedict, hash browns, and coffee. Yum!

The family hugged me and said their goodbyes after breakfast. Mom stayed with me and we sat at the tables outside the restaurant and waited for my other visitors. Mom's friends Kaye and Glenda arrived first, later joined by Jolene from Unity and another good friend, Bryan Edington. Bryan's eyes told me he was glad to see me looking as good as I did.

Bryan and I have worked together for a long time. He played stellar guitar on most of my CDs and, from his home recording studio, also produced the first ten CDs I released. (including the Vocal Lesson set, as one project). When I lived in South Bend, Indiana, we gigged in the '90s. Bryan would sing harmony with me, and I with him. After Phil and I moved to Bloomington in 1999, we reconnected with Bryan and his music at the Wheatland Music Festival.

Regarding Bryan: I met the most wonderful people in my travels. My visit to Cincinnati in 2000 created another best friend, Janet, a fellow soprano and another lover of laughter. A nurturer, she took great pride in her job of cleaning other people's homes. After several years she obtained her massage therapist license. That's when I introduced her to Bryan.

He moved to Cinci and lived with Janet happily–ever–after until Janet was diagnosed with kidney cAnswer. She died slowly under the care of hospice during December. After that, Bryan moved home to South Bend to heal and redefine himself. So I found it important to be able to provide a different memory of cAnswer for him. I promised him I wasn't gonna die, even though two weeks ago, I looked as if I might at any moment!

At Farmer's Market, South Bend, IN   *Farmer's Market Stool*

No, it's not a smiley face. Those two indentations are from my butt bones. Since I've always been concerned with a big butt, not having one is weird. I'll have to shape it the way I want with yoga and walking,

Mom and I stopped for a gelato before leaving the Market. On our way out we spotted Nanci Sanders. We almost missed her. It pays to stop for dessert.

I included Nanci's "bio of our friendship" earlier. She played organ for my college recital. She faithfully followed my posts and encouraged me to write my experiences in a book and include others' journeys as they weave into my own. Her excitement and energy supported me when I said writing would be an opportunity to make a difference in people's lives.

"More than you will ever know." She beamed at me the same way my mom would when watching me perform. I took her words to heart and I'm fascinated to watch it unfold.

We stopped next at Milton House Retirement Home to visit a friend I knew since the early '90s. In 1992, I earned my degree in Music Education and landed a job teaching in three different schools every week. I loved the kids' energies and interest when I instructed them to move, sing, and learn by "doing." I taught for thirty minute periods in a gymnasium that doubled as a music room. In this first teaching experience I encountered discipline problems with my students. The combination of the gym and the freedom in my class as compared to their quiet math and English classes, encouraged terrible and disruptive behavior. It took too much of my energy to maintain discipline and I couldn't teach in my usual manner.

Heaven came to my rescue after a wondrous, magical holiday stage show including all ages. The principal, who reminded me of Captain Kangaroo with his white hair and mustache, called me into his office. I thought I was to be reprimanded as so many teachers had complained about my energizing effect on their students. Instead he informed me that the school district had decided to give me a promotion to the high school. They were *demoting* the current music teacher to my job. This entirely political move caught me in its tide.

At Michigan's Niles High School, my opportunity to initiate real art excited me. I choreographed a play and danced with the kids to Janet Jackson's music. I managed a 120 member mixed choir, a 60 member girls choir, and a 24 member show choir.

Best of all, a professional costume designer served as my assistant, my secretary, my sounding board, and my best friend. Evelyn Bolton had worked with the music department since the '70s, initially as a volunteer, then as a paid employee. We spent the spring semester together until I was laid off. She retired, and the former teacher moved back into his space. After a solid, action-packed year including every kind of vocal music and teaching at every level, I knew for sure I had finished my experiment with teaching.

As in everything, many gifts came out of that year. Meeting "Mom" Bolton was the grandest. After all these years we have remained friends. Now she lives in a nursing home. During our visit she wondered why, at age 92, she's still here. We have always talked openly about God, living, and dying. I didn't have an answer for her. I love her dearly, however, after all the visiting I had done, I grew weary. As we hugged goodbye, I noticed the similarities in our delicate frames.

My mom and I returned to her apartment and she poured me into the anti-gravity chair. She played Rogers and Hammerstein's *Cinderella*, then *Carousel*, then *Hair*, then *Oklahoma*, and finally our favorite, *Jesus Christ Superstar*, on the piano for as long as I could stay awake. I sang along on this familiar, magical, and therapeutic musical journey, at times pulling my stitches on the high notes. I loved singing again, moving air, breathing deeply, and creating sound. Because we sang when I was healthy, I felt healthy again as I sang once more. Many songs moved us to tears facilitating wonderful releases. Another layer of healing and forgiveness of old situations peeled off in the therapy provided by the melody and the songs" symbols.

One example is Simon and Garfunkle's *Bridge Over Troubled Water*. That song first came out when Mom and Dad had been fighting, creating unhappiness for everyone. To me, the song meant I was the bridge to keep the peace, to support my mom, and to pacify my dad. Much later that song triggered tears when I remembered how miserable I felt during those past events. But with my forgiveness work of consciously releasing old feelings and beliefs, that song and many like it no longer give me that emotional charge. In the dance with cAnswer these songs shifted me into a new level of forgiveness and healing. I appreciated that Mom gave us the gift of music. At every party, no matter what, we would sing.

I dozed while Mom fixed my favorite meal, hearty beef stew in a rich tomato base accompanied by drop biscuits smothered in butter. I looked forward to the flavors mingling in my mouth when I woke up. Alas! I was not relishing the flavors I remembered and loved. The broth tasted bitter and too salty, the meat flavorless. The biscuits tasted like cardboard slathered with Crisco. Chemo/Dreamo may not have made me sick, but it stripped me of my taste buds. What a weird thing!

After eating a little, I slowly climbed the stairs with Mom behind me for support. Sleep came easily, as it did all through the journey. I slept deeply throughout the night in my mom's guest bedroom on the bed my husband and I used many years ago.

Sunday Mom and I visited my original home church, Unity Church of Peace in South Bend, Indiana. I had missed Unity Church since my last speaking engagement at Unity in Pensacola on April 1st. Rev. Sandy announced my presence from the pulpit. I imagine I looked odd with my short hair, now thinner than ever with a mostly shiny scalp.

Attending precious Unity again allowed me to experience people's tangible love and support. So many followed me on Facebook. Everyone hugged me, some with tears in their eyes. Rev. Barbara, my first Unity minister, was all smiles and hugs. Another friend said what most were thinking, "You look a whole lot better than I expected you to look. Is that appropriate?"

I told her it absolutely was appropriate. It occurred to me that perhaps my visit was as much for my friends as it was for me. How else might they think about someone healing from cAnswer except tired and weak? What a great visit it was!

That evening, I went to Indy with my dad. We spent time with cousins Jon and Nit and their daughter, Alyson Powell, who had recently undergone gallstone surgery, and son, Adam. Alyson and I must have sounded like two old biddies comparing scars and healing stories. Adam gave me a hug. He's a fine young man excited about his future at mechanic school. How nice to have family nearby! They took great care of Dad while he stayed with them each time I was hospitalized.

Recreating a new "normal" taught me to embrace and appreciate impermanence.

—Lauren Lane Powell

July 23, 2012 FB Post

I shared a synopsis of the previous information on Facebook.

SHARRON: Thank you for sharing your beautiful self with us once again, Lauren. Keep basking in the love and healing energy of your family and friends. Soak it up and feel your own energy rising, expanding, filling you with strength and well-being beyond your imagination.

SCOTT: Hi Lauren, I don't know you. Sought you out to ask you to sing on my new CD. Yet I must say that I am touched by your perspective and beautiful spirit.

DIANA: I am so happy for you; you inspire me and give me courage!

JOHNNIE BETH: Very Good! Very Good! YEAH! I am proud of you! Welcome to the survivor's club! Yeah! I am so tickled pink for you! I know your spirit will rub off on me.

CHRISTINE: Lauren, thank you for sharing with us about your process and strength retuning. I love how you tried to memorize how it felt to be healthy again. Holding you in prayers for vibrant health restored, by divine grace and design! You are my hero!

ELAINE: Was just wondering about you and was going to look you up on FB, and there you were, right under Armand...I'm glad you're doing, feeling better and better. Many love you and see you whole. Blessings and appreciation,

JUNE: Love and Light to you. Thanks for sharing your story of recovery and life.

SUE: Glory be dear Lauren...the peace of God and joy are witnessed in your story and your image

So Many People Walk this Journey with Me.
It Makes it All that Much More Magical.

~ Lauren Lane Powell

July 24, 2012 FB Post

I want to dispel the myth of the "Horrors of Chemo." IU Med does it differently in that they give me a lower dose every week. Every third week I get two chemo drugs instead of just one. While it is an all–day event, I find myself looking forward to the imposed rest. I listen to my meditation and my and my sister's music during the actual treatment. The rest of the time is preparation.

Vitals, blood drawn and read, premeds then the chemo. I have only been nauseated once in the hospital and once at home. The meds work, but I don't take them unless I need to and I don't need to. My fatigue feels less and less evasive as the days pass. My appetite is awesome. I eat every two hours to gain weight and get to eat anything I want. My hair is slowly shedding. Eventually I may lose it all. Even that's ok now. I'll paint my head! I'll be creative!

I've met the nicest people, the nurses who are so attentive, so authentically loving, and so professional. I want them all as my friends! I request the same Chaplain who saw me inpatient, from the beginning. Lorraine prays with me and anyone who is there (nurses included) that wants to pray, and sings to me. I can finally sing again after three months!

So even chemo therapy can be magical! After yesterday's double dip, I have so much energy it's difficult to sit down long enough to get on the computer. I've got things to do!

JOHNNIE BETH: I so appreciate you proving that attitude is everything. I believe in miracles and asking for them, too. Praise God from whom all blessings flow. I flow gently and easily w/the River of Life.

SOPHIA: I'm so glad that you're sharing this journey with us. You really are a light!

OLIVIA: You continue to inspire us all and light the way!

ELSIE: What a love–filled post. I'm blessed by your writing.

KATIA: You can be very proud of yourself.

LARRY (Dad): She means it. I was with her during the last (7th) chemo.

JANICE: Our Granddaughter called it Nemotherapy***

JOHN: Thanks—best post of the day—to hear you doing well. We pray you get well. You are not done yet. Lots of love.

JEANINE: So wonderful to hear you are back and receiving such good care from everyone, cause we are all behind you. luv u.

KATERINA: You are an amazing person and if they could bottle your courage and strength they would make you millions You are always in my prayers.

HENNIE: Thanks for sharing your story; it's inspiring.

LEANNE: Lovely. You are inspiring.

SANDRA: HOLY KISSES! Thanks for sharing! Keep up the great DIVINE working order! Luv Ya!

EDNA: I am so happy that you are doing well keep your spirits up. When we talked right before you started all this, I knew that you would make it and survive just like I did when i went through all of the treatments.

STEVEN: I don't know you but I am so glad that you are having a positive experience with your chemo, as I know that many do not. You are very fortunate and blessed, and I admire your spirt and attitude. You seem like a very strong and positive person and I want to say God Bless You. Good luck to you .

EVAN: I went through chemo 20 years ago, before they had all these wonderful anti nausea drugs that they have now. I was soooooo sick for months, but my stage 4 brain tumor is gone, and has been for 19 years now. That makes all the sick days worth it. I am alive!

SALLY: This is fantastic news. Very encouraging about Chemo as well.

CHRISTINA: You are an amazing inspiration to many!

SPIRITUAL TOOL
Music to Create Peace

I wish I felt up to singing more often. I desire to play a more active role in my healing but, for now, the best I can do is listen. Listening keeps me in a place of peace and acceptance. I can feel a difference in my body before and after my meditation. That solid hour or more of breathing and feeling healing tones enter my body through my ears continually amazed me.

My inner peace extended out into the room. Upon entering, nurses would mention how good they felt. As that palpable peace expanded, everyone returned it to me, amplified.

Finding the place of surrender and gratitude grew easier. Every week I allowed my music to wash over me, wrap me up, take me deep, lift me high, and carry me away. I celebrated healing with my dad and, on the prior weekend, with friends who loved me that I loved in return. The song that stood out on my iPod this week was *Healthy Are the Ones.*

My numbers were so good I danced. I played the Black Eyed Peas' song, *I Got a Feeling* and danced in celebration like a ninny. Dad filmed it. When I look at it now (healed and three years future) I remember vividly how good it felt to know that I was healing. Between the Chemo/Dreamo, prayer, Reiki, my own meditations, and my body's willingness, I was healing and the numbers proved it! CA–125 from over 2400 down to 77 with only seven treatments…and three surgeries.

Healthy are the Ones

by Lauren Lane Powell

Healthy are the Ones who love me

Healthy are the ones I love

Healthy from within, without,

Below, between, and up above.

Healthy is the air I breathe and

Healthy is the water that I drink

Healthy is the food I eat and

Healthy are the thoughts I think.

July 24, 2012 FB Post

7th chemo of 15 and blood work shows everything normal and CA125 (cancer indicator) down from 2000 to 800 to 400 (last week) to 77! Let me point out that my father is 77, this is 7th treatment and the reading was 77. I guess our lucky number is 7.

Larry Powell uploaded a new video, Lauren Lane Powell Celebrates.

https://www.facebook.com/larry.powell.3975/videos/4435226967059/?pnref=story

TERI: Doing "The Happy Dance", that's awesome. I love you Lauren!

DIANE: You are such an inspiration, Lauren!! Love you and your wonderful energy!!!

SHARRON: You, your spirit, and the video. Way to go, Lauren!!!

JULIE: Cutest video ever!!!!!

KELLY: Happy, happy, happy! And I'm happy for you!

LINDA: Wonderful! So good to see you celebrating the great news!

JUDY: Hallejala Jesus. Don't know you, but I am thrilled for you.

RUTH: This is another one of those times when FB needs a "love" button in addition to the "like" button. :))

VERNON: In numerology 7 is the Christ number.

KAYE: NO like, love

SALLY: It was so nice to see you when you visited in S.B. You are amazing with your positive attitude and great spirit. It would help others going through similar circumstances to read about your journey

Chapter Nine
Oceans of Emotion

My Aunt LaRue from Texas bought me his beautiful satiny robe with two–piece matching pajamas. However, I didn't receive them until my mom and I discovered the set, still in the wrapper, when we cleaned out Aunt LaRue's house after she passed away. She called herself "Aunt Purple" after the color of almost everything she owned.

I caught my purple fever when I was eight years old from my Aunt LaRue, my Aunt Purple. This love is reflected in at least three-fourths of my wardrobe and I surrounded myself with my favorite color while I healed. The more I wrapped myself in my favorite things, the more peace I felt.

I adapted well to my new normal but not to Lucy. I tried to personify her, and to not take it personally when she insulted me with the pain, noise, and stench. I received new brands of bags or appliances, and adhesive or deodorizer two or three times a week; followed by phone calls from salespeople asking about my fit. I eventually realized that Lucy would never truly fit well. I would have to tolerate her until she was reversed. Reversed! Hmmmm. I couldn't go there now. One day at a time.

This beautiful matching scarf arrived from my sister–in–law, Karen. Talk about perfection!

July 30 2012 FB Post

This is a great "Good Morning" post. On my way to Indy today for Chemo/Dreamo #8. More than half way through!

July 31, 2012 FB Post

I sure do love and appreciate my parents! As a kid living through mom and dad's break–up, I was amazed when they both came to every function, every event, every performance. It would have been easier on them to skip it.

Now at 50 years old, to see them both at my bedside along with my stepmom, I learned again how much I am loved by them. I am so blessed!

DIANE: It was later when we had a family crisis that my kids came to understand that my husband and I both would always be there for them united. I thank my lucky stars we were able to get to that level. You are committed as a family through it all....warts and all.

ERICA: I've had something of a similar experience. My mom accompanied me to many many of my chemo appts. I have a greater tenderness and appreciation of her than I've had before. My dad. Well, I never told him I had cancer and he passed away while I was in radiation. I didn't feel like he could deal with it, and I didn't have the energy to deal with him not dealing with it.

DIANE: What you said brought tears to my eyes, Lauren.

FRANCES: It is so true that those we call friends can when the going gets tough and you need support...not really be there...not in the same way and...it will most always be your family who is by your side, forever and always

KRISTEN; We have always been so blessed. How wonderful to feel it even more fully! Loving every family member! Thank you all for your presence!

Susan: I am so glad they are there for you and I know you are also there for them

I remember the moment I noticed the shift begin. In 1984, my sister won a pageant in Bloomington. where she was crowned Miss Hoosier Hills. She sang Barbara Streisand's "Everything" from the film, "A Star is Born" with beauty and grace onstage. While she accepted her title and was briefed on her new obligations our parents and their significant others had gathered together at a round table outside the auditorium. Mom and Mary Ann sat next to each other; and Dad and Randy, mom's boyfriend, sat together. All appeared earnestly interested in each other. I memorized the feeling of healing from that moment, a decade after the divorce, that Holy Shift. The extended family has bonded since that time. We've all traveled together and spent holidays with each other. I'm grateful to be a part of such a happy, healthy family after what we went through in the '70s!

July 31 2012 FB Post

This week, everything in the blood–work looked good except the immunity, bone marrow. So instead of getting premeds and Taxol, they sent me home. My body will build more strength without chemo for a week.

The best news this week is that I weigh 100 pounds now. Yeah baby! My lowest was 89 a month ago...! Thank you all for your prayers. We know prayer works.

Huh, turned away from chemo. I didn't know how I felt about that. It wasn't worth the trip to Indy. I wish they could have informed me to stay home instead of waiting until I arrived in Indy and then telling me to go home. Oh well.

My home sanctuary provided a safe, green, blooming, loving, and healing space. The country isolation allowed a quiet energy to nourish my body and soul, away from the hustle and bustle of too many people. The only germs I experienced there came from our animals, and I considered cat and dog germs as deeply healing. So instead of curling up with chemo, I curled up with a couple of dogs and a kitty cat or three. I thanked God for the place I call Home.

August 2, 2012 FB Post

At the center of my being I have the answer. I know who I am, and I know what I want. Now I listen to that center and move forward.

CARLA: Wonderful, thanks Lauren! I will share this!

SCOTT: EXCELLENT POST LAUREN! I lost sight of this. Perfect. I woke up and tears fell, I chose right then to just believe. I found a that the treasure was buried inside me and that it wasn't very deep.Then I found the power to just....be. The power of eternity. All fear of death left me and I fell in Love!

ALISA: LOVE JOY PEACE LIGHT!!!! Thank GOD I AM ALIVE!!!

SALLY: It was so nice to see you when you visited in S.B. You are amazing with your positive attitude and great spirit. It would help others going through similar circumstances to read about your journey

August 2012 Energy Journall

It's August and I'm almost half–way through Chemo/Dreamo treatments. My hair comes out in thick gobs. Every morning a light brown film covers the pillow. Each shower rinses off more. Merely running my fingers through my hair results in a wad on my hands. I knew what to expect, but had not fully prepared myself for how I would feel about this. I had become used to having short hair. Now I'm heading toward baldness.

I still sleep a lot. I can sleep in the morning easily until 9:00 or 10:00. I take a nap on the couch before *Curious George* on PBS. I move to the big recliner in the late afternoon. I find myself looking at the clock at around 8:00 PM. Is that too early to go to bed? But I am grateful to be alive and growing healthy!

Myrtle Filmore, my hero, healed herself from tuberculosis by reminding herself, "I am a precious child of God and therefore I do not inherit illness. I am a precious child of God and therefore inherit only perfect health." She and her husband Charles founded Unity after she healed. It is from these teachings that I drew my strength and wisdom. The practice worked when I practiced! Hmmm. Imagine that!

August 4, 2012 FB Post

My precious caretaker, housekeeper, chef, pet lover husband has done it again! And I forgot gardener! Last night he made the best zucchini bread from seeds he planted in his garden. I look forward to doing more for myself, but until then, I learn more and more about receiving as he never grumbles, never gripes. He doesn't even roll his eyes! Four months and counting. We are both so grateful he was laid off/retired the first of the year. Divine Timing at it's very best! So here's to my wonderful best friend and husband who manages to juggle everything in our world with grace and love!

KATHY: He looks and sounds delightful. Wishing you the best as always! Hard to learn to receive, but a valuable lesson for us all!

CARRIE: A wonderful reminder that there are no mistakes in life. What a beautiful, heartfelt tribute to your loving partner! xx

ALISSA: After both broken legs and T12 and L345... my beloved still picks up after his self.. 83 years young and counting...I AM blessed!!! We are both blessed... thank you ...LOVE, JOY, PEACE, GRATITUDE!!!!

DIANA: Wow that man has a great spirit about him. Like you

My life partner, my lover, and my husband remains my best friend with our marriage an extension of that friendship. I'd been home full–time since April, give or take the hospital visits, and found life with Phil 24/7 to be comfortable. Although Phil and I had spent 12 ½ years with major alone time, being back together 24/7 had been great. I couldn't wait to see how we related when I healed.

Moment by moment, hour by hour, day by day my body regenerated, nourished by my refuge in sleep. During my waking hours I practiced gratitude, actively appreciating my surroundings. These mini–meditations would often deeply relax me back into sleep. I moved my body around the house as a welcome change in scenery because changing my position when lying down was impossible. Lucy and all the surgeries required me to lay on my back. Side sleeping could be faked with a plethora of pillows piled behind me, enough to fool my body and mind into believing I sustained some comfort. I moved from the bed in the bedroom to the couch in the living room, and from the recliner opposite the picture window to the futon in the den. Each different space provided a unique cocoon.

I dreamed of health and my old self with long hair, when I slept; not much of a story line other than feeling good and whole. cAnswer never entered my dreams. I revisited life as I have always known it. Then I would wake up to empty Lucy, give myself a shot, and redress my incision. Once a week I rode an hour to Indy and back for Chemo/Dreamo treatments. I continually reminded myself that my life was shaped in a new way. I would consciously love, bless, and release any hope of getting back to how my life ran in the past. *Everything is different now.* I sighed to myself as I accepted my new reality.

Letters from strangers arrived and, many times, those strangers became new friends...at least on Facebook. These friends cheered for me and rallied behind me to remind me that I was never alone. Because I was such an extroverted social butterfly in person, having new and old friends love me on social media felt similar to touring, ministering, and loving people in my past. When I didn't post for a few days, friends inquired as to my well–being. When I learned something about myself through this dance, I shared it. Others would share that inspiration and more new friends appeared.

What are some of the things I might do with six or more months of healing time? I'd love to work with stained glass again. I inherited all my Grandmama's glass and equipment. I'd love to sew or do beadwork like I did as a kid. I kept all the supplies. Now those rainy days I had been saving up for had arrived. However, I had no energy. Doing anything at all simply wore me out. I stood at the sink to do dishes and lasted upright for about five minutes before fatigue overtook me. I followed the flow of energy as it became available and rested as needed.

Before cAnswer I would hear that people on chemo were tired all the time. I imagined they felt awful, confined, and terribly uncomfortable. Now, as I moved through the lack of energy, I experienced none of those feelings. I wasn't torn away from something I wanted to do. My "To Do list" featured one thing, rest. Just rest. Nothing else mattered but healing.

Down Memory Lane

Aug 4, 2012 Journal Entry

While I can do little else, reflecting on the past is easy, especially the most colorful experiences made more vivid by Dad's photography.

This day I revisited my trip of a lifetime with Dad. He promised me a trip to Europe when I graduated from college. It took six years to earn my degree in Music Education in spite of taking 19–21 credit hours per semester. Dad probably wondered, as I did, whether or not I would ever graduate. When I finished school in 1992, I took him up on his offer. These became two of the finest weeks of my life, and enhanced by the bonding between Dad and me.

The melody of my song *Paris Waltz* was born two years before our trip. I could barely play it on the piano, but the lilting melody hung in the air like crushed lavender on a cool day. I assumed, because no words took form, that it would remain a simple instrumental...until I went to Paris with Dad. As soon as we returned home the song grew a second life.

Paris Waltz by Lauren Lane Powell

Paper hearts, candy thoughts, silver moon,
Castle walks, river talks, golden noon,
Velvet sky, pure July, misty mornings,
This is Paris, this is Paris

Ferris wheel, carousel, flowers bloom,
Amber wine, hanging vine, sweet perfume,
I'll remember as long as I live
The lovely gift only Father could give

Watch the river wander
Waltzing to the sea
Under God's blue heaven
As my father waltzes with me

Picture perfect daydreams
Follow as we live
Picture perfect Paris
What a gift to give

The Europe trip provided a memorable, remarkable adventure with the heart of my heart, my Dad. Five years later, I chose *Paris Waltz* for our father/daughter dance to bestow an enchanted moment in the midst of another enchanted event, my wedding to Phil.

Among my most enchanted experiences in that trip to Europe was singing *Beethoven's 9th* in very broken German, on the bow of a boat cruising down the Rhine River as we pulled out of Bonn, the composer's birthplace. We hiked through vineyards, over steep terrain in the Italian Riviera in Burks and flipflops. We almost missed the train coming back from Florence because we lost our way and missed Florence. We drank beer in Munchen, wine in Nice and

fantastic coffee everywhere. Dad's favorite cognac nightcap made him snore like a banshee, so I drank a little from his glass so to reduce his intake. It worked! Either he stopped snoring, or I stopped caring. For that reason, I developed a taste for Courvoisier. In all, we enjoyed a two–week whirlwind of fun.

As a reminder of those happy times, *Paris Waltz* is one of the songs on my Chemo/Dreamo set that I listened to every treatment.

Often what accompanies sweet old memories are those that are less happy. This time of reflection and contemplation brought everything up for review, the good, the bad, and the ugly. So I caught myself getting teary–eyed when thinking about that trip to Europe with Dad, because the sweet memories are coupled with the negative ones.

After many, many counseling sessions, thirty years of Spiritual practice, and an ongoing ritual of releasing toxic emotions through forgiveness, I've come to welcome and embrace all of the emotions.

As I Release
I Feel more Peace.

~ Lauren Lane Powell

When emotions overwhelm me and I can't sing, meditate or pray them away, I know I'm on the **Verge of a Purge.**

SPIRITUAL TOOL
The Primal Purge

Even though I know...I believe I will be ok, even though I know...I believe I will survive this, "What if I don't?" is still a real life question. When the "What ifs" become too heavy, when the fears out weigh the faith, when the tears lay ever present in my throat, I know I'm on the verge of a purge.

Today it's enough to deal with the here and now. I yell at cAnswer, "I hate you cAnswer for invading my body! I hate you cAnswer for infecting my ovaries! I hate you cAnswer for scaring my mommy!" It feels like I'm spewing pure venom when I say these words—when I feel these words.

I do this on purpose, to get the toxic emotions up and out of my physical body so when I used the letter "h" in the word "hate," I am pushing out those nasty vibrations from the core where they were buried in the first place.

Then it's done, at least for now. Now I feel empty, depleted. Now I say aloud and on the breath, "I forgive you cAnswer for invading my body! I forgive you cAnswer for infecting my ovaries! I forgive you cAnswer for scaring my mommy!"

The reasons I purge:

1. This technique for emotional release works for me.

2. It makes sense to my logical mind that I hold unacknowledged and hidden emotions in my body. *The issues are in our tissues!*

3. The purge allows me to release feelings of lack, inadequacy, pain, sorrow, anger and fear.

4. While "I hate you" feels dramatically drastic and, while those words create a low vibration, they are the very words that conjure up the next required release.

5. My conscious mind makes no sense of this practice. I don't really hate anything or anyone. Yet bringing those words out into the open allows hidden angst to be revealed and healed.

6. When I'm finally able to say, "I forgive you for..." there is a tangible clearing. I can feel healing strengthen within with every purge. During the forgiveness part of the purge I often wind up crying all over again. Then sweet tears flow and soothe me.

7. When it's over I feel giddy, filled with anticipation. I experience miracles within a day or so of a purge.

8. This clearing allows space for inspired ideas, divine realizations, and deeper understandings.

9. I delight in the recovery of repressed memories that emerge due to the purge. For example, I buried strong pain and anger deep down inside me towards Mom's old boyfriend, Dave, because I witnessed him hitting her as I was growing up. The fights terrified me. As I purged, over and over again, that negative energy dissipated. As I forgave him, over and over again with this practice, precious nuggets of good shined through the shit, happy memories that had been blotted out by the not so happy ones. Now I think of Dave, as well as many of the traumatic instances in my life, with little to no emotional charge at all.

Through this process I see how everything in my life has happened for a reason, to bring me to this point of seeing the perfection in the imperfection of all things. I remain eternally grateful for this powerful tool of release and my ability to share it.

Releasing all that was, in order to embrace all that is, making room for all that will be, is not for the faint at heart.

Purging allows me to see
the perfection in the imperfection of all things.

ALAN: Lauren, you have been on my mind and in my heart for the last several days, and while knowing the utter magnificence that you are you still find ways to WOW me. You are my Hero, thank you. I love you.

CAROLYN: Thank you for posting that lovely flow. I feel great. Your communication feels great to me because you are willing to share the space in which you are in resonance. The words that make impressions on me- First heart, then magnificence, WOW. Hero. Thank you. Love. Sweet. Nice, Hear.Oh my. This all sounds delightful. Let me just tune in. I'm looking to feel where we share VISION. We have many common interest. 1.) Meditation: any particular for of meditation ? When you ask, who can I forgive and you listen, what are some possibles responses do you meet in resonance? You really feel to BE resonating PEACE. Thank you. I am VERY interested in your Forgiveness Workshop on CD. Where would I be so delighted as to locate one. I am delighted with our connection. My Circles are Growing. I am in the Manifestation flow of at the point of integrating and actually building form. We are in total alignment. I love your choice of name. Harmonics of Healing is PERFECT, of course. That's the gift of this awareness. Thank you for sharing your GIFT and talents to this point in consciousness. Welcome to my world. Oh, this is GREAT !!Namaste

MY REPLY: Thank you! When I tune in and listen for the answers to the question "Who can I forgive now?" often the answer is "yourself." Other times it's mom, dad, both...Sometimes the answer that comes to me is "God!" What in world must I forgive God for? Then I remember, I get to forgive the god of my old understanding...the god with a small "g" who did not keep mom and dad together, the god who lets bad things happen. I know better now of course, but when I formed those core beliefs god did not answer prayers. It is that god that I forgive to truly align with God within and everywhere present. Does this make sense as I'm getting treatment as I write this?

MY AFFIRMATIONS

It is Natural for My Body to be Well.

My Only Job is to Relax and Heal.

I am in Very Good Hands. I will Relax Now.

This is what
108 pounds looks like!
Doctors are thrilled!
Who in the world gains
weight during chemo?

Chemo/Dreamo
Illumination Treatment
#8 since last week's
was cancelled.

Adding an Abraham-Hicks
meditation to the mix.

Then to South Bend!

I'm giving my husband a
whole week off
of care-taking!

OLIVIA: That's our girl! You're on your way. Body made over by God...Toned muscles to match that beautiful smile! Whoopee! I love you.

STEVE: You are indeed capital spirit. Onward and upward.

STEPHEN: I see your truth, healthy, and complete a life with spirit! Looking great!

CECILIA: Oh Lauren you look BEAUTIFUL! Love your T–shirt. Was thinking about you with a full heart just about two hours ago. So happy to see this posting and see your Goddess-ness!!!!

EVAN: You look wonderful! I wished that I looked that good during my chemo!

LAUREN: Things always work out for you! You are a healthy, wealthy child of God!

CHERYL: You are amazing and so very beautiful... And news and outers! :-)

PATRICIA: Follow the evidence of healing and let the illusion of anything less than perfection float away.

KALAR: Dear and sweet Lauren, you are looking so good and radiant. I am thrilled to see you reflecting better health and feelings. I love you.

PETE: Hello Lauren, I think singing is medicine too! And you sing beautifully. I would like to sing again and my wife says I should practice more. What do you think? Love and Compassion,
(Pete is my friend and long ago former voice student. He married another dear friend of mine and soon after experienced his own healing journey of the heart and mind.)

MY REPLY: Pete, If you were to practice these exercises in this order you would strengthen your core muscles, relax your throat, increase your range and enrich your tone.

1. motorboating: three notes, "Do Re, Mi, Re, Do" up and back—thru your range
2. ooh, same three notes but pushing more wind thru to strengthen your core-then
3. yawn and sing an ooh. same three notes thru your range. Then
4. finally sing a song...with the motorboat first. Now, not only are you warmed up, but you have practiced too. Twenty minutes or so everyday.

PETE: Thanks Lauren, I will practice those tips. Pam and I hope all is well, as it is, with you and Phil. God bless you Lauren!

Chapter Ten
Hair, There, and Everywhere

August 6, 2012 From Journal

This past week I barely know myself because I am more like the old me than ever, bursting with energy. On Saturday the 4th, I cleaned, organized, and shuffled stuff and found no time for journaling, a daily activity since D day, diagnosis day. The next day, Mom visited and the three of us went out for pizza—not a big deal any other time. But now it is a big deal to feel good enough to enjoy going out.

I let a few friends know why I wasn't there this year and asked them to hold the high watch for me. I'm grieving.

I'm welcoming the distraction for another reason. This is the week of my beloved Michigan Womyn's Music Festival. For the last three years, I had participated; pitching my own tent for camping, setting up my wares, and selling at the Festival. I presented my Harmonies of Healing program four times during those eight days of camping and company, earth and sky, song and dance, and friendship and frolic.

At my booth, people placed their feet inside the big bowl. Then I played the bowl and toned with my voice. They instantly relaxed and their pain lessened. People have regained sensation after years of neuropathy and have relieved other foot, knee, and hip issues by later working with the bowls by themselves.

August 7, 2012 FB Post

Insight! This is an "Aha" that is probably a "Well Duh!" But I'm going to say it anyway!

Might it be true that some of us are *afflicted* or *gifted* depending upon our perceptions? I overheard a conversation about someone losing a limb. The discussion was about the attitude this person retains and how they inspire others. Perhaps one of the big pictures in life is just that. We all have opportunities to whine, grumble and complain. I have done my share and I do know there is a place for such "human–ness" but as soon as I can, I look for and find the gifts in every situation.

Perhaps that is what we are all learning and teaching one another. Maybe this is why we attract such "gifts." Ideas?

JOHN: When our minds and hearts are open, we are able to receive amidst all life's little twists and turns!

DEBRA: I have found that I cannot just stop a behavior. I need to replace it with another. My joy is a way for me to focus on the good in my life. It doesn't mean that I don't feel the negative energy experiences but that I accept them as they are—messages from Spirit that I am out of Harmony with my true self. I can then release the stuck energy from my body and start to share my joys! I usually do this in song like you do!

EDIE: I believe your perception is right on. Sometimes we go through experiences (gifts?) that on the surface are very challenging and scary to our humanness but the soul growth for both ourselves and others can be immeasurable. The most important lesson I learned through a disabling illness at age 37 was that to be healed I had to forgive everybody and everything. That took some time, but I did finally receive the gift of healing following a Unity Village retreat. That was years ago, but I still am in awe of the experience and forever grateful to God for the blessing.

JOAN: Well, I know one thing—I always get something out of what you have to say—you make me think and that's hard to do.

PAT: You are the best teacher!

Another song I played in my Chemo/Dreamo treatment meditations was *Angel Flying*. It took me to a place on high where my healthy self waltzed with my sick self, a beautiful dance between two different parts of me. One night, I dozed in and out of sleep. In that state, I saw my healthy self pass off my sick self to dance with another recognized, beloved friend, and then another. Pat Mawson was among them. It seemed like I danced with every woman I've ever known. The only two men who came to dance with me at the very end of the vision were my daddy and my husband. Ever since that dream experience, the song holds new meaning. I felt such indescribable love while I danced with these angels.

Angel Flying
by Lauren Lane Powell

When I was young no one
told me it could not be done.
So I had friends, the celestial kind.
We would walk on the wind at night,
Following stars as our guide.

Once upon a time I used to fly with angels.
Higher than the trees,
Much higher than the clouds.
Once upon a time I used to fly with angels.
Angel Flying, once upon a time.

And as I grew my attention turned to other things.
I soon neglected my family with wings.
Time made me jaded. My memory faded.
I seldom remembered my dreams.

Once upon a time I used to fly with angels.
Higher than the trees,
Much higher than the clouds.
Once upon a time I used to fly with angels.
Angel Flying, once upon a time.

When I'm an old woman preparing for my rest,
Will I see my family of angels from the past?
Smiling faces tell me that I'll not be alone.
Winged graces beckoning. They'll come to take me home.

One upon a time I used to fly with angels.
Higher than the trees,
Much higher than the clouds.
Once upon a time I used to fly with angels.
Angel flying, once upon a time.

www.harmoniesofhealing.com

August 8, 2012 Journal Entry

I feel Angels within, without, and all around me as my constant companions, my friends, my healers, and my team.

One of my earliest compositions written in 1996, is a song that actually wrote me, *Angel Flying.* It flowed through me with ease and grace. This song contains interweaving strands of melody in the chorus, one of my favorite songwriting tools. Each melody stands alone. When combined, they create magic in motion!

A childhood memory inspired the lyrics. When I was six years old, I used to hover above my bed. I remember floating about six to eight inches over the sheets and looking down at the indentation of where my head used to be. Then I'd be gone! Never alone though. My companion Angel, an enormous figure of golden light, shimmered, glowed, and illuminated our way. I was never a bit frightened. We traveled in overwhelming beauty. I learned to look for and see the magnificence of all things in this place of peace. And I felt love all around me. I could touch it, hold it, spin it around, wear it, swallow it, and then become it.

One time we didn't fly. We just sat on the fence in my back yard. We didn't speak. It wasn't necessary. It felt good just to *be*. So normal. I didn't have to do anything. That presence felt warm and wonderful.

A few years ago, my dad and I took an eight hour road trip. He was just getting over a sore throat, so we opted not to speak for the duration. We spent the time in silent holy communion, being with one another with no words to get in the way.Those precious moments brought back how I felt as a child, sitting on the fence in the backyard with the angel held in the wings of love.

One day I told someone I flew with angels. She said that was impossible. I thought she must have been right. After all, she was a grown–up. I never flew again until the day I danced to this song one twirl at a time during treatment. It felt new and fresh, and at the same time comfortably familiar, to dance with all the people I love and allow them to love me back to health. I can still feel the light breeze we created as we waltzed.

 Laughter Lightens Life's Load

On Mom's turn to care for me, we met halfway between Bloomington and South Bend at Ruby Tuesday's. In the past, we would go inside the restaurant, order a meal or an appetizer, and spend a few hours talking and laughing before going our separate ways. Not these days. These days, Phil drove my frail, tired body the obligatory two hours. We waited in the car if we arrived first. This time, Mom sat waiting for us. Phil transferred my belongings, my suitcase, my cosmetic bag filled with meds, Lucy's supplies and bandages, a cushion for my bony butt, and lots of pillows.

I never knew how I was going to feel or how much energy I would have when traveling in between chemo sessions or to see Mom. I couldn't predict how Lucy would behave or misbehave. Living with so much unknown was interesting, to say the least.

Progressively feeling better, I returned to my normal talkative self. I would have loved to have recorded our conversation because our humor surfaced and we were off to the races. I remember well this particular tangent. Our family is quick to notice happenings that others might call coincidences. We call them synchronicities; for example thinking about someone and then they call, or humming a melody and that song comes on the radio when getting into the car. This time, getting silly, we started playing with the numbers on the clock versus the numbers on the speedometer. They were nowhere near the same. And "Look at that bike! I wasn't thinking about bikes at all!" At the same time, she and I decided there needed to be a word for that—two things happening completely unrelated, the opposite of synchronicity. "Synchro–*not*–city." I thought I'd rip my stitches!

We found more examples of unrelated things and our giggles turned into hysteria. I thought Mom would have to pull the car over as she laughed so hard she cried. I laughed so hard I thought I would wet my pants and/or burst Lucy. Then I realized this was the first time since before April that I had laughed like that. From my wounded, poked, prodded, sliced up belly, came this deliciously dear, old friend of laughter. The real thrill came when I recognized I could laugh this deeply with no abdominal pain whatsoever. *That* was worth celebrating!

August 8, 2012 FB Post

Another milestone! Yesterday on our way to visit my sister, Mom and I started laughing and couldn't stop. I realized in the middle of true hysteria that I felt no pain at all. Here I have been wanting to watch funny movies, needing humor in my life to heal, and having a hard time finding anything really ha ha funny. But then when I did finally find something that tickled me, it hurt my incision and my stoma! (colostomy). But yesterday, there was NO pain! I can laugh again! Wow! How healing!

CHERYL: Your beautiful smile and powerful laughter has always created healing energies around you. Love that *you* could experience it too!

JUDY: God keeps blessing you. Thank God! hahahahaha!!! wonderful!!

THERESA: Is it possible you didn't think about incision in those happy moments?

August 8, 2012 Journal Entry

Too true! At the age of 50, I finally loved my body at its healthiest, fittest, and thinnest. How conditional! Now, I have to heal my life of self–loathing as an adolescent and young adult. I was never good enough, fit enough, pretty enough...blah blah blah.

I would love to share with young girls the importance of loving *where we are now, as we are now*. It's time to love *what is*.

Your Body Believes Every Word You Think! Stay Positive

Time to forgive myself more for all those years growing up that I hated parts of my body. I remember detesting my breasts because they weren't big enough. I was driving somewhere in my early twenties and I railed at God for shortchanging me in the boob department. My sister was amply endowed. It wasn't fair! As I whined out loud I was almost sideswiped by a kid in a pickup truck. It was as if God said, "Enough already!" At that moment, I started appreciating my "Itty Bitty Titties", as I subsequently referred to them. "I am so sorry, my sweet body, for ever hating parts of you. Please forgive me. All of you is beautiful. Even now. Especially now."

I made peace with myself over and over again, for many things that now seem silly in the grand scheme of things. I made peace with the impermanence of my body that was small and frail. I accepted the scrawny arms and bony legs I saw in the mirror. I made peace with the skeleton I had become. It was a lot to ask. It was a lot to do. It was my job.

August 9, 2012 Journal Entry

What brought me peace while dancing with cAnswer? Creativity. Putting together something like this little graphic kept me occupied. Art of any kind kept my mind going and gave me a source of expression and something else to focus on other than cAnswer.

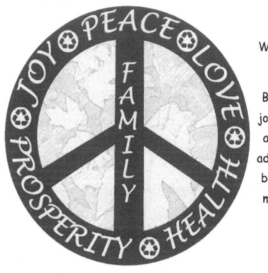

What brings you PEACE?

Besides family, joy, love, health, and prosperity add cats, nature, beauty, singing, meditation and friends!

August 10, 2012 Journal Entry

This has been a long week for me. I am not used to all of this activity. Mom came down on Aug. 4th but forgot her meds. That put us in South Bend two days before we planned on being there. She already had my anti–gravity chair set up and blankets and pillows nearby. We met Kristen in Merrillville on the 7th. When she worked during the day, I would sleep, work on my laptop, eat a bit, and sleep some more. Mom read. Very peaceful. When Kristen finished her work, we all went out to dinner. That was enough energy to expend.

Mom and I had returned to South Bend on the 9th for more rest and visiting with friends and family. A high school friend, Cheryl, who reconnected through Facebook, arrived at Mom's to practice healing touch and some other modalities with me. A gift lovely to receive! Her brother had received a colostomy going through cAnswer a year ago so we had a lot to talk about. When we attended high school, I thought the only thing we held in common was long, long hair. I was so wrong! We shared so many similar childhood stories, we were amazed. I am so blessed with her friendship, another blessing because of cAnswer!

On Sunday, August 12, I decided to attend Unity Church of Peace, in South Bend. I wanted to see everybody and have everybody there see how well I was doing. Or, at least, better than anyone expected. I wore hats to cover my very thin hair. Soon I would be shaving it off. The air conditioning in most places left me chilled, so I carried a scarf for a wrap. Since Lucy often bubbled loudly, I sat near a bathroom.

August 11, 2012 FB Post

I finally grew cajones to change my profile picture. I guess I was still attached to the long hair. (you think?) Well here I am, the way I am now and learning to *love it all!*

Thank you God for the valuable lessons that teach me.

RHONDA: Amazing! You still shine!

CHERYL: Beautiful and Precious!

MICKEY: You are lovely and inspiring!

MICHELLE: Had the Blessed joy of being able to visit with Lauren yesterday. Lauren you look amazing, I pray for your strength to continue coming back, I pray for healing.. just looking at the glow in your eyes tells me you are. Chemo will not keep you down! Tom and I are so grateful for having had you in our girls' lives for so many years..their voices will always be mixed with yours.. you are an inspiration, fabulous vocal coach, friend and a lovely human being. I love you my friend! God Bless You.

MONICA: Your beauty was never in your hair.

With all contingencies covered, I enjoyed the message of Spirit speaking, as Rev. Sandie Vanek, and the music of Spirit sung, as Melanie Gabris. I felt cherished like I did the very first time I entered a Unity church. I felt so embraced, so healed, so released, so joyful, so sorrowful, so grateful, so peaceful, and so prayed for. Many found me afterwards to tell me just that. "We've been following you on Facebook. You are in our prayers." Over and over and over again. It was heartening to know just how many followed my journey.

August 13, 2012 Journal Entry

We all know now how laughter is healing. The lesson today by Rev. Sandie was perfect, "Finding the humor in all of Life." Lightening up and having fun with God. So appropriate!

We met Phil in Kokomo for the reverse transfer. The laughter from that week with Mom left me stronger. I was able to sit at the restaurant and enjoy a light meal. I walked to the car that was pointed towards home all by myself. It was starting to feel like real healing now.

I Have Chosen to be Happy because it's Good for My Health

August 13, 2012 FB Post

Music is healing me *now*. Ask me what music I listen to during my chemo/dreamo treatments.

DALE: Which songs do you listen to during your chemo/dreamo treatments?

ME: Hi Dale! I listen to Kristen's "Holy Spirit" and "Love is All There Is," Karen Drucker's "Blessing to the World," Lisa Ferraor's "Face of God," Amy Camie's harp music and my own CD called "Metamorphosis," with singing bowls and voice.

ROBYNE: That is so funny you said that. Our Metamorphosis CD helped me to experience spiritual metamorphosis, so when I read your question I hoped you would be listening to Metamorphosis. It is a masterpiece in my humble opinion. You are a gifted composer. Love and Blessings to you.

Sweet Spirit
Show Me How to Have Fun With This

~ Lauren Lane Powell

August 14, 2012 FB Post

It's time to post this picture.

This past week I showed my mom this photo for the very first time. We wept long and hard together. I didn't let her come see me for three weeks after my final dismissal in June. I wouldn't even Skype my dad. I didn't want anyone to see me like this. It was upon my sister's insistence that I took a picture at all. I was very resistant. I didn't want to have this weak state documented. I am glad I did.

When Mom did come to help care for me, I was five pounds heavier, not nearly so emaciated. Seeing this photo, she knew why I kept her and Dad away. I was trying to protect them. Understanding that, she thanked me, admitting that had she seen me at my thinnest, she would have panicked.

June 5, 89 lbs.
Just after third surgery

August 11, 108 lbs.
Before Chemo/Dreamo treatement #9

When you know the essence of who you are cannot be threatened, you're not afraid to heal.

Kristen won an award for this from MyPeaceTV Contest, Feb 2013.

OLIVIA: Through tears of joy I smile and am so blessed to know you. Thank you for making us all part of your family and allowing us to share this journey with you.

JUDITH: And Spirit will transcend every time!

RICK: Amazing what prayers and positive attitude can do—letting your light and natural beauty shine through! Keep it up and write a song about it.

CAROL: You are a blessed and divine demonstration of how to use Spiritual Principles to heal.

DAVID: You are an example for us all of holding the Truth in spite of appearances. Thank you Lauren for you being you and sharing yourself with us.

CAROLE: Dear lady, you are an amazing woman indeed. Thank you for sharing such an intimate picture and showing your amazing strength.

RENE': Sweet Darlin', you have been in my heart and prayers from the community from the first moment I heard of your journey. Our entire community has been holding you in the light. You are the most courageous, brave, and beautiful woman. I am proud to know you... You are loved!

DALE: Lauren, I think you are amazing and I am grateful you are sharing your powerful message of healing that will help many people.

SUE: Thank you for sharing who you really are. Your Spirit lives on! Ego would have us believe different. No denial here! Only LOVE is REAL! I/We love you! Sue and Edith

ALLAHKARA: You are the bravest person I know. I've never seen anyone face something this difficult with the beauty you have. You are inspirational as well but, then again, you always have been. So you have proven to be not only true to your heart but true to your walk... Good for you Master! P.S. I am sharing this by the way I pray you don't mind, but your story is just too amazing!

SOPHIA: You are a brave, amazing woman with a lot of spirit—thanks for sharing!

ELLEN: Thanks for sharing this photo of yourself. How brave of you! It reminds me that we are our physical body but so much more. You are a good example of that philosophy. I see your physical and spiritual body as one, working together in love, peace and harmony. I see you standing in the light, whole, perfect and complete, a beautiful example of God's love and grace. I thank you for the courage to share such a personal experience in such a public way. Much love I send to you.

AL: You are still the same wonderful, powerful, beautiful, inspiring soul I have known and loved since eighth grade, my dear friend. Your energy remains one of the most incredible forces I have ever encountered.

DONNA: You are brave to share and you are an inspiration as you live your truth. I am touched and honored by your spirit.

Mary: You look great. Hoping still to gain more weight too. You are an inspiration.

JOHN: All God's blessings for continued recovery and spiritual enlightenment!

SHERRY: Thank you for sharing your journey and your amazing spirit! Sending you love.

MARCELLA: Wow...you are beautiful! We are with you! Thank you for your courage!

DEDRA: Wow! What a difference! Spirit in you is strong!

SUSAN: Oh my gosh, Lauren, what Grace and Will have achieved... You are a miracle.

HELENE: You are love in motion! Xo

MICHELLE: My hearts aches seeing the first picture but it sings seeing the second!

SPIRITUAL TOOL

Being the Observer

Watching myself at my lowest weight of my adult life, looking like an Auschwitz victim, feeling very frail and vulnerable. As I become the observer, I can stand aside and watch. I can be less judgmental from afar. I can be more compassionate as I see myself as someone else.

I am growing to love that sweet, delicate little body; her wrinkly skin hung in folds down her thighs from her saggy, bony butt; and her scarred tummy protruded like that of a starving child.

Her knees and elbows appeared freakishly enlarged by comparison. Her breasts hung in a vacant chest. Her visible ribs lay in ridges under thin skin. Feeling sorry for her was easy. But I didn't want my pity. How could I love her like that? Hmmm...How could I not?

As I continued to use my reflection as a gauge with which to measure my newly reborn and now necessary self–love, I felt my heart melt open again and again, learning and relearning to love this healing child of God.

I love myself the way I am.
I love myself the way I am.
I love myself the way I am.

Daddy drove me to Chemo/Dreamo treatment #9 in Indy today. When I began receiving the Taxol drip, I turned on the music and closed my eyes. Dad went to the cafeteria to leave me undisturbed. I felt this good because I was not trying to do more than I could. I understand some people go to work while undergoing treatment. I am convinced that part of the reason for my rapid healing is due to allowing mysef a lot of rest.

HAIR STAGES

In January, three months before I was diagnosed, I had my hair cut for Locks of Love, a charity that creates wigs for cAnswer patients with donated hair. I have donated three times now. They require ten inches or more and no gray. So I knew that, since I was beginning to see streaks of silver near my temples, this might be my last time to give.

In April, before my first surgery, I cut it shorter yet, and more so when I started Chemo/Dreamo treatments. Each time I went to the Academy for a haircut, I met someone different. Each sytlist expresse understanding and gentleness.

My "Bob" this time My hair thinned so much that it made me feel elderly.

After ceremoniously shedding one hair identity at a time, losing hair at this stage of my treatment, proved less traumatic. However, I still freaked when I watched swirls of long hair go down the drain, and woke every morning to a pillow case covered with fine five–inch strands. Seeing my hands furry with hair after I touched my head nauseated me. My husband cleaned the screen in the shower because I couldn't bear to do it.

I try to believe *"I am not my hair"* but who am I without it?

My hair was longer at age two than it is now.

Hair, There, and Everywhere

I have had long hair all my life.

In 1980, I performed in a local production of *Hair*, the rock opera, at a well–known bar and grill. My hair fell well past my waist. In the show, I adorned my mane and proudly exhibited my dancing prowess. My dancing focused on my hair. I would spin and my hair flew. I lunged over and whipped my head spirally and my glorious, shiny hair splayed like rays of the sun around my body.

"Gimme a head with hair. Long beautiful hair. Shining, streaming, gleaming, flaxen, waxen."

My hair had been an extension of myself like my arms and legs. Fifty years is a long time to love it, then lose it.

I came by my love of long hair honestly

Chapter Eleven
Growing Bold, Growing Bald

August 17, 2012 FB Post

I needed this post today. Another reminder that I am not alone! Thank you.

WHEN "I" IS REPLACED BY "WE," ILLNESS BECOMES WELLNESS.

August 17, 2012 FB Post

This was so much fun! I spent an hour talking with Dale Worley and sharing my music and the cAnswer dance. I know you will enjoy it, too.

DALE- Lauren Lane Powell was my guest on *Music Speaks Louder Than Words* and she shared an amazing story of healing. Hear her theme song at https://www.youtube.com/watch?v=IjSRvxxCcrA&list=PL0DF1550033873C87&index=1

Download a podcast of today's show at www.unity.fm/program/musicspeakslouder.org

JONIEBETH: I'm so glad you are putting yourself on here! I can just go to your timeline and get my morning lift. I love you. I'm so glad you were born and most of all that you are still here with us and on Facebook! Step, Step out on it! Best way to build an audience. And less expensive than traveling!

AMY: Lauren, I listened to this show and your beautiful voice and positive attitude helped bring back my spark. Thank you for your gift!

DIANE: I just watched the video of your theme song and the tears flowed… I've heard your song before but it touched my heart so much more deeply this morning…

*Lauren Note: *Some May Tell You!*, my theme song is a dedication to my mom who encouraged me every step of the way

August 18, 2012 FB Post

Nice cool weekend in Indiana. On today's schedule: dead head the butterfly bush, organize the back room (where the innards of my van lie), fill out financial aid forms, yoga, and rest. What a life!

I am not doing what I used to do, what I loved to do—tour the country teaching people how to sing and use the voice for release and relaxation. I am blessed to be surrounded by nature. I am learning to love doing nothing, resting, and healing. My life is full of love, prayer and fuzzy creatures. I am so blessed!

DEANNE: What a great picture. You and Phil and cats are all chillin. Great healing technique for everyone.

SHARRON:Sometimes the soul as well as the body needs rest in preparation to continue the journey.

MONICA: This reminds me of the time I spent with you guys. Even with the pain you were experiencing, I felt the peace and love wrapping us all up

PAT: Love love this pic! So sweet.

MELODY: You are doing what you always do. Teaching us all through example. You are a beautiful spirit.

DONNA: You are SUCH a blessing and an inspiration to the world! Sending you healing hugs and love!

CHRISTINE: You are blessed, Lauren, and so are we every time you count your blessings with us! Blessings of Love and Light to you!

JUDY: Lauren, You are so not doing nothing. Always love,

August 18, 2012 FB Post

How's this for productivity? A newsletter on Wednesday and a Radio Interview on Thursday. Both came so effortlessly I nearly missed the fact that something big had happened. My energy level is high and has been for 14 days in a row. I am doing yoga again, 15–20 minutes a day to start. It's cooler outside so I can spend more time in nature. Feel the healing energy? It's a nice Holy Shift isn't it?

The Gifts of cAnswer

Greetings!

Many of you know that I have been blessed with the gift of cAnswer.
I mean that very lovingly. Dancing with the diagnosis since April 2nd I have learned many things. I have experienced many miracles. I have received many contributions. I have witnessed much love!

One of the Spiritual messages I received early on is "Have fun with this!" Right! Have fun with cancer! How does that look? The first thing I did was change the spelling to cAnswer! It changes the vibration for me the writer and for anyone who reads it!

Another Spiritual message was to STOP doing what I was doing and do it differently. I loved traveling the country. I learned to love to drive. I learned to love to set up, tear down, lift, haul etc because I had to. It was what I did. Now I know I get to work smarter not harder. I haven't a clue what that looks like yet but I am open to suggestions.

The latest Spiritual message came in the form of trying to gain weight for the first time in my life. Having reached my goal weight in September 2012, my 50th birthday, I was fit and lean. I did yoga almost daily. I had 7 months of "perfection" then THIS! 3 surgeries took me down to 89 pounds! I cut my long hair very short anticipating loosing it during chemo. It has thinned a great deal, but I still have some. Between the weight loss and the hair loss my sense of "perfection" looked like nothing more than false pride.

I need to love what is, in the now, scarred and exposed, all of it. Tall order, but that's my job for the moment!

Sincerely,

Lauren Lane Powell
Harmonies of Healing
singforyoursoul@aol.com

Join Our
Mailing List

Accepting Contributions

Phil was laid off over a year ago and is now retired. I am self employed.

I haven't worked since the beginning of April. Even with no health insurance I have received the best medical care available. IU Hospital and Simon Cancer Center has taken very good care of me.

Medicaid is STILL pending! IF you wish to make a donation towards medical bills you can mail a check to:

Lauren Powell
PO BOX 1
Stanford, In 47463

OR Paypal singforyoursoul@aol.com

Anything is gratefully appreciated!

In This Issue

The Gifts of cAnswer

Changing the Way Healing Feels!

Actively Increasing Internet Biz
Instructional CDs and DVDs
Music for Meditation, Music for Fun
Goddess Dresses, Singing Bowls
Freenote Wing Instruments

Changing the Way Healing Feels

Can you find something to giggle about in the midst of grief? Can you sing your way out of depression? Can you meditate your way into merriment? Can you create joy where others see only travesty?

YES! You Can! Yes! we Must!

Working smarter, not harder the opportunities are endless. I see traveling less and reaching more people. I see using the internet more effectively. Perhaps I'll be working with families of patients helping them heal through expression, laughter, singing and fun. Any ideas are welcome! I am open!

Music and Meditation for Releasing

This is a great Package CD set.
2 Hour Workshop on 2 CDs $35.00
AND a 3rd CD of Forgiveness Songs for Meditation and Release. $20.00
Vibrations of Forgiveness
Package $45.00
Save $10.00
Free Shipping if ordered before Sept 2nd,
Lauren's 51st Birthday

Instructional CDs & DVDs

With Lauren's 5 lesson CD set singing on key is just moments away! With her no-fail techniques vocalizing is fun and healing!
$59.99

Watch Lauren In Action on her Harmonies of Healing Workshop DVD. A 2 and 1/2 half hour teaching video. A "must have" visual of the Vocal Visionary! $39.99

Meditate, relax and receive the pure tonal vibrations of the Singing Bowls and Lauren's authentic, angelic, healing voice mixed with the transporting sounds of the Freenote Wing! Lauren's 90 minute CD "Metamorphosis helps you sleep, uplifts and inspires, repairs and relaxes, embraces and heals. $20.00

Each sold separately. Buy as a package for only $99.99 and save $20.00!!

Many GREAT techniques to enhance your voice and it's healing qualities.

HarmoniesofHealing.com

Music for Fun
Natural Affirmations
Money's Flowin' In
Acting in the Play
Future Recollections
Somethin' Special
All Original, All Fun
All Uplifting, All Lauren's

MELODY: Hi Lauren. I just found you on FB. I so miss our times at Wheatland. I'm sorry to hear what you have been going through but am so grateful to hear you are doing better. You always have such a positive outlook and beautiful spirit. I'm so glad I found you here. Love, light, hugs and healing prayers your way.

August 19, 2012 FB Post

Did anyone else wake up thrilled and excited this morning? It is as if I was given a wonderful gift. All I had to do was open it.

As I started my morning, my heart grew warm when I was shown an infinite number of possibilities laid out before me, not just for today, but for my future. I have so many choices. All of this I have done before, but which deserves my focus the most?

What do you see me doing to truly serve the Universe and to stay healthy and whole?

I can go to a Bluegrass Festival every weekend and do a workshop; sell my voice lessons, DVDs, and dresses; and introduce healing with music to a whole different audience.

I can stay home and work with individuals on Skype. I call it Karma Coaching. Enhancing your voice enhances your life. Singing on key is just a side effect.

I can finish the book(s). "Sing For Your Soul", "Vibrations of Forgiveness," and "The Dance of cAnswer." All three are underway. (Now called "Holy Shift! Everything's a Gift!")

I can serve the cAnswer community and their families, to change the way cAnswer looks and feels. Hospitals, cancer centers, etc.?

I can serve New Thought centers like before, but differently...maybe spending a longer time at each, doing fewer events over two Sundays, and working with individuals during the week.

I can upload my DVDs and lessons, etc., to make them more accessible.

I can relax and see what life has in store for me next.

I can do all of the above. I can do none of the above. I have choices.

I can relax and be led. I can follow God's guidance.

LIZ: Which option brings the biggest smile, the very thought enhances your joy. Take a deep breath and "follow your bliss.". Namaste

LAUREN :That's just it Liz, every idea brings a smile to my face! Each one makes me happy!

LIZ: You are truly blessed, and a blessing. So, we can have it all. You know your right first step will "magically" appear. Namaste

JAMIE: I am keeping fire for a sweat lodge today and it will most likely be raining. Most of the time I dread those conditions...but today I woke up excited that I get the opportunity to tend fire while liquid life touches my skin and blesses Grandmother Fire!

DEANE: I see you simply being you and allowing spirit to show you the places and spaces that need your 'joyful, grateful' heart. Each place may need a slightly different version of your talent. You will know!

DEBORAH: Says it's a new moon in Leo, and time to shine. Sounds like you're on it.

JUDY: My father read a book entitled Thank God I Have Cancer. I believe that I now understand that title.

MELODY: I've missed you. I love reading your optimism. Just reading this post has opened up my possibilities for my day. Thank you for the gift of you. I think of you often. Particularly, this time of year as we get closer to Wheatland. I haven't gone in so many years. I miss it.

DEANE: Lauren check out Anita Moorjanai's book "Dying to be Me" a near death experience that is so spiritual and how she ended up being encouraged by Dr. Wayne Dyer to share with the world. She also sees cancer as cAnswer.

KIRA: Tell your story...about the music! Everyone can relate, but I wonder if they really understand how healing sound (vibration) can be, especially infused with love. I think you were born to tell that story.

MY REPLY:Thank you, Kira. My first memory of this journey was requiring my family to sing me thru surgery. They sang in the waiting room instead of worrying about me. No one knew then that they would have to sing for two more surgeries, but they were troopers. I believe it helped those singing as much if not more than me!

KIRA: You and your family...amazing! Grace!

JOHN: Give it time— just some—you will write a book and a song. You know that

MELODY: Lauren, that was beautiful. Some of my favorite songs are yours. You are living proof that it's the story that you give to what is happening in your life at any particular time. You can choose to look on the dark side, which helps no one, or you can look at it as a gift and make the best of life, which helps you and everyone around you.Thank you for the gift of you.

Life is a Gift
Have You Opened Yours?

August 27, 2012 FB Post

"Premission." Just before it's officially remission. God is so good.

This morning as I was waking, I thought about all the miracles that have blessed me because of, not in spite of, Canswer.

I am eternally grateful for my family for singing me thru three surgeries, by my request. They sat in the waiting room and sang my songs and others. They couldn't focus on fear or drama while they sang.

I am eternally grateful for the very hot summer. I didn't miss anything by staying inside. Phil couldn't work outside so he stayed in too. Such quality time! We watch "Curious George" together every day at 3:00.

I am eternally grateful for Phil being retired and taking such good care of me all summer. I am eternally grateful for time spent at home. Being on the road for 12 1/2 years kept me away for three weeks at a time. I was home a week at a time. Now I have the entire summer to spend at home.

I am eternally grateful for the flowers in the garden that I would have missed if I were still on the road, the hummingbirds that play all day on our deck, and the tons of butterflies in our yard.

I am eternally grateful for my mom's singing during a depressing, degrading colostomy blowout. I am eternally grateful for my dad reading to me—just like when I was a kid.

I am eternally grateful for all the friends I've made at IU Med Center. I am eternally grateful for my rest all summer. I am eternally grateful for the Chemo/Dreamo treatments and the side effects I have not encountered.

I am eternally grateful for my rapid recovery. I am eternally grateful for my smiley face scar.

I am eternally grateful for Lucy, my colostomy, for working so well and allowing me to witness to bodily functions that I never knew I wanted to see.

I am eternally grateful for finding humor wherever and whenever I can.

I am eternally grateful for time out and time off of "work."

I am eternally grateful for having to stop working so hard. I am eternally grateful for nudges from the Universe that push me lovingly toward a bigger dream.

I am eternally grateful for being able to eat whatever I wanted to gain weight. Time to slow down a bit since I am 113 today.

I am eternally grateful for prayers and love from my Facebook friends and fans. You help keep me going. I am eternally grateful for you all. This list is just a drop in the bucket of the blessings that have been bestowed me.

Thank you! Thank you! Thank you! Thank you! Thank you! Thank you! I am eternally grateful for all the cracks that let the light in.

OLIVIA: And I am eternally grateful to know you and to call you friend. You are such an inspiration to us all. You have taught more than you can know about Living Life Fully and Wholly with Joy! Bless you. Feel the love overflowing from everywhere!

MARTHA: Love you Lauren! What a gift your cAnswer has been. Love that new blended word! What a blissing you are. Like that word, too?

LARRY/Dad: The aspect of cAnswer has been profoundly changed seeing it through your eyes. Thank you.

BARBARA: You not only teach our Souls to Sing. "You Light Up Our Lives".

CHRISTINE: This is amazing, Lauren! Many thanks and blessings to you for sharing your story!

August 21, 2012 FB Post

For the last two to three years, I have consciously been working on receiving. The more I opened, the more I released the fear of feeling helpless. The core of that feeling helpless also relates to my resistance to having children. A *huge* part of that is the helplessness that comes with being a mom. Another huge part is the helplessness that comes with being pregnant. Helplessness, i.e. loss of control.

Throughout the experience of cAnswer, I gained control by changing my diet, dancing every day, Facebooking for prayer, meditating often, and staying creative as best I could. All of that helped, but especially my active participation.

There is a time for activity and it helped. But then came three major surgeries in a row. The hospital stays: four days in, three days out; ten days in, three weeks out; nine days in. Plenty of time to truly experience "helpless." I needed help to pee. I endured vulnerability by having to stay positioned on my back. Every four hours I had to *trust* that what the nurses were doing to me they were doing for me. Not sleeping added to the deep emotion of it all. I needed help to walk at first. I was on my back then at home, weak, fatigued, yet healing. My husband had to do everything for me for what seemed like forever.

It is so cool that the core of this was released with a hysterectomy—birthing, creativity—all lower chakra stuff. The core of feeling helplessness was such a cellular piece that all the work I had already done around it consciously was merely preparation. Two or three people at every event for the past two years told me I needed to be open to receive. I'd wrinkle my nose and think, "I thought I was." I had done some awesome deep work throughout 2010 and 2011 and, as you might suspect, I was receiving more at the beginning of 2012.

I was receiving more help with the websites, with unloading and loading the van, and I hired a virtual assistant to help with data entry. I felt like I was on my way and open to assistance like never before. Still my ego said "It's not happening fast enough."

The Universe replied, "Your wish is my command." Now I really am open to receive by default. I was opened up three times and have a hip–to–hip smiley face scar that is healing. I am open to express my bowels in ways I never knew possible and receive waves of humility and gratitude with every movement. (tmi?) I am open to and I am receiving funding now because I am open to and receiving the best medical care on the planet, with no health insurance.

August 21, 2012 FB Post

So, I am proof that when Spirit knocks, let her in, listen, act, and listen some more. Oftentimes, there are many things I will be guided to do, read, etc., to reach our highest potential. But sometimes, what is there to release is bigger and lies deeper than where I can go or do. That is where willingness comes in. I continue to be willing to truly receive. Wow! Look where that willingness brought me! What a gift!

Thank you, Friends, for being part of this awakening. I love you.

MICHELLE: Lauren, you inspire and teach us. We are honored to be part of your journey.

MICKEY: Lovey, you need to write a book—seriously!

AMY: YES!

HENNIE: I agree with Mickey!

LARRY/DAD: You are an inspirational book waiting to be written.

JUDY: Lauren, I am simply astonished at what your spirit has done, how it moves you, in seemingly all the right directions. He carries you every step of your way, He cradles you softly, and you are his baby, siempre, siempre...

EMIL: Quite the powerful life lesson.

KIRA: Absolutely extraordinary. You go and keep going, Girl!

ALLISSA: ASK and IT shall be Given...Be open to all POSSIBILITIES...LOVE, JOY, PEACE, GRATITUDE, SORRY, LOVE, FORGIVE, THANK YOU GOD. To make it right...TO Heal Every Person, Place, or Thing...LOVE is the answer for me! Lauren your life is an open BOOK... Thank You for Sharing it with us.

CHRISTINA: Your journey touches me so deeply that words fail me.

JEANNIE: Today's Daily Word was "Praying for Others." You were on my list and will be receiving prayers throughout the day. Enjoy!

DEB: Beautiful Lauren. I'm so glad to know you even if just a little. You so inspire me!

KALLIE: I agree with Mickey!

VERNON: Lauren, thanks for sharing your journey. You are inspiration, indeed.

CHERYL: Wow, Wow, Wow! You have articulated your feelings and thoughts so well. I love you, am grateful to have been and hopefully continue to be a part of your healing. As most have said you are a true inspiration and proof that sending and receiving positive energy truly does help one and all. Until we meet again (in person) you're always in my heart each and every day. xoxoxoxo

JOANNE: It's been a while since Unity in Edinboro has held a healing/toning circle with the bowls. In June, we included a circle in our Wednesday night class that was so well–received, we decided to hold one again after service on a quarterly basis. Last Sunday we had about 12 people join us. It was wonderful! We began the circle with YOU in our center and toned words of health and well–being. Thank you for bringing us this practice and allowing us to serve you in this way. You are loved.

When "I" is replaced by "We" Illness becomes Wellness.

August 23, 2012 FB Post

I have restored hope. 1. I am learning so much more than I ever thought I wanted to know about financial aid for medical services. This morning I learned that I can go to the Social Security office and receive a document of income — or lack of income, which may offset what our tax forms say we made last year. 2. I started working on the cAnswer dance book yesterday and I am excited. I didn't know how many friends of mine were not on Facebook. So I'm turning my Facebook documentation into a book, complete with all the comments. What fun to reflect! Should be out in no time at all. 3. Going on the third week in a row of feeling good. Thank you God! 4. Divining new ideas for service and income. Don't you think Cancer Centers of America would embrace my story? I believe I can help other patients and their families heal through singing positive thoughts, reframing cAnswer, and having fun with it all. Where do I start?

JULIE: So many times I've wanted to respond to your posts. the video your Dad did of your dancing in the hospital gave me Hope. When you posted "something to giggle about", I was confident that Everything, yes. Each item was going to be fine cuz the Lauren I know & love is Back!! Fully present & joyful in the Now moment regardless of the moment's content!! Much love to my lovely lady!!!

JULIA: Go for it! Your songs are inspirational. You will inspire many with your own story. Your path has many lessons in it. Thank you for sharing.

SUSAN: Sounds DIVINELY INSPIRED, Lauren, God provides in the midst of your creativity to hold one again after service on a quarterly basis. Last Sunday we had about 12 people join us. It was wonderful! We began the circle with YOU in our center and toned words of health and well–being. Thank you for bringing us this practice and allowing us to serve you in this way. You are loved.

August 25, 2012 FB Post

Good Morning Friends! I don't know many cAnswer patients other than those I meet here. I know even fewer who deal with a colostomy. Mine came during the second emergency surgery after a bowel weakened and tore. Making the best of things, I named her Lucy. She has her own persona—instead of calling it "my bag." So when I have a night like last night, I just exclaim that Lucy kept me awake all night. That explains everything.

This morning I found a site of support for colostom–ized folks like me. Videos are plentiful on changing the bag, making it more comfortable, stinky leaky problems, allergies, reversals, etc. I found a new group of friends. One young gal made a video about wearing her bag proudly with her bikini after she decorated it. How cool! I am learning so much.

Would it be helpful or gross to include a discrete photo of my own?

CHERY: Lauren, good for you. Everyone needs a little support in their lives. Even Lucy. Continue keeping the faith and humor, it's done you well so far. I can picture Lucy without an actual picture Love you

EVAN: My dad is considering the surgery. Any advice/warnings?

MY REPLY: Yes, tell him to have fun with it. I understand it helps heal IBS and is necessary for Krohn's disease. Once I learned how to change the bag, it's no big deal. Have him try out all the samples they will send him. Ask questions. My skin seems to developed an allergy of sorts to the adhesive. When I'm home I let her breathe by going without a bag and carrying around a roll of tp just in case. Boy, you sure get used to dealing with poop quickly! Check out the Colostomyland Facebook site.

JUDY: Girlfriend, do it!!! Yes!!! You are loving yourself, and every extension of yourself. Don't leave Lucy out. Let her shine and be!! Let's all heal together!!! Let's make it fun!! Lov elots, Judy

BRYAN: I don't think I would want to see your A%^ hole, now would I???

MY REPLY: Yea Bryan, I got it! My father threatens to introduce me as the daughter with two a–holes. In teasing of course.

ARMAND: I say anything that you do that supports you in embracing all of you, is helpful.

JONIEBETH: When I was a teen I had a friend who had one of those. She will have to deal with it the rest of her life. I must admit it was difficult to ignore the smell, obviously this was in the 50's and technology has changed a lot since then. It was tough for her as a teen to be accepted.

BARB: I think it would be very gracious of you to share if it might help others.

MADELYN: I've always been curious about what they look like.

MICHAEL: Our church manager had one of those. Our minister said he accessorized with it. He had it in a purple bag and he just carried it around. I'm thinking the design of the bag could be outstanding! You always post those interesting colorful pictures. Could you consider having a carry bag du jour, i.e., orange for Monday, blue for Tuesday, etc?

EDIE: I'm so happy to hear about your support angels and whatever you want to share is fine with me.

SUE: Post any pictures you feel led to Lauren! Of all the things one can view, pictures of our 'communication device' aka 'the body', and it's miraculous capabilities would be viewed as what it is intended to be, a learning tool. I am all for it dear One

JANICE: LUCY!...you got some 'splaining' to do! ~Love Desi

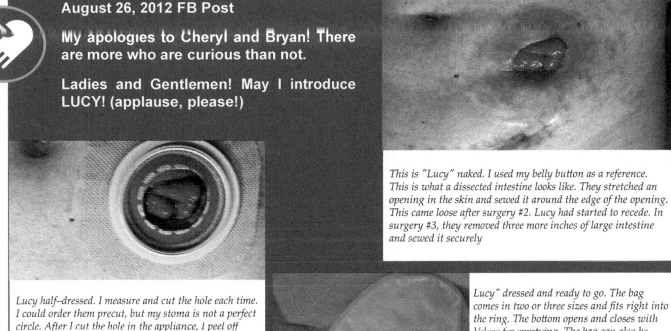

August 26, 2012 FB Post

My apologies to Cheryl and Bryan! There are more who are curious than not.

Ladies and Gentlemen! May I introduce LUCY! (applause, please!)

This is "Lucy" naked. I used my belly button as a reference. This is what a dissected intestine looks like. They stretched an opening in the skin and sewed it around the edge of the opening. This came loose after surgery #2. Lucy had started to recede. In surgery #3, they removed three more inches of large intestine and sewed it securely

Lucy half–dressed. I measure and cut the hole each time. I could order them precut, but my stoma is not a perfect circle. After I cut the hole in the appliance, I peel off the sticky backing and slap it on. I previously used an adhesive that looked like toothpaste, but I think that is what irritated my skin. It holds fine without it.

Lucy" dressed and ready to go. The bag comes in two or three sizes and fits right into the ring. The bottom opens and closes with Velcro for emptying. The bag can also be lifted off the ring to allow air to escape.

Is this more than you wanted to know about Lucy and I? My humble apologies if I offended anyone.

ALLEN: Courtney and I got a chuckle naming her Lucy. That's our dog's name. How apropos.

MONICA: Lucy's looking good!

JOHN: No offense taken Lauren Lane Powell ! This is what we all need to know to make what you have been through a reality. This is one example why I have created "Lightworker Support Group" .. If you would like to post it there please do so !

MARTHA: Compassionate sharing of something many people live with. Thank you, bless you.

JOHN: Things we all need to know.. removed from the texting and virtual reality .. Reality like this is Like Ice down your back.. wakes you up.. We all Love you so Much Lauren Lane Powell!

DIANA: I am not offended and I thank you for sharing this event. I am no longer so afraid but accepting.

JULIE: I think Lucy looks great!!!

AMY: Gives new meaning to "I Love Lucy"! Thanks for sharing, Lauren.

LISA: My brother had this, too. Is yours reversible?

ME: YES! Yes! It is reversible. Surgery #4. In a couple of months

EDIE: You are beautiful and so is Lucy! Thanks for sharing. Sending a hug.

CHERYL: Very informative and since it has blessed you with LIFE saving qualities ..... I am pleased to meet Lucy!! (who of course was a redhead too!)

SHARON: Applause is for you!!...thank you for sharing and introducing us to your friend Lucy and your incredible spirit.... I work as a Life Coach and it is your courage that is an inspiration to more people than you realize. Blessings to you and my prayers of light and love for your continued recovery!!

BETSY: You are such an amazing light being! I love and appreciate your courage and your sharing.

MELODY: How amazing and brave of you to share Lucy with us. I've never seen this before. Interesting and amazing all at the same time. Hmm, just like you!

KALAR: Glad they have something to help you and sorry you had to go through this.

ELIZABETH: Whoa baby. Such courage you demonstrate!

MICKEY: I am such a fan of yours. Thank you for sharing the miracle that allows you to live and be well. We are much too squeamish about body functions and too slow to bless them for the magnificent jobs they do. Thank you!

CLAUDELL: Pink and healthy! Thanks for the education. I have another friend with this necessity. It's good to be alive.

JUDITH: Bless your courage and Thank you for your Inner Light that shines so bright

JUDY: You got real chutzpah, girl. Cool. Very, very cool.

BETH: Wonderful! I had an ileostomy named Gut Butt. Your post brings back a lot of memories!

OLIVIA: In my mind's eye I see you smiling and laughing putting this together. NO ONE but a giant spirit like you would do it! And, again, I echo those who applaud your courage, your openness, and most of all your demonstration that there is absolutely NOTHING we can't find humor in. You made some cringe, some gasp, and most of us smile at the Light you are. Thank you Lauren, and thank you Lucy for baring yourself to us...pretty redhead indeed. She certainly deserved a name and Lucy is perfect.

LARRY/Dad: Lauren, you have removed much of the fear surrounding this procedure, for me and many others. Mickey was right on when he observed how most of us take the routine bodily functions for granted until they stop working. So many blessings received every day.

ALAN: Hollister also makes that wafer in a form to fit version. You don't have to cut it you simply mold it to the shape you want. It then turtlenecks the stoma.
carry bag du jour, i.e., orange for Monday, blue for Tuesday, etc?

EDIE: I'm so happy to hear about your support angels and whatever you want to share is fine with me.

August 27, 2012 Journal Entry

Love this! Next week I've decided to make 51 a *real* birth–day. Starting anew, the birth of my next 50 years. I am a wide–eyed and excited infant, seeing everything for the first time, born into blessings yet uncounted, and an empty vessel ready to be filled with love. I can hardly wait to see what happens next!

August 28, 2012 FB Post

I can't keep it in! I was going to post this after the fact, but I am too excited!! Last week I made the decision to shave the rest of my hair off. It's falling out very slowly now and I may not even lose it all. As long as it's combed (brushing is overkill!), it looks ok. But when it's blown and separates at all, it looks like ca–ca. I told my family as soon as I made my mind up, so I wouldn't back out of it. Now I can't wait! I've been up since 6 AM. It feels like Christmas. The timing is cool, too.

On Sunday, I'll be 51. A starting point for sure, of a whole new life. What better way to be reborn than balder than I was when I came into the world!

I CELEBRATE EVERYTHING! I invite you all to join me. Pictures soon to follow.

ERIKA: Hooray, Lauren! When I lost all my hair it felt both like a monk deepening on a spiritual path and an opportunity for rebirth for myself. I hadn't been bald since I was a baby and I got to consciously experience my next state of evolution. My hair is now very curly (a big departure from the straight locks I had before)—a beautiful, daily testament to this blessed reincarnation. Here's to your powerful transformation!

JOSEPH: I heard someone say one time: "God created a few people with perfect heads. The rest She covered with hair." Celebrate your beautiful head.

MICHAEL: You're not even a mature woman as of yet according to the Cherokees! At age 52 you graduate to "maturity " so you still have a year to be a kid! Although I know you're a kid at heart!! You teach me courage each day! And have inspired me to get my tuning forks out! Big and bigger hugs and healing to you sweet child!

MADELINE: Can't wait to see the bald, beautiful you.

BETTY: The hairdresser in me wants you to know it will also look so much better when your thick again regrowth comes in. You won't have to deal with thin sprigs having to be cut down to blend with the new growth. Here's to freedom and new beginnings. Thank you for reminding me to make the most I can of every day!

LARRY/Dad: Your bald head will be beautiful...but not so beautiful as the girl inside.

August 28, 2012 FB Post

Updated Profile Picture

DENNIS: Goddess!

HELENA: Sassy!

ALLAKARA: Seriously beautiful

MARYANN: Perfection.

MARY: Radiant!

KAREN: I like it so much. I think I'd feel free!

HENNIE: You are Amazing!

MICHAEL: It looks really hot! No kidding.

JAMIE: Words cannot describe what I see!!!!

CATHY: What a beautiful head you have!

JUDY: Wow—you look HOT!! Great pic.

MARIE: You GLOW!!!! Beautiful!!!!

LYNN: Yep, you're one of those with a BEAUTIFUL head! Love it and you!

JUDY: Wow you can really see your beautiful eyes!

LOURDES: You look beautiful Lauren. Radiant! Love the do.

MAUREEN: Wowwza ..shining and bright...very attractive..U wear it well for sure...

MELODY: How beautiful you are. Not too many can pull off the bald look, but you look great!

JON: Looking Healthy Laurie, your eyes are bright, you look as if you've gained weight. Keep going kiddo!

HELENE: You are incredibly beautiful!!! Your Spirit is showing!!!!

LISA: You look BEAUTIFUL!!! How freeing is that!

ELLEN: You are totally rockin' that look! And it emphasizes your beautiful eyes!

JUDY: You are beautiful, Lauren!!! Hair is really overrated. It was really a freeing time, when I was bald and wore just a tattoo on the back of my head. Good for you for being free and not hiding under a wig. Sending love and light from one sister to another. You go, Girl!

OLIVIA: Woohoo! Sexy lady! I knew you would be one of those exceptional ladies who could pull off baldness. I AM ENVIOUS! You are beautiful!

JUDY: Jeepers creepers, where'd ya get those amazing peepers? To look hot with a shaved head....wow. You've got somethin' out of this world!

LIZ: Lauren, you are absolutely, radiantly beautiful. Look what all that hair was hiding, shine on!

TOM: I just saw this picture and my first thought upon viewing it/you is...... "Wow! Radiant!" .... and that was without reading any of the other comments above!

LARRY/Dad: She could not wait for her birthday on Sept 2nd to get rid of the thinning strands. As always, she radiates love and enthusiasm. Thanks, God, for your ever flowing blessings.

JOHN: THANK YOU. YOU ARE SO MUCH THE LIGHT THAT I WANT TO BE—SING ON—SING ON

DENISE: My sister released her guilt when she shaved her head for a fund raiser, she was so grateful ...

Lisa: You are glowing! as I see your aura in yellow/green. Your amazing courage and strength shows in your eyes! Behold your strength especially in times of doubt, and know that you are love and are loved by so many!

WILLOW: Wow. STUNNING

KAYLE: Absolutely a Beauty :))

NAOMI: Yeah I was just going to say your head is perfectly shaped for this look, also love love LOVE the earrings. Love you beautiful lady.

ELLEN: I've thought for a long time that, if we all were bald, it would make life less stressful & give women a lot more time to do necessary things! Lauren you are & always have been beautiful!

ERIKA: You are radiant! A pure expression of light and love. Keep shining!

CAROLYN: You are beautiful. Are you going to shave it all the time or is this temporary? Just wondering, Lord I wonder if my head would be shaped as beautiful as yours if my hair was shaved off..

MARYANN: With a face like yours, anything looks great!

August 28, 2012 FB Post

WOW! I am so surprised! I love it! If feels awesome! Peach Fuzz!

JOSEPH: Lovely! Continue to celebrate your life and yourself! You are an awesome inspiration.

RAMONA: You are gorgeous! What freedom is expressed here.

SARA: Love these pictures! Such a beautiful head you have! It matches your soul and your smile.

JOY: Beautiful! Surely there is a peach fuzz song. So soft and sweet. I remember my last workshop before the diagnosis. Gina in the audience asked me if I was afraid of surgery. At the time I was convinced I had a hernia. My reply was wide eyed: "Well, of course I'm afraid of surgery!" She just sighed, as if she knew. That moment, I too knew. I MUST face that fear somehow to get beyond it! The next thing I knew, I was hospitalized, getting a total hysterectomy, facing chemo and a colostomy. I was learning to surrender in a whole new way!

August 30, 2012 FB Post

This was fun to put together. Quite a study!

REV. LAUREN: What a fascinating retrospective on your hair styles—you're equally lovely in all of them, but frankly, I like the new one. Time to simplify!

JODY: All beautiful!!!

MITZI: All beautiful—the latest is completely stunning. You are glowing with love, beauty and Spirit!

CATHY: You are beautiful no matter what length the hair is. Not many can pull that off!!! BEAUTIFUL !!!!! Inside and out. You Always have been even as a child. Lol

JAMIE: Bald is freaking awesome! You are beautiful no matter the length of your hair...but dang girl...you are awesomely beautiful bald!!!

CHERYL: Namaste ~ We Love and Miss you our Beautiful Goddess Many Blessings

SHERRI: Eyes, you have always been beautiful, and your radiance literally shines forth in the latest photo!

KAYE: Your other friends said it again and again, Beautiful, Beautiful, Beautiful.

MIKE: Adventure...enjoying too that the smile remains unchanged.

JANET. You actually look fantastic with no hair! You Rock!

MELODY: You look beautiful in all your lengths of hair. You have such a perfectly shaped head. You actually look really beautiful bald!

MARY: Perfect in all "mane festations"

CAROLYN: Very very interesting indeed..Only you could pull this off! As you did !

CHARLES: And in each and every picture your beautiful soul shines through!!!!

TRISH: Beautiful at any length - it's in the smile and the eyes.

JODYREA: What's in a hair???? You are too beautiful.

MARIENNE: Love the new look. It's a renewal!

MICHELLE: A year of transformation and growth!

MARYLOU: Beautiful! Now we can see you first.

CECILIA: Lovely Locks Locked in your TRUE SPIRIT! Shedding that fur let the light shine! So beautiful. Truly.

DENISE: My sister released her guilt when she shaved her head for a fund raiser, she was so grateful ...

LISA: You are glowing! as I see your aura in yellow/green. Your amazing courage and strength shows in your eyes! Behold your strength especially in times of doubt, and know that you are love and are loved by so many!

WILLOW: Wow. STUNNING

KAYLE: Absolutely a Beauty :))

NAOMI: Yeah I was just going to say your head is perfectly shaped for this look, also love love LOVE the earrings. Love you beautiful lady.

ELLEN: I've thought for a long time that, if we all were bald, it would make life less stressful & give women a lot more time to do necessary things! Lauren you are & always have been beautiful!

ERIKA: You are radiant! A pure expression of light and love. Keep shining!

CAROLYN: You are beautiful. Are you going to shave it all the time or is this temporary? Just wondering, Lord I wonder if my head would be shaped as beautiful as yours if my hair was shaved off..

MARYANN: With a face like yours, anything looks great!

My hairdresser, Jesse and I. I was in good hands. After the shave, I received a scalp massage. Ooooh Baby!

Oh Lauren,

You are truly a living example of what we all could be and should be, with your powerful positive attitude that only comes from faith. I am so happy to hear that you have conquered this life–threatening illness. But, my what a whirlwind of events that you have stood up to and the journey you have been on! I had been wondering how you were doing. Every Christmas I get out my CD of *Jesus Christ Was Born Today* and I thank God for introducing you to me, because if I had not met you, I would have never had the courage to write that song. You and your wondrous music abilities are so inspiring.

Lauren, you are such a beautiful person, with such a lovely spirit and calming way about you and I truly miss those music lessons! Thank you for accepting me on FB....I read through all your posts last night in just complete shock, but with happiness, knowing that you are on the road to a healthy recovery. Please keep me posted. If you come up this way, would love to visit with you!

Hugs and Blessings to a very dear friend, even though we haven't seen each other in a long time. You made quite a lasting impact on my life, helping accomplish a very important goal!

Janis Williams

Chapter Twelve

Drama? What Drama?

In September, I headed for the final few rounds of Chemo/Dreamo treatments. I thought I'd be done with them when I turned fifty–one. But I had miscalculated, and planned for fifteen. Instead, six rounds of three equals eighteen treatments, not fifteen, proving math wasn't my strong suit. Bummer. So I went deeper into my fifty–first year in treatment. Sigh.

My favorite poetess and good friend, Pat Coughlin–Mawson sent a poem to me the day before my birthday, brightening my day.

What a lovely poem and beautiful tribute! I felt so loved and eternally blessed by the ways in which that love out–pictured itself over and over again throughout this journey.

By this time I had gained strength, weight, and improved health due to and, in spite of, Chemo/Dreamo treatments. Chemo/Dreamo was helping me heal—my Truth and I was sticking to it. Period. My head now looked bald as a billiard ball, and I experienced fatigue as my only other side effect. So I slept a lot. I started waking up in the middle of the night around 3 AM with creative energy. Often I'd write a song or work on an earlier composition. I'd create a graphic on my MacBook to post on Facebook. Sometimes I'd stoke the fire in our wood–burning stove and gaze into the flames. I loved these meditations in the wee hours. By 7:00 or 8:00, I returned to bed and occassionaly napped until noon if I didn't have medical or other appointments to keep. I cherished those days with nothing to do and

LOVE WILL ALWAYS LAST

I didn't know the strength I had
within my heart so deep
until the magic carpet
was pulled out from my feet.
I didn't know that I could stand
on my naked legs
amd learn to walk through miracles
beyond my mind or head.

I didn't know that illness
from the many books
could come so deep within me
and change my hair and looks.

But I do know that I never
lost the ancient song
singing to me lullabies
of how I do belong.

And on the other side of this
I see the colors bright
reflecting right back to me
my wondrous laugh and light.

And I do know now with wisdom
as changes do take place
that it's my choice whether sadness
or joy come through my face.

So for everyone who joins me
on this journey of my path
sing with me a new song
LOVE WILL ALWAYS LAST.

Pat Coughlin–Mawson

For You Lauren Lane Powell, You are an inspiration to us all. Today this "came" to me for you!

no place to go. I found myself rotating among padded bed–type things all afternoon and into the evening. I'd slump from the antigravity chair, to the couch, to the rocker, to the couch in the workshop where the wood–burning stove warmed the room, then back to the living room couch. I would watch the clock, waiting for 9:00 PM, stretch, and go to bed. Going to bed before 9:00 seemed uncivilized.

I spent my birthday leading songs at Unity Bloomington with Ginger Curry and other great singers. No better place to be! During the meditation, I played the Freenote, a xylophone–esque instrument that guided the group as I spoke. A treat!

Another microphone, positioned perfectly over the instrument on a pedestal, rose about waist high. I listened and played gently. Then it occurred to me who else might be heard on the mic if she decided to speak—Lucy! So, while everyone else surrendered to deep prayer, I was thinking, "Lucy, please stay quiet. Lucy, please stay quiet. Lucy, please stay quiet." She cooperated and stayed quiet with no gurgles, burps, or farts. I never thought about those things in the past. Why would I? The entire congregation could have heard music from the colostomy bag. Can you imagine me saying, "Take a deep, cleansing, healing breath. Exhale and relax," with Lucy's chorus, "Rumble, gurgle, burp, fart?" How embarassing!

On Facebook that day, I received scores of Happy Birthday greetings and appreciation for my increasing health. I felt so incredibly blessed to be alive and to feel all right, Lucy notwithstanding. Another birthday gift was postponement of Chemo/Dreamo by a day due to the Labor Day holiday weekend. For me September has always meant new beginnings, the start of school and fall. This year it meant a new path to complete health.

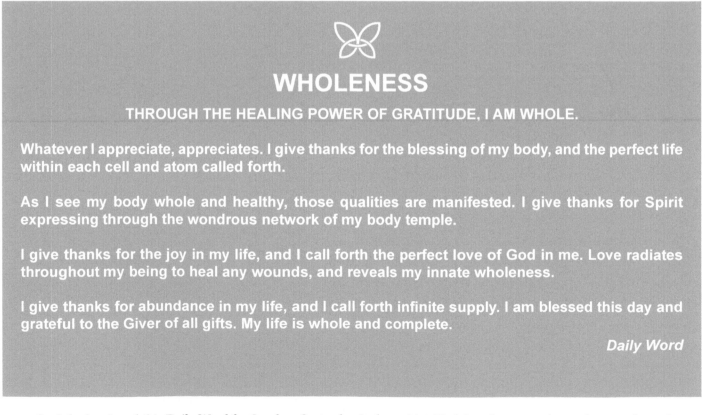

WHOLENESS

THROUGH THE HEALING POWER OF GRATITUDE, I AM WHOLE.

Whatever I appreciate, appreciates. I give thanks for the blessing of my body, and the perfect life within each cell and atom called forth.

As I see my body whole and healthy, those qualities are manifested. I give thanks for Spirit expressing through the wondrous network of my body temple.

I give thanks for the joy in my life, and I call forth the perfect love of God in me. Love radiates throughout my being to heal any wounds, and reveals my innate wholeness.

I give thanks for abundance in my life, and I call forth infinite supply. I am blessed this day and grateful to the Giver of all gifts. My life is whole and complete.

Daily Word

I cried when I read this Daily Word for Sunday, September 2nd, my 51st Birthday. So appropriate and so true for me!

Drama? What Drama?

September 3, 2012 FB Post

Morning everyone. Happy Labor Day! Today is *mine*. I can do whatever I want. I think I'll organize, clean, straighten, recoup, and regroup today. Starting over every day is so much fun. I recreate *me* every morning.

Music in the soul can be heard by the universe.

— *Lao Tzu*

September 4, 2012 FB Post

Now that I've had five months of rest/healing, I can redefine myself. I am a composer, songwriter, singer, vocal coach, and motivational speaker. An now an author. Using my passion for the voice and its healing powers, I see myself talking to cAnswer patients and their families on not only surviving, but *thriving* through singing, meditation, self–expression and having fun in the midst of it all, because if we look...*Everything's a Gift!*

Last week at Chemo/Dreamo I went in with the intention of booking speaking engagements about my new life after cAnswer once I'm fully healed. The very first person I spoke to told me about Camp Bluebird, a weekend long campout for cAnswer patients and survivors held in September and April. I signed up to attend that afternoon. Next, I spoke with a nurse and the head nurse. Both gave me a contact or two and were excited about what I have to offer. Life is *good* all the time.

BARBARA: What you offer with your spirit, your voice and soul will be healing for all who enjoy your space.

MICKEY: It's so true. Everything is always in Divine Order. It's up to us to recognize it.

NYELA: So many will benefit from you sharing your gift. Life is good.

JANIS: Lauren, yesterday at Unity of Ft. Wayne a person was wearing one of your articles of clothing. Today I see this message. You are a gift and your experience will be a gift to others. May God bless you.

LIZ: Thank you for being the gift... Namaste.

ANDREW: Lauren, I find you inspirational. As I don't know you personally I'm sure your positive attitude is just one of your many assets.

KATHY: It is amazing what can happen when the Holy Spirit is at work in us.

DIANA: Strong words from a strong friend, Lauren. I'm happy to hear you are in a loving and positive space, sister. Know I am sending you strength over the miles.

SUSAN: LAUREN, you have a blessed path ahead of you even while you've been on a blessed path all along. You ARE blessing.

DEBBIE: You are such a gift to the world. I would love to get to know you better.

169

September 4, 2012 FB Post

Calling on puppy prayers! Our 5–year–old basset/lab mix was just diagnosed with a compressed vertebra. Steroids may bring back the back legs? She's dragging herself around now. My heart goes out to her. When I get home from chemo, I'll do some Reike on her. Please help me pray for her and for my husband's peace. Thank you!

ALIANNA: Oh Lauren!! Do you remember Forrest??? He is definitely available and helping your beloved four legged!....Remember to give her some Rescue Remedy, if you have it, and arnica too.

JOHNIEBETH: Oh, poor baby! Has she gone to the vet's? Sounds like dysplasia, mine has that but not that bad. The first time he went down with it, it scared me to death. He had a pinched nerve along w/the dysplasia. Now, I'm advised to give him a whole aspirin 3 Xs a week, which helps some but may have to pick up his Remedy if he doesn't improve after a few days rest. Have hubby massage her hips. I do Bojangles' as well as my little girl, both were stressed from running in the hot temp. However, they mainly stayed in the water. But the little running they did Not so good. So, yes, when I massage my babies I'll have yours in my golden light of love and healing. So sorry to hear about your precious one.

DIANA: Light and love send to you and your family and four–leggeds. She is young to have this vertebra abnormality…maybe the vet can give her a block shot to keep her from climbing the walls or maybe acupuncture.

BONNIE: Praying for you all and sharing with my friends.

SOPHIA: You got it. Puppy prayers on the way.

CHERYL: Love, Prayers, and Healing Energies for All!

BARBARA: This is a major medical emergency with light at the end of the tunnel *if* you act *now* and get proper treatment. If you haven't gotten her to a vet do so ASAP. I have a lot of experience with special needs doxies.

ERIKA: My doxie mix responded well to acupuncture—lived another 12 years. We had to monitor pain, which she hid, and prevent her from doing activities that could damage the spine further. She's in my prayers. And ditto what Barbara said.

PAULA: My love and prayers are sent to you, your husband and your sweet fur baby. May you all find peace and good health in the days ahead.

JUDY: Get the kitty to lick the doggie's back. Sprinkle a little catnip on him. The loving licking and the nearness of kitty will be very healing.

JUDY: Prayer for a Sick Pet is awesome. Done.

ALISA PEARL: Prayers of LOVE JOY PEACE GRATITUDE…I will do Acupuncture for my little cat eleven years young.. Prayers to all of you..It is done So be it.

JANE: Healing prayers going out for you, your sweet baby, and your family.

Drama? What Drama?

KIRA: Oh my...she's just a baby. Healing energy on the way.

JANE: Healing prayers going out for you, your sweet baby, and your family.

ALLEN: Prayers, knowing God's right where you are. I declare peace, the peace that passes all understanding. This peace melts away all.

TAMI: Poor puppy!! The kitty in this adorable picture looks just like my kitty. I hope ur doggy feels better soon xoxoxoxo

JUDY: Happened just recently to our poodle Brandy...she is walking now, but no jumping or running.

September 5, 2012 FB Post

Thank you all for your prayers! Upon taking Rory to the vet, she discovered that our 60 pound basset/lab has a compressed vertebra. Sweet baby! I've received many great ideas to help her. This morning I'll buy some Rescue Remedy (she's crated for the first time and hates it) and arnica for stress. Thursday we'll take her to an acupuncturist. Ice? I'll continue to tone and give her Reike. We are grateful for continued prayers.

ERICA: We made ramps to help our guys get up on the bed/couch and in/out of the car. The stairs and jumping out of the car were the two things that seemed to make it much worse. Acupuncture was like a miracle—she was paralyzed and shaking, and then...she wasn't.

JUDY: Lauren, arnica was one of the first words I learned from my homeopathic physician dad. And Rescue is something one of my relatives used when her child was suffering from anxiety. Both remedies work exceedingly well, as I am sure you know. God is loving your dog.

TERRI: I will hold Rory in prayer! Our poor baby, Sparky Barker, is struggling, too. He ruptured his ACL in his "good leg" and is not getting around very well. We are giving him OsteoBiFlex and Vetprofen. Have thought on and off about ending his misery, but I still see that spark of joy in him. And he does seem to get better. He is 12 years old.

September 7, 2012 Harmonies of Healing Blog

Is Detached Love Possible?

Many lessons to be learned on the journey to health, not the least of which is all about Love. I understand cognitively the concept of detachment. To love without attachment seems to be the goal, because to be attached is to set up grief and pain when the object of that love is here no longer. After years of contemplation and, now with a new awareness, I believe that attachment is a part of love. My being passionate and intimate with people, events, animals, and my body means to me that I love everything around and within me deeply. When those things I love disappear, naturally I grieve. It is my honor to grieve.

Now I do not feel that way about everything I love. I love every sunset I see and do not grieve its passing. I love the rain. I do not grieve when the sun shines and dries it all up. I have been taught to appreciate everything in my life and I do. I have been taught to be grateful for everything and I am.

So now my precious body heals, my hair falls out, and my life is forever changed. How do I now love what is and not miss what was? I remember practicing loving my body on purpose and, as I cherished it, I knew love would make it stronger and healthier. I remember practicing loving my hair on purpose as I brushed it. I knew love would make it stronger and healthier. I remember practicing loving my life on the road on purpose. As I embraced it, I knew love would make my life stronger and healthier. I became very adept at loving what is, so much that now that it's all different, I grieve… again…and more.

Love without attachment? Not for me! I choose to love the grief that makes me so incredibly human. I choose to stay passionate and love deeply, even if it leads to pain at its loss. I choose to grieve the loss of my beautiful hair. Now I can embrace my baldness. I choose to grieve the loss of my beautiful body. Now I can embrace my scars. I choose to grieve the loss of my beautiful life on the road. Now I can embrace the new adventure.

Today, I give myself permission to be fully human and to love with attachment knowing full well that the other side may hold grief and loss. I choose to feel it all, because every emotion contains its own deliciousness.

PAM: Yes, when one understands what detachment really means.

ME: Pam, I thought I knew what it means...?

SHELLY: Detach: to be separate, to disconnect. To disengage, withdraw.

MY REPLY: That's what I thought it meant! How can I love deeply and be separate, disconnected, disengaged and withdrawn? They don't seem to jive!?

SUE ELLEN: I think it is to be disconnected and disengaged from expectations. Love deeply with no thought of outcomes.

MY REPLY: My Dad posted a reply on the blog site. He said, "How many of us are so afraid of feeling the pain and grief of a loss that we do not allow too great a love? Somehow Lauren has learned the secret of "loving recklessly." Isn't that the way God loves us?" Thanks, Dad. I love you recklessly.

JULIA: My dear Lauren, you are the 2nd woman who has inspired me to shave my own hair. I've not done it yet….currently at the spike stage. AND IF IT WILL HELP and/or COMFORT YOU, i will Shave my Head also as I, TOO, LOVE & Grieve INTENSELY while praying for what some call DIVINE DETACHMENT !!!!!!!!

September 7, 2012 FB Post

With this feeling of contraction, something wonderful must be forthcoming. Right!?

Does anyone else feels like screaming? Ready? One, Two, Three!

AAAARRRRGGGGHHHHHH!

ERIC: Ahhhhhhhhhhhhhhhhhhhhhhhhhhhhhhhhhhhhhhhhhhhhhh!

JANE: Argh is the pirate sound, and Sept. 19 is Talk Like a Pirate Day! http://talklikeapirate.com/

AMY: Welcome to the energy of LIBRA!

JULIA: Oh yes….and then you know you have a Surround Sound of loving people, angels, spirit guides to get you thru this!!! You my Dear are a Warrior. Much Love !!!

MARCY: I prefer to ROOOOOOOAAAAAAARRRRRRR!!! hee hee.

JOHNIE BETH: Birthing a new creation? Wow! I can hardly wait as I know it is a good one!

THERESA: I did end up screaming yesterday. So glad to know it wasn't just me.

September 8, 2012 FB Post

OK, what does it mean to up to my armpits in poop? My sweet Lucy (my colostomy), has been acting up and now our beloved dog Rory, temporarily paralyzed from the waist down, is releasing her own wherever she can...ugh!

ALLAKARA: What in the wide world of sports is going on energy wise lately? Crazy weirdness. My dog had a crazy poo accident. I clean all that up. Get to the school and a student has a crazy poo accident. I clean that up. I get to a client's house that evening and I change her adult brief three times for poo. I love that you look at things metaphysically..lol

KC: releasing toxins..yay =}

MARTHA: Everyone's getting rid of their sh%#!

JEANINE: Yes, I have been feeling the weirdness for a while, and mentioned to several intuitive friends. They noticed too. All the more reason to live life with gratitude & love and counter act the negative vibes in this world.

DEBORAH: Releasing all that no longer serves you and Lucy's following suit. You are such an amazing teacher. It's all blessings—though some are in disguise more than others.

September 9, 2012 FB Post

I got it! The definition of Divine Timing! Divine Timing is the puppy who waited until I was strong enough to lift her, to become lame. Divine Timing is the husband who now is available to care for the puppy while I drive myself to Chemo/Dreamo. Divine Timing is the ability to move our Michigan trip to October without incurring additional costs. Divine Timing does not mean clear sailing, it means that when the storms come, I am ready. Thank you God for Divine Timing. Fun Revelation!

KAY: Fun revelation, indeed! As the Lauren I've known you continue to flow with such creative play. Continued Godspeed and looking forward to viewing what is next.

DOVE: Hi Lauren! Wonderful to "see" you doing so well! Are you continuing to sell crystal singing bowls?

MINNETTE: You are too cool my dear friend! Loving you!

KRISTEN: Wonderful wonder filled you! I love you so very much!

MARSHA: I love your openness and honesty.

OLIVIA: Brilliant!

SUZAN: Love you.

LARRY/DAD: WOW, ain't that the truth. (with apologies to Ruth Price, my grade school English teacher).

MELODY: Back home from Wheatland. What fun hanging with Cindy. Good food, great company and lots of wonderful music and dancing. I'm not used to being out in the hot sun though. I got a little sunburn and a headache from the sun/heat. Still had a great time anyway. Missed you.

MY RESPONSE: Yesterday was a sad day, knowing we could have been at Wheatland, but we made the best of it. We rigged up wheels for Rory and she likes them! I'll put a video up soon! See you soon, I hope!

"Go Within and Trust Divine Timing."

—Wayne Dyer

September 10, Energy Journal

Enough of this nonsense. Today I plotted a graph of low/high physical energy times, sleeping versus doing things. I expected to see a pattern. Chemo day, then sleeping; or up at 3 AM, day two—anything I could plan around. *Nothing!* No pattern emerged for any given day. So much for my energy journal!

Drama? What Drama?

September 10, 2012 FB Post

Someone told me yesterday that on CMT, the country music TV station, they have a show called Bayou Billionaires. The first show of the season featured healing modalities for one of the family members that included a Singing Bowl! They had the guy put his feet into a big bowl just like I do! Great ideas circulate quickly, don't they! Are you ready for your very own bowl?

Jeannette and Sophia Srivastava
2011 Michigan Womyn's Music Festival

ERICA:That is so cool! You'd suggested the idea to me—I haven't gotten hold of a big bowl to put my feet INTO, but a friend loaned me her small brass bowl with a really nice tone—I've been sounding it near my feet and seems to help

September 12, 2012 FB Post

I'd like to place a Divine Order, please. I'll have some perfect peace, a side of abundance and a grande latte of love. Oh, add some joy for dessert. That will be all. Thank you!

CARLA: And so it is!

OLIVIA: Make that two please. Oh, and while you're at it, please rustle up enough for everyone..... OH, you already have? Well, in that case, THANK YOU!!!!

CAROLE: It is done!

LARRY/DAD: You already have it all. Revel. The Universe

PAM: The great part of this is that when you get all this—so does everyone around you!

PETE: I agree with my wife, Pamela, the more you give the more you receive.

September 12, 2012 FB Post

I've been thinking about Grandmama lately. I learned Monday that my last Chemo/ Dreamo treatment is on her birthday, October 15. I'll post this again next month, but since she's so present today, I'll share the blog I wrote about her and a link to her song now. Enjoy!

My beautiful, wonderful Grandmama made her transition March 1, 1997, at age 87. I am so grateful to have been close to her. Therein lies the story, her story, our story.

She made a living as a fine artist and art teacher, raising my dad as a single parent long before it was popular. She made sure everyone knew her life was hard.

I grew up knowing her to be very judgmental, unforgiving, and hypercritical. As much as she loved life and appreciated the beauty of everything around her, she seemed to dislike people in general. Her rare hugs felt cold and prickly. She didn't understand me at all as I grew into a young woman, and she could hold a grudge as if it were a trophy.

When I was twenty years old, I moved to Sarasota, Florida. Our relationship changed. I wanted a good connection with her as she was my only living grandparent. I decided consciously that I was going to make her love me. Because she lived in Clearwater, an hour away from Sarasota I was able to visit her every other weekend. I pushed my way into her heart. I loved her into gentleness.

I shared "hug therapy" with her. She softened and opened within the year. She learned how to hug without pushing me away at the same time. In fact, before I moved back up north two years later, she made two sets of stained glass hugging bears from the little book called "Hug Therapy" and gave them to me. I treasure them today.

In 1994, she was slipping and was willing to move north for the family's care. God Bless her! I flew down to move her and her belongings to Indiana. We left Florida, the home she'd know for thirty years, on her 85th birthday, bittersweet for her. That trip proved to be an adventure worth blogging about later. For the next two years we both lived in South Bend, so I saw her often. I videotaped some of her stories and we grew closer.

The last week of February, I left for a Florida tour. The day before I left, she had fallen again, and was hospitalized a block away from my home. I knew then, that I visited her for the last time on this earth plane. I rubbed her feet. I brushed her hair. I told her goodbye. Later that day, the doctors discovered the inoperable brain tumor that had been causing her falling. She would be fully cognizant one minute and out of it the next, something she was aware of, and it pissed her off! She had been mentally stable throughout her life and now she would be moved to a nursing home.

I drove to Florida, stayed at her old condo and, all of that week by long distance, I gave her permission to go to God. "It's OK, Grandmama. You can let go. I'll miss you but I'll be OK. It's your choice. I love you so much." I continued all week long. On March 1st the call came. "Thank you God!" was my first response.

September 12, 2012 FB Post, continued

That night, she came to me in my dreams and thanked me for her room. I didn't understand.

She said "Just look at this place!" Out of the mists a palatial estate formed!

"Why thank me?" I asked.

"You taught me how to love! I wouldn't be here if it weren't for you! You changed my Karma!" Wow! Just by loving her...Wow!

DEBBIE: Lauren. That was beautiful. Thank you for sharing. The pictures are amazing too. You have a voice like an angel. Keep blessing us please!

LYNN: I hope I'm that kind of Grandma when my time comes.

JANET: This is beautiful! You are lucky to know a grandmother. I never knew mine, they died while my parents were still children. We have pictures, and so many wonderful stories though.

ELVA: Beautiful, Lauren! Remember when you sang this in Playa under the Palapa? Awesome!

LARRY/DAD: An omen. She is with us helping.

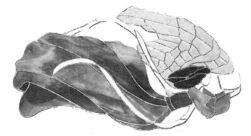

Isn't it Amazing to Find the Hidden Gifts

Sometimes Buried Deep Within the Holy Shifts?

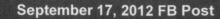

September 17, 2012 FB Post

Chemo/Dreamo #14. Today, I post my original song called "Chanting Around". Very fitting today. Great number of perfect health and well–being. In April the infamous CA125 reading was 2600+. Five and one–half months, three surgeries and 14 Chemo/Dreamo treatments later, the reading is 6...*Six!* Can you believe it? Whoopee!

JOHN: OMG! Beautiful, Lauren !

KAY: I'm with you for perfect health and a GREAT number. You are a lovely well being.

SANDRA: Dearest Angel, I am with you with great expectations and I see you in perfect health.. Keep up the great harmonies of healing!!! Luv Ya!

OLIVIA: You are a joy to behold and hear! Your song is enchanting. Can't wait to sing it with you.

ALIANNA: Purely angelic offering...thank you Lauren!

MELODY: Beautiful. Angelic. I love the chant. It's so great to sing. Very uplifting.

PAT: What a sweet example for all of us to see. I am so proud to know you

I Have No Limitations
I Have All that I Need
I Have Great Expectations
I Will Succeed

Chanting Around by Lauren Lane Powell

September 17, 2012 FB Post

Cool photo of Dad. We Skyped today during my treatment. What fun! It made the time fly by. Thanks Dad. Love you.

Yesterday's Chemo/Dreamo treatment must have stirred something up. At 3:00 AM, I was wide awake, full of energy and cleaning! Who am I and what have I done with Lauren? I may have a nap attack later, but right now I'm lovin' it

September 17, 2012 FB Post

I celebrate many anniversaries in my life this time of year. First, my birthday, September 2, then the divorce of Mom and Dad in October. I celebrate the oncoming cold, the change from green to brown, and then the beautiful snow. Our move, with ten cats, to Bloomington from South Bend on my birthday in 1999 demands another recognition. The last of our South Bend cats hangs in there at the age of seventeen, but the time to say goodbye will come soon.

Now, as my hair comes in white, I'm reminded of the transition in my own life as I start my 51st year. Our 15th wedding anniversary comes up on October 11th. Everything has changed, Holy Shift! Big stuff!

HELENA: YOU are amazing and so powerful—so glad you are writing that down of others!

GWYN: This is a message that needs our attention.

SHIRLEY: Holy Shift! I love that.

SHELLY: Girl, you be amazing!

ANN: You are such an inspiration! HOLY SHIFT! I love that!!!!:)

LARRY/DAD: I am glad to be around to watch the miracles and marvel at who you have become. I love you. Wish it could have been easier but then you wouldn't recognize your self.

JUDY: Embrace the grey...I went from mouse brown to jet black to nearly white (silver).

SPIRITUAL TOOL
Gratitude

How can I be grateful for "this"? "How can I be grateful?" is the right question. With gratitude added, great grief turns warm and sweet. Being grateful transforms into a tool, an exercise, a prayer that deepens, enriches and enlivens every aspect of life...including death.

September 22, 2012 FB Post

I have felt awesome, high–energy and pain–free, since early August. I have been grateful and thrilled. Now...not so much. Thursday I woke with what felt like a charlie horse in my left side. You know a stitch–in–the–side kind of feeling. I thought maybe I had pulled a muscle. My doctor is concerned about infection around Lucy. My immunity #S were low Monday. I am on antibiotics. I see myself feeling better and better. I am releasing a slight fever. Continued prayers will be wonderful. Thank you all.

DEBBIE: Absolutely! Calling Silent Unity (800-now pray) also. Love you!

DAVID: Holding you in the healing Light!

ALIANNA: I see you standing in your activated Light Power.

CHERYL: Love and Prayers in the midst of another level of healing and release!

RAMONA: Continued prayers and love your way. HUGE [gentle] hugs.

CATHY: Lauren, Elaine S. played at my church today and did a Ho-o-pono-pono thing. Then Marie at the church talked about your version of it and how much she loves your CD and listens to it in her car every day; and we were all talking about how wonderful you are and sending you love and light.

KATIE: All is releasing in Divine Order. Love, Love, Love

In the midst of all things medical on Setember 23, Phil's 63rd birthday, came and went. No party. Thank God for his good health. Had to get ready for Chemo/Dreamo the next day.

Chapter Thirteen
Reeling in the Drama

 September 24, 2012 FB Post

Enough with the drama already! I feel better today and I will receive some blood because my counts are down. *That* is not the drama. Two of our sweet fuzzy four-legged kids are still not well. Rory, the 5-year-old short-legged dog *still* can't move her back legs. My husband has been in overdrive caring for both of us. Our 16-year-old favorite kitty is on his way to God... but that's not the drama.

This morning, my Daddy fell in his driveway, hit his head and broke his neck. *That's* the drama. I learned during chemo that he'll be okay. He now has stitches in his head and a neck brace. Then, in treatment, the last five minutes of my Taxol went all over the floor. Hazmat team came and everything! That's the drama! NO MORE DRAAAAAMMMMAAAA! Affirmation: I am so grateful that my life moves smoothly, perfectly, effortlessly. Thank you God.

SOPHIA: Joining with you in affirming...Smooth, perfect and effortless day!

PAT: It's just a story. Tomorrow it will be a different one! Love you SO MUCH! FEEL IT?!!

JOHNIE BETH: And so it is! Keep breathing.

MITZI: Peace now! Thank you God!

CHARLES: Just remember Lauren, breathe in, breathe out. I affirm only the best for you, healing prayers.

SALLY: Seeing you drama-free, surrounded by peaceful thoughts and beauty, continuing to heal. Love.

DEBBIE: The light of God surrounds you!

DONNA: Let's affirm a calm and peaceful day tomorrow.

BETSY: How does it get any better than this? Just ask the question.

DEBORAH: My heart goes out to you. I am visualizing a day of light and joy. I so appreciate your attitude and perseverance!!

SUSAN: PEACE BE UNTO YOU, LAUREN.

RENELLE: I like your affirmation, Lauren. Of course, life is tough and heartbreaking, with a new challenge and necessary adjustments around every corner. I envision you as flexible and resilient, bending calmly in the winds, accepting loss and your own and your loved ones' challenges with the grace, wisdom, and courage you have been showing throughout this ordeal. And continuing on as an inspiration to all of us who love you.

JEANNE: I find it amazing that drugs that go in our bodies require HAZMAT to clean them up after a spill. Wow. Drama be gone!

JANE: Seeing you and your life as the perfect expression of Spirit. Holding you in serenity.

MARILYN: The universe just affirming and showing you how strong you are! Love and light to you and family!

MARIE: Enough of the excitement. Make like a windshield wiper and wipe all that ugly energy away. Then Picture a beautiful white cloud filled with crystalline light and energy pouring down all over you.

September 24, 2012 FB Post

This is not a big deal in the big scheme of things, but on top of everything else... a little chemo got on the favorite sweater. They took it! Even washing it several times is not safe! WTF! Done with the drama! I say it again!

CHARLES: You are surrounded by Light, Love, and the Universe. Your friends all LOVE you and support you.

SHELLY: Amen amen amen

JOHNIE BETH: Keep breathing and get still. Peace!

MICHELLE: "Drama, Drama go away. Grace and Ease are here to stay!"

JANE: Spirit is guiding you to a new sweater, and giving you opportunities to embrace and love drama!

   MY REPLY: I'm working on that Jane...Loving the drama!

"Don't waste time on what's not important. Don't get sucked into the drama.

Get on with it: don't dwell on the past. "

— Allegra Huston

September 24, 2012 FB Post

OK. I got it! PERSPECTIVE!!! Sitting in a new–to–me part of the cAnswer center, filling up slowly with new fresh blood, I struck up a conversation with two sisters. The one receiving the blood had been in remission for two years and had a really good time. With the leukemia back she needs blood daily to stay alive. Without it, she has 4–5 weeks. For quality of life, she now has to choose...God bless her. No more complaints! I promise!

MELODY: It's ok to complain if it helps you to get the negative emotion out of your system. But then, as you did, we get perspective and move on. Love and blessings.

MY REPLY: You sound like me talking to me! And you are right! Thank you.

MELODY: Hmm, I like that comparison. Love you!

ERICA: F****ing cancer. I don't think being frustrated and upset with a sh*tty situation is the same as 'complaining'—sitting in the sh*t isn't helpful of course, but experiencing and authentically sharing feelings is totally NOT complaining and is productive and honest— also reminds the folks who love us about the day to day realities we manage. Yes, it could be worse —AND some aspects of what is are TERRIBLE and hateful.

JOHNIE BETH: It is good to get out of yourself and listen to what other patients have to say about their disease, but do not take it on, shield yourself with the loving light and be a blessing to someone who might need your "transfusion" of love and light as well.

CHARLES: It's all a matter of perspective.

September 24, 2012 FB Post

You all have a good point, of course. You need to know that before I ever post anything less than positive, I do live with it for a few days. The physical pain started onThursday morning. I didn't ask for prayer until Saturday. Here on Tues AM, I feel good again. Phil played the bowl for me once and I received many prayers. And through my resting, I felt the feelings. Love you all!

MARY: Lauren, I've been meaning to let you know that the toning circle continues monthly, although now only at United Life. We feel great appreciation and a strong tie to you and the healing techniques (and bowls!) that you brought to us. BTW for the last two months, we have dedicated our toning time to you! Blessings to you.

MY REPLY: I am touched and healed by your love and singing support! Thank you so much. You are a Blessing!

You are a Blessing!

September 26, 2012 FB Post

Daddy's in surgery for his neck at 1:15. When he fell on Monday, not only did he land on his face against an SUV bumper, but he fractured his C5, front *and* back. No paralysis, thank you, God! Just a 4–hour surgery. Anyone who can and is willing, please join us in song anytime between 1:15 and 5:00 today. Thank you! My sister and I will be singing away. We know music heals. Thank you for adding your voice. Lots of love!

KALAR: Oh my goodness, Lauren, I send you prayers and ask the angels for special blessings for you and your family. I love you.

BONNIE: Prayers in a song ~~

JENNIFER: Praying for my Favorite Uncle!!

LIZ: Singing prayers.......

BERNADETTE: "Every little cell in my body is happy ..."

BONNIE: You and your family are completely wrapped in the loving and healing arms of our magnificent Universe.. Namaste

ESAM: I still see in you the fourth grader I met years ago...very beautiful, excited, and open to life.

PATRICIA: Singing to the sky for you and dad, and the rest of your tribe.

JERILYNN: Oh wowser darlin, SO grateful there is no paralysis and joining my voice to yours!

SUSAN: Lauren, music truly speaks louder than words. I sing for my soul every day on my gazelle and I think of you and smile. I remember when my head was bald and yours wasn't and my precious Demetri had such a crush on you and that makes me smile too.

CHERYL: Still singing prayers and loving gratitude for answered prayers!!!

GIEO: My thoughts are out there for your dad. Sorry to hear. I am holding healing energy for him

TRISH: Sending prayers your way -- the musical kind.

TERRA: This is at EST, correct? And SO IT IS!!

AMY: Sang and prayed for you both in synagogue yesterday. How is your Dad doing? How are you feeling?

OLIVIA: My prayers are sent with the angels surrounding him. How is he doing today?

JODY: Praying for you and your father, sending musical healing energy... love you!!!

Update on Dad. I guess it was a pretty tentative surgery, but he came through it. That night they watched his heart closely because it was doing weird things. Last text from my stepmom said he was better and resting. Thank you all sincerely for all of your prayers and singing. We are all surrounded by angels!

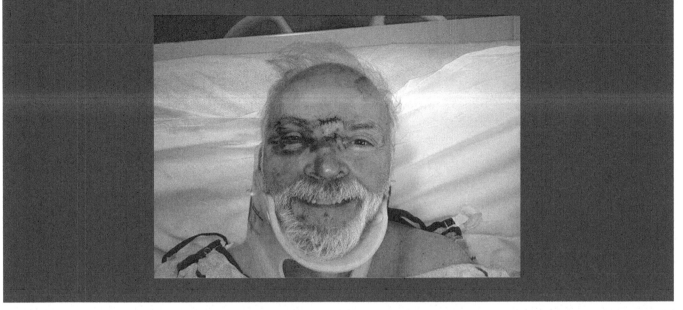

I waited to see what was mine to do, if anything. It wasn't easy. I wanted to be at Daddy's bedside every minute. I wanted to help Mary Ann. I could do nothing but stay put and continue to heal. Kristen stayed overnight with Dad for several nights. He did not do as well on the morphine pump as I did. It put me in la–la–land, relieved the pain, and helped me sleep. It gave Dad terrible hallucinations. Without Kristen at his side, he may have hurt himself further, as he was trying to get up in the middle of the night because of the feces on the wall or the rats and bugs that he swore were crawling around. They sent me this picture to show that Dad still smiled. Obviously I get my attitude from him. I wish I could've been with him.

While I could not go see Dad and my sister, I was, however, headed for Camp Bluebird, a camp for cAnswer patients in all stages of their healing. I wondered how many actively underwent chemo like me. I thought, once I was healthy, I could serve others in this place; and talk about meditation, attitude, singing, and prayer. Perhaps next year. This year I went there to participate.

Because I was off the pain meds, I could drive short distances like to the camp, an hour away. My cousin on my mom's side sent to me a Flat Stanley that I was only too happy to photograph and post for him from camp.

I drove tentatively and parked as close to the sleeping room as I could. Then I saw the sleeping room, a dorm room with bunk beds and very thin mattresses (if you want to call them that) and wafer–thin sheets. The bedsprings looked old, stiff, rusty, and questionable. I felt my bottom lip begin to quiver like it did whenever I hovered between frustration, disbelief, and fatigue as a little girl.

Before unpacking, I attended a meet and greet where I joined the circle of about sixty women and a few men, young and old. They took turns speaking, one at a time, about their cancer. Oh, they owned it! They didn't know any better, but after five or six stories of umpteen surgeries and recurrences, job loss, pain, and side effects, I wanted to run. We all needed to vent and this place provided a forum, but Holy Shift! I heard *nothing* positive. I sat dead center in the circle and had brought my Freenote wing with me. I resolved to bring some peace to this place. Before my turn though, the gal right before me said, "I've been studying a little bit about meditation and how my autoimmune disease could get better if I didn't have so much stress in my life."

When she finished it was my turn. I introduced myself and said "I teach meditation." Then I played the Freenote wing, a wonderful, lightweight, toning intrument that rings like angels sing, very soothing. I talked about loving what is, finding the gifts in the shifts, and making peace with change. I may have reached a few, but when I finished, the second half of the Woe–is–Me circle picked right back up where it left off. However, I made a fast friend that day, Rachel, the gal before me wanting to know about meditation.

As the circle closed, she asked, "You're not going to sleep in the dorm room on those beds are you?"

Did I have a choice?

"I have an extra queen–size bed in my hotel room on the premises. Come stay with me."

I knew this angel had answered my prayers!

Nothing at camp mattered except meeting Rachel. I imagine those who lived in the city and had neighbors, enjoyed getting away to the woods as a nice vacation. I couldn't wait to get back to my own woods. I received a text from Mom as I prepared to leave. Her brother, my Uncle Larry, had passed.

He and his wife celebrated their 50th wedding anniversary the previous December. Confined to a wheelchair from polio since age fourteen, he recently suffered a number of strokes. At last he walked on the other side with Mom's mom and dad opening their arms to greet him.

As I hung up the phone, Phil called. "Max died today."

Holy Shift!

A Little About Max and His Place in Our Lives

Max, our fourteen–year–old miracle kitty stood at death's door several times, then came back to perfect health. His teeth troubled him so we removed several over time. Once Max jumped down from a ledge and dislocated his hip bone. That incident resulted in a ballectomy in which the vet removed the hip ball joint itself. After surgery, Max jumped and ran like his old feline self within a month.

Another time I arrived home after a tour and found Phil weeping in the bedroom next to Max. Max had been failing fast for no apparent reason. I've learned that when I'm still and tap in, sometimes I can hear the animal's voice. I asked Max, "Is it your time?" I heard/felt a definite "NO!" We rushed him to the vet to find out his liver was shutting down and his kidneys were failing. No answers as to why. When Max messed himself, the technicians shaved him. They discovered two tiny ticks burrowed deep in his inner thigh. Apparently, the ticks had sickened him.

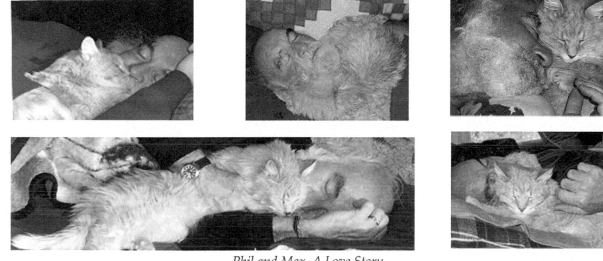

Phil and Max, A Love Story

I received my share of Max kisses

The clinic kept Max for two more nights and loaded him up with heavy–duty antibiotics. After five meds a day for a week, he came back from death's door to enter his cuddly energetic second kittenhood.

His love of prowling outside resulted in dreadlock type knots in his thick coat. Every spring, he endured the indignity of

almost–shaved choppy fur. I had to believe he felt better. Hairless or fully fuzzy, this love of our lives showed us multifaceted love. He knew when to deliver a good cuddle. Standing on a table, he would reach up either paw to our shoulders for a full body hug. He slept with my husband in an orange ball on the foot of the bed, or curled up behind his knee. Every morning presented a photo opportunity, because they loved each other every night!

Max shared well with others. He didn't seem to mind the rest of the menagerie piling on, as long as he assumed the prime spot, up front and in Daddy's arms!

The four times he came back from the brink of death, his energy renewed and he appeared grateful to be alive. He knew where to lie and apply his special purr therapy.

Max loved Phil, and Phil loved Max. As much as I would love to be number one in Phil's life, I know how much he loves these fuzzy babies of ours. I'm happy I receive half of that love.

As I packed, I noticed the absence of the intense grief that often accompanies such news. For me, deep satisfaction filled its place, knowing that this time, Max was ready to go. He had bounced back to us many times and blessed us beyond all prayers with many good healthy years. So I felt no grief. None at all.

At home I expected to feel a hole left by Max's passing. Phil and I felt no hole, aware of how light we felt about it. We buried Max in the backyard in our kitty cat cemetery and thanked him for the many blessings that he had bestowed upon us so deeply and for so long.

Max's Shrine

When I called my mom on the way home from Camp Bluebird, I realized that I experienced gratitude and peace around Uncle Larry's passing too. He had been in and out of the hospital for months, most recently for six weeks. He coherence allowed some good visiting and expression of great love. His 78–year–old body lingered long enough that relief predominated over emotions of grief and shock. I found it curious that our favorite cat and Mom's only brother died on the same day, just hours apart.

With that, September ended with a bang. At least I felt more human as the weeks passed. The fall colors emerged from a sea of green. The air held that camping–outdoors–in–a–tent kind of crispness in the evenings that grew longer each night. In addition to necessary warmth for my bald head, wearing hats became part of my purposeful fun.

October 1, 2012 FB Post
I started a new photo to the album entitled "Many Hats for a Bald Head."

MELODY: Did someone make the hat and shawl for you? They are beautiful, just like you.

ME to Melody: I found the hat at a consignment shop years ago. The prayer shawl was made for me by Christine Baldwin in OKC. They just happen to match!

LANA: Great picture. You look fabulous!

SOPHIA: Love these pictures!

KATHLEEN: That's my girl :)

SPIRITUAL TOOL

Processing

Processing that weekend required many tools from my Spiritual Toolkit to find peace, feel better, release judgment, and stop crying. When I felt the need to weep, I did. At first I did not attach to the tears. Then tears were assigned to the people in camp who suffered. Driving home, I pulled over in a private place and allowed my body to sob as much as it wanted. By that point, I no longer felt sorrow in my mind. My feeling body let loose everyone's pain, including mine.

October 1, 2012 FB Post

Home from camp last night, filled to the brim with gratitude for all kinds of things! New friends, healing, good sleep, new opportunities to serve, good food, *kittens* everywhere. The weekend was awesome and awful all at once.

I heard *way* too many horror stories of other people's illnesses. I would have liked to hear more of their miracles of healing, gratitude, etc. But the first evening's event was a sharing circle. At least 50 people talked about their disease like they owned it. I wish I had a thicker skin. It took a long time for me to process. I woke up the next morning in tears, practicing Ho'oponopono. I know how to love everyone where they are, but I see a need for a Holy Shift of energy.

The weekend put things into a deeper perspective for me. I realize just how blessed I am. Even with Lucy, (my perfectly functioning colostomy) I am healing very well. No chemo horrors, no radiation, no nausea stories. *Thank you God!* I am so blessed!

Now I look forward to the next Camp in April, at which time I will be more able to shine my light and share from the heart how to sing ourselves back to health and speak our truth with words of love and affirmation. For now, I can love us all to peace. Thank you, God, for my understanding of truth.

ERICA: I TOTALLY get what you're saying about people owning the disease. I NEVER speak of "my cancer" and I always speak of it in the past tense— like a bad tenant who was evicted, I'm doing clean up—and am moving back into my house. That was a HUGE amount of energy to be around—sounds intense. I've been super careful about being around the "sick people." I just started attending an "after breast cancer" class. I think it will be ok. The energy felt pretty good And YES, our entire human species is ready for a Holy Shift of energy. This disease is TELLING US THAT—it is time time time to shift it, release it, heal our Mother, and we will be healed right alongside Her.

PAM: THANK YOU both Lauren and Erica for expressing the positive with the diagnosis of cancer. I have never 'owned' breast cancer (8 years ago) and now squamous cell cancer on my vulva. I always found the same situation with the groups, some friends, and others that they seem to focus on the dis–ease instead of the positive aspects. I am not a victim and hopefully never will be. I also went with alternative care after BC and didn't do the usual western chemo and radiation as was suggested. Now, I'm looking at surgery again soon and hoping this will be the last one. Yea! Thank you both and blessings in abundance!

FAYE: You are amazing and a true blessing to all.

LINDA: Such a leader for us all: you learn, you share, you teach.

ANNE: YOU ARE SUCH A BLESSING AND INSPIRATION!

SHIRLEY: Lauren, you are such a bright light and I know you will shine that light to assist many in their travels with illness. It is a shame that some own their illness and the stories around it, but unfortunately that is the way it is. That is their free will to do that. I find that in my healing practice, some really do want to heal and with assistance they do. Others however cannot let go of the stories and what was done to them. It used to really bother me that my healing sessions didn't work for everyone and I blamed myself, but then I realized I was just there to give what I can, so that others can receive what they can.

REV. LAUREN: This is probably your first big taste of a whole new PFE — Purpose for Existing for you—to get people off of the subject of what's wrong and over onto the subject of what's right. But unfortunately, before they will listen, they have to be able to tell their story. So— Let me teach you the balloon trick. Whenever someone starts to talk about something you don't want to hear, just imagine a playful little balloon floating between your face and theirs —you can still seem attentive and interested in what they are saying, but actually, you are playing with your little balloon. Change its color, make it do fun things like flips, twists and circles—shoot up and drift down—and then the things they say will not impact you. They will feel heard and you will feel untouched by their particular problem. Let me know how it works.

MARYANNE: So different when you are in a place where people are victims. It really allows you to see how much you have grown past that. I am so proud of you my friend. I Love YOU!!!

ERICA: LOVE THE BALLOON TRICK Lauren OMG!!!! That is so great. An energy worker and mentor taught me to surround myself in golden light before I stepped into public—I'm a librarian and was working all the way through chemo—and that nothing harmful to me could enter my energy shield. The nurses were always amazed. "You're working with the public and you've never been hospitalized with an infection?" they'd exclaim, as they looked at my blood counts and got my chemo infusion ready. Of course, besids my golden shield, I also TAUGHT myself how to be OCD about washing my hands and not touching ANYTHING the public handled as much as possible. But I did it. I got through without infection. I'm still amazed at what I've been through!

ME to Erica: Me, too, Erica! Thank you for being an inspiration to me!

ALISSA: OUR LIGHT does SHINE very BRIGHTLY You are a BLESSING TO us all who know you LOVE JOY PEACE GRATITUDE.....

DAYNA: Sometimes God needs us in odd places. Your love and light must have been needed for all those folks identifying with their miseries....I can't imagine, but I'm glad you were there for them!

JODY: Just thinking of you, and wanted to send you some flowers! Love, joy, and blessings sister!!! xxoo

October 3, 2012 FB Post

More prayers please! Dad didn't pass his swallow test and may not be a candidate for a feeding tube as that is more major surgery. He says he feels weak and is aware that he hasn't eaten in quite a long time Of course he's being fed via IV. I ask that you send him peace and stillness for his ultimate healing. I'll be with him tomorrow and I'll sing. I think when he can yawn and hum, working it slowly from the inside out, the swallowing may be strengthened. I thank you in advance for the many miracles created by so many angels' prayers! Thank you Facebook friends!

CLAUDELL: So many prayers are coming your and your dad's way. Peace and wholeness and an ease through this experience.

FRANCESCA: Praying for your dad and your family, so sorry about his fall.

JIM: Knowing that all is well and that healing is revealed.

CHERYL: Namaste ~ Always sending Love & Prayers your way Many Blessings

EILEEN: The beauty of your singing will flow through him, healing and harmonizing his physical being.

DIANE: May peace and stillness be with your dad...

KALAR: Sending you prayers for healing and love.

ALISSA: I Pray for your Dad ... My 83-year-old beloved husband had to be given a tube. It was so hard to see him like that; so painful, but needed. Blessings to you and your family. Be well, stay well. Beautiful songs of Healing to your dad....LOVE, JOY, PEACE, GRATITUDE.

JOAN: Sending love, peace and healing prayers....

CARMELA: Sending much love and light.

SHIRLEY: My dear friend, it is not uncommon to not pass initial swallow tests. so...... repeat after me..... Dad has not passed the swallow test YET, all is in Divine Order, Dad's throat is healing now..... I envision smooth swallowing, Dad is healing now.

JIM: May The hand of God touch you this day.

JOY: Holding your dad and the entire family in thoughts of well being.

ALISSA: AMEN.

SHIRLEY STALLINGS: Everything is in DIVINE ORDER...

JEANIE: Sending prayers and love to you and your Dad.

DOROTHEE: Sending prayers and seeing him whole and complete. Love and blessings.

SONDRA: Sending LOVE and healing prayers for your dad. Blessings and strength for you XO

JENNIFER: Both you and your dad are two of the most positive people I know! Prayers and songs are coming from the Missouri cousins! We love you all!!!

CHRISTINE: Much healing energy for your father, Lauren, and comforting presence and peace for you and your family!

KANTA: Love and light to you and to your dad. Affirming healing and comfort for him.

CHERYL: Sending lots of love and healing prayers for your dad. Seeing a wonderful miracle of restored health and strength for him

GWYN: My prayer is for your father's highest good to be met in all things.

ALYSON: Prayers going out for Uncle Larry

SOPHIA: Prayers coming now Lauren.. surrounding your Dad in love and light

ELIZABETH: Praying for your dad and you!

MICHELLE: Lifting your father and your family in prayer.

KATHI: Lauren lots of prayers and love are going out for you both. What an incredible time these last few months have been for you all, and what a special spirit you have maintained.

CHERYL: Praying, Loving, Beholding the Healing! Amen!

JAY: I send my love to your father and family. You are in my heart.

SUSAN: Prayers for healing and light.

RUTH: Love and prayers being sent to your dad, and to you and all of your family!

CECILIA: Blessings coming his way.

CARLA: Seeing him at peace and swallowing easily.

MARIAN: Angels on the way!

SALLY: Standing with you and your family, Lauren. Adding my prayer to the many surrounding you and yours with love, peace, and healing.

JOAN: Prayers of strength to boost your dad's healing ability sent his way. I see him perfect, whole and complete, responding to your beautiful songs.

BRENDA: Prayers and Blessings coming your way ~

DESSINA: Sometimes it's hard being human. Never ever give up. You will never be alone. God loves you too much, as well as all the people that love you and your family.

MARY: Sending smooth swallows songs!

October 4, 2012 FB Post

Thank you my angels! Your prayers are so powerful! Dad started swallowing yesterday and was eating real food when I got to the hospital today. You work fast! We are all very grateful for your love and support—another demonstration that prayer works and love heals. I am so grateful for all of you!

DONNA: Great news!!!

PAT: Wonderful! I rejoice with you!

MADELINE: And so IT IS!

SHIRLEY: I expected nothing less!

RAMONA: Exciting news! THANK YOU! THANK YOU!

CHARLES: Of course, and the prayers continue

October 10, 2012 FB Post

Even though I felt less than perfect, spending time with Dad was precious and put things into perspective. I chose to be there for him, like he was for me while I was hospitalized. Such a nice three days! Phil and I will stop on our way back from Michigan for another visit before we go home. So grateful Papa's healing.

Thank you for your prayers!

Chapter Fourteen
Remission

Doctor Schilder said "no" to camping at the Wheatland Music Festival, because my low blood count numbers would compromise me in crowds. No camping at Wheatland upset me, but no vacation at Saugatuck upset me more. Every year after the festival, we extended our vacation another three days in Michigan at a sweet little "Boat–tell" overlooking a river that eventually flows into Lake Michigan. Phil suggested that we move it to October, before the really cold weather, to celebrate the end of Chemo/Dreamo. I added that the trip would double as our wedding anniversary celebration.

October 10, 2012 FB Post

We came up to South Bend after Chemo/Dreamo #17 and spent the night w/ Mom. Then a short drive up to Saugatuck, MI. Chemo was awesome. So relaxing! I listened to my meditation music, dozed a bit and thanked God they are almost over.

ERICA: I too find chemo incredibly relaxing. My blood pressure drops about 20 points every single time

Love is All There IS
by Kristen Hartnagel

Love is all there is.
Love is what we're here for.
Nothing else could matter.
Nothing else is real.
Only Love is real.
An expression of, or cry for.
And when we know
It can't be threatened...
We're not afraid to heal

When we know
Love can't be threatened...
We're not afraid to feel

This is the last song of the set on my Chemo/Dreamo meditation mix. What a way to get going again!

October 10, 2012 FB Post

Next big event is sending Lucy home, maybe as early as November—last/final/healing surgery. While I've learned to love Lucy, I am so ready never to have a blowout again. I am so ready not to smell so bad. This trip is so hard for both of us. I am in constant pain. I am so ready to poop normally and feel good. The things we take for granted! My sweet husband is so patient.

They say that couples start looking alike after a while. We are celebrating fifteen years of wedded bliss tomorrow. This picture is awesome proof of growing alike together...Phil said that he was expecting long thick locks of hair....

"Sorry, honey! I'm lookin' more like you instead of the other way around!"

JUDY: You are a patient, healing example for us all.

JOHNIE BETH: Intimacy. Into you/me I see. Funny guys. Yours will grow back, but I don't have much hope for his to grow back.

LEAH: You are both shining, radiant beings of light.

MICKEY: I know you enjoy every day you have together!

BRENDA: Happy anniversary! I remember the day. It was beautiful!

ALMA: Happy Anniversary from Florida Study Group on Friday nights. You and your Dad are still very much on our prayer list.

SUSAN: And aren't you glad to be celebrating? Have fun and Happy Anniversary.

MICHELLE: It seems like just yesterday when we were so Blessed to celebrate your wedding day with you...love you!

OLIVIA: As long as you don't grow a beard! LOL. Congratulations on 15 wonderful years!

MADELINE: Happy Anniversary. A beautiful and handsome couple. Much LOVE

DOROTHEE: Congratulations! I wish you all the best, love and blessings.

CHARLOTTE: Happy anniversary. What a beautiful couple!

MAUREEN: Happy Anniversary. We Love you and miss you guys.

YVONNE: Lauren, How do you make bald so beautiful? It's an inside job, isn't it?

MELODY: Wow, 15 years. Continued love and God's blessing on you both.

LINDA: Congrats! Yes, you two do look alike.

CHUCK: I wonder what you would look like with a beard??

ELLEN: You two look beautiful!

COLLEEN: Omg, you r beautiful! What a lot of energy from such a beautiful two

COCO: Congratulations and many more

While I certainly wasn't up for much visiting, I *had* to see Pam and Pete, two of my favorite people on the planet. Pete's medical journey includes a stroke, multiple heart conditions, many hospitalizations and ultimately a pacemaker. The lovely, low–key visit, provided comfort I needed. They sang to me and Phil, then served us homemade banana bread and all natural jam.

October 11, 2012 FB Post

Sunset last night. on our wonderful, *Cold* vacation in Saugatuck, Michigan.

No agenda, no expectations, just being together was perfect. Sigh! Celebrating our fifteen years of marriage. How nice just to *be* together! So sweet. So easy. God bless my best friend, my husband, my soul mate. I love you so much. You help me heal just by loving me. I am so blessed.

TERRI: Congratulations, Lauren! This photo looks like the heavens celebrated your milestone of love too

HATTIE MAE: Your words are so precious. Even more precious than this beautiful sunlit sky.

SOPHIA: I really like your Anniversary gift from Spirit. Thanks for sharing it with all of us.

JOY: So happy for you both, and wishing you many more healthy, joyous, fulfilling years together.

CHRISTINE: Thank you Lauren, for sharing Love, Light, Life and Laughter! oxox

VICKIE: Hi Lauren. We have missed you at Unity/Gainesville. Would love to see you if you find yourself headed this way.

SARAH: Interesting and beautiful. My honey and I have been dating 30 years. Married 20 years and he still calls me his bride. I wore your shirt today, the one with "I sing because I am happy because I sing"!!

FRANCESCA: And I was there! In fact, I just came across the program from your wedding a couple of weeks ago! Love to you both!

JOHNIE BETH: What a good thing it is to appreciate another for loving you. Like my brother said to me, "Everyone should have someone to love". A lid for every pot.

DIANA: What a gift to share, Lauren. Absolutely out of this world. . .thank you for sharing and happy fifteen years of love and bliss. . .love is what we came here for. . .you know what I mean. . .

DEANE: I remember that day (your wedding) and trying to get all your cats into a portrait.
Fun, and a first for me.

COLLEEN: Omg, you r beautiful! What a lot of energy from such a beautiful two

COCO: Congratulations and many more

MY REPLY: Great pics, too, DEANE. Our favorites! OK, I have to find those photographs. Oh, Here they are!!

Phil has a son, Dylan, who is grown and living in Oregon. I am childless by choice. So our kitty cats are our children, all fourteen of them when we got married. It was only natural to have photographs taken with our fuzzy kids! Even our cake topper was a set of two dancing cats in medieval garb!

LINDA: Congrats! Yes, you two do look alike.

CHUCK: I wonder what you would look like with a beard??

ELLEN: You two look beautiful!

Our vacation experience differed from past years in that no Wheatland preceded it. Because Lucy gave me fits all weekend, I felt like the stuff filling her bag. All I wanted to do was snuggle up inside. Braving the cold, I managed to get out for a few hours. We made our rounds from the boat–tell to downtown, stopping in all the shops until we headed to our favorite breakfast place four blocks away. I struggled with this usually easy walk,and replaced my once brisk pace with nothing more than a meander. This strain was not due to cAnswer or surgery, but to *Lucy*.

As soon as I sat down and felt a little better, I apologized to Phil for being such a stick–in–the–mud. He reminded me of what I had recently endured. Still, the entire situation pissed me off. I had so much wanted to have fun. Oh well, next year. At least now I can say that with conviction. Next year! I know I'll be here that long since Chemo/Dreamo worked.

Instead of lingering with a requested late check–out time, we left for our six–hour drive home at 11:00. My body wouldn't get warm and my baldness added to the challenge. Lucy hit the warpath and I was running out of supplies. I felt crappy. Time to go home.

No energy to talk, I shuffled into the moho, holding a pillow on Lucy, and went right to bed. Holy Shift! I was grateful for our Michigan vacation, but I felt bad about feeling bad.

The following few days I geared up my mind for the *final* Chemo/Dreamo treatment. So far, I had handled them all lovingly and peacefully. I had befriended the process. I had mentally accepted the chemo as medicine and not poison. Through it, I made new friends along the way. But I'm *done.* No more. With all of the above intact ninety percent of the time, I knew I could have done it all better if it hadn't been for all the damn surgeries. This would have been so much smoother without Lucy. It would have been easier if I had weighed more than 89 pounds when I started. But I was mentally finished.

Mom—With me every step of the way

Mom accompanied me to my very last Chemo/Dreamo treatment. I wanted to make it as big a deal as possible. At the infusion center, a big bell was mounted on the wall in the entrance to the chemo room for us to ring, to signify our last treatment. I planned to bang that thing off the wall! Lucy had recovered from our vacation diet and I wanted to celebrate. Covered in my warm blanket, I laid out my crystals and put in my earbuds. I managed to obtain a private room so I would be able to stretch out fully on my back and prop my head with a big fluffy pillow.

Sitting upright for the premeds, I ate the graham crackers and drank the chocolate milk we brought with us. The nurse paged Chaplain Lorraine for me. When she came in to pray with me, I cried, knowing this appointment ended our weekly visits. This ended my regular visits with all of the nurses and techs who had taken such loving care of me for five months. I cried again, saying goodbye to all of them, and then I realized, *I'm grieving Chemo/Dreamo treatments*! How silly! When I hugged Lorraine goodbye, I settled in for my last trip into my music at this depth. As much as I would have loved to meditate with it like that when I'd recovered full health, I knew myself—a few songs at a time maybe, but a whole hour—wasn't gonna happen. So I gratefully luxuriated in the bubble bath of sound once more.

October 15, 2012 FB Post

From my treatment bed. Last Chemo/Dreamo today. Hold the high watch. Last, final, ending, done and any other synonym that means this is the last treatment. I am *sooo* grateful for *all* of it! I will miss visiting with my new nurse friends, but I know where they work, so I can visit anytime. I will meditate now.

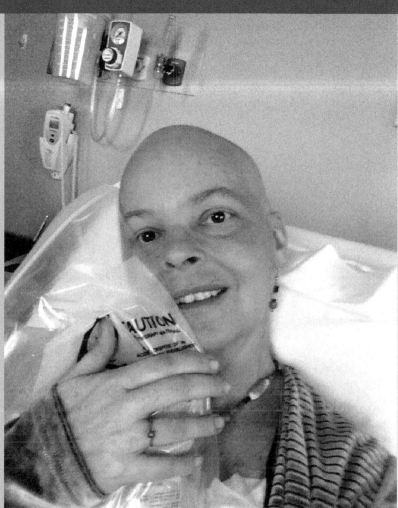

SONJA: You are the Spirit ..

ELAINE: Perfect and whole and full of Light.

SOPHIA: Whoopie! That's great news!

MADELINE: The best news.

MARY: Hallelujah!!

DIANA: We are all meditating for you!

CHUCK: Yeeeeehaaaw

PATRICIA: Such wonderful news!!! So glad you said, "I will meditate now".

CARLA: Ahhhhh. Blessings to you!

JUDY: May the wind be always at your back.

JOAN: Blessings, Lauren...and continued healing. I look forward to hearing your lovely voice at Unity of Melbourne again.

PAT: We are so proud of you and the inspiration you have given!

BRENDA: You are looking radiant in your pictures! Congrats on your last treatment.

CHARLYN: And holding the intention that it is the last you will ever need!

CAROL: As in all you do, this process will bless the world through you.

DAVID: It's so good to hear that you've gotten to this point. I'm visualizing health and joy for you.

DOROTHEE: Great that you finally got through it. Love and blessings!

MERRILEE: Hugs! Keep on the sunny side of life. You deserve only the very best of God's Love, Life and Joy!!!!!!! Nothing can separate you from your divine birthright

October 15, 2012 FB Post

Mom videotaped this ending to a chapter. Very emotional during the meditation earlier, we hugged, cried, and realized what could have happened if the cAnswer had not been caught in time; if I didn't keep my attitude up; if I hadn't received prayer; if I didn't trust the process; and if the infection that caused my second surgery hadn't been caught in time. Yes, we went down that rabbit hole of "I could have died!" then went to the other side with gratitude and celebration. What a whirlwind of emotion! What a gift to go there with Mom! God I love that woman! I am sooo blessed to have the mommy I have. She drove four hours all the way down to Bloomington. She just had to attend my last treatment. What a mommy!

JORDAN: Dance on, Sister! For all of us!

LAURA: Moms Rock!

JEAN: Bless you dear for being so REAL!!!

SUE: We are all blessed by you, Lauren. Great dance! Thank you for the honor, Sister.

GINA: Way to go Life isn't about waiting for the storm to pass, It is about learning to dance in the rain.

CECILIA: LOVE YOU GIRLFRIEND! You got the groove on for certain!

JOHN: Congratulations I know that this was a long road and I am very happy that you are done. Time to Celebrate.

DANA: YAY!!! You Are Amazing and so Brave! Thank you so much for sharing your journey with us all.

MARILYN: I am joining you in support of your celebration dance! You have been a true inspiration! Congrats...and now on with LIFE!

CAROL: Oh how you make my heart smile! You are such an inspiration to so many and I share excitement in your victory. You are a true overcomer!

DEBBIE: This is so inspiring.... have to share. Thanks.

CAROLYN: Ok....so the tears are flowing but they are tears of joy and celebration for you. What a blessing you are to all of us. Thank you Lauren, and thank you God.

CLAUDELL: You are a light in our path! Thank you so much for your sharing. I want to dance like that!

JOAN: Love our moms and those who stand in for them after they are gone. Their prayers and love sure do sustain us in our journeys.....good and those not so good.

JULIA: Seeing you dance makes me Happy! AND driving 4 hours to celebrate with you IS what mummies do!

CONNIE: We celebrate with you... Yay! Your smiles and laughter are magnificent!

DESSINA: A Mother's love is endless.

MICHELLE: BIG HUGE HUG FOR YOU BOTH!!!!!!!!!!!!!

GLENDA: How wonderful the God healing you have HAD. May he bless you in your positivity! It's just not your time, Lauren. God has plans for you.

OLIVIA: Plans AND Plans! Now all the questions about the "why" of it are clear. You are now able to be an even better instrument for God and your real ministry is just now begun!

KATHY: You have honored your mom all along, too, with many songs and things you have said when in the public eye. Great relationship!

JODY: The journey to wellness is incredible—embracing it all and walking through the fire and out the other side heals us—and you have done that! So grateful for you!

When I sat in the quiet and allowed the stillness to speak to me, now that I was out of chemo and starting over, one of my messages from Spirit was to do it differently. Do *life* differently. Before my illness, I toured the country for three weeks every month. I set up and tore down the workshop space, sang, and conducted workshops, up to four times per week. I should have been exhausted. But I thrived! I *loved* my life on the road. At first, I didn't love the driving, the booking, and the shlepping so I learned to love it all on purpose. I practiced loving all of it until I really loved it. Now, post cAnswer, I had been told to do it differently. Okay. I am listening. I am open.

The day after the last day of chemo, a very good minister friend of mine from Oklahoma City stopped to see me on her way home from visiting her folks in Virginia. Shelly and I met in Playa del Carmen, Mexico on a wonderful retreat I've written about earlier, one that Rev. Roy Fisher organizes for New Thought musicians, the retreat my entire family enjoyed. Shelly hit it off with me and my family. I visited her in Oklahoma City and spoke and sang at her church many times.

Shelly and I could have explored beautiful downtown Bloomington or driven through Brown County (noted internationally for its autumn allure), but we stayed on my land and played in our own leaves. I appreciated her friendly, grounded, and nurturing presence.

What a nice visit from my friend Shelly from OKC. The trees are at their peak and it was warm in Bloomington! Awesome!

SHELLY: I had such a wonderful time with you and your Phil in your beautiful sweet sanctuary. I am blessed. Thank you.

Positive I was finished with chemo, I booked a gig in October. I attended the yearly Gathering of SHE the last several years, where I presented my workshops and sang. Gillian, our hostess, treated me like royalty by providing a great room in which to sleep and awesome meals. She would add a very nice stipend and a coupon for a selection of incredible crystals with written information next to each stone that she lovingly laid out on a table. I looked forward to this weekend so much that missing it was not an option. But with Lucy? So close to the end of chemo?

Kristen made my trip possible as she was able to join me traveling to Gillian's in North Carolina. She had just undergone elective surgery to remove a large benign fibroid tumor in her uterus. It hadn't caused her much trouble and removing it was costly; but after my diagnosis, she held a family history of cAnswer, so she arranged a complete hysterectomy in September. The tumor proved to be microscopic and left her with only two tiny scars on either side of her navel. Her minimal recovery time allowed her extra time away from her job to travel with me.

October 19, 2012 FB Post

My sister and I are taking our first trip since our respective surgeries. Please hold us in the light for safe travels, plenty of energy, good weather and feeling good. Thank you again for your prayers of love and support.

The Prayer for Protection
by James Dillet Freeman

The light of God surrounds us;
The love of God enfolds us;
The power of God protects us;
The presence of God watches over us;
Wherever we are, God is!

www.unity.org/prayerforprotection

BARBARA: Love this prayer from Unity!

PAT: Love and Light surrounds you both on your wonderful trip!

ALISA: So Be It. All IS Well.... Be At Peace on your trip. Love Joy Peace Gratitude.....Lots of fun and laughter on the way....

GEORGE: You are there and sending much love with it.

SUSAN: You Got it! Have FUN!

FAITH: Safe journey and tender mercies.

PETE: Just listened to your CD songs on healing and oh my God! They are beautiful, just like you, Lauren.

CHARLAINE: So proud of you for the courage to come to retreat this weekend. Every time you sang, I just had tears flow down my face. Such a gift that you chose not to leave your body at this time. ♥♥♥ Excitement in your victory. You are a true overcomer!

DEBBIE: This is so inspiring.... have to share. Thanks.

I'd driven the familiar fourteen hour drive to the Smoky Mountains by myself every year for twelve years. This time I sat in the passenger seat of my own van while Kristen did all the driving. Once we arrived, she did all the unpacking, setting up, and arranging that I had once managed. I wrapped myself in a blanket and sat watching her. Chemo had left me sick, weak, and always cold.

I drew joy from this awesome event for several reasons: 1) I was alive and out in the world again for the very first time since the diagnosis, 2) I was reconnecting with friends who had been following my journey on Facebook, all so glad to see me. I saw love and relief pour from their eyes as we met and deeply hugged. Each hug I received said, "I'm glad you are alive." Each hug from me said, "Me too! Thank you for your prayers." 3) The mountains possess a healing quality and the weekend focused on healing our feminine selves, 4) At this point in my healing, I attended as a participant, a unique role for me. However, I gave a talk from a space so deep inside of me, that we were all transformed; then Kristen and I sang together, 5) Best of all, at that awesome event, was the company of my sister.

During childhood, Kristen and I continually sang together and also with our mother. In our adulthood, our busy lives rarely allowed us an opportunity to sing together, maybe once a year. Mom said she went to heaven every time we sang together. Just to send her there with our voices was reason enough to harmonize. To see the look of love on her face, pride, and overwhelming joy during every song we sang...Well, if she were the only audience member (oftentimes true back in the early days), that was enough for us.

Kristen

Although she could not physically attend, Mom's spirit joined us during this trip, in Spirit, and we called her often on the phone to fill her in on the fun. Many women remembered her from other events, and sent their love.

My only negative was dealing with unhappy Lucy. While everyone else stayed up late talking and partying, I soaked in a hot bath, sans bag, to baby my painfully inflamed stoma. I was so angry at the pain that I sobbed allowing the pain to drain out my tears. It must have worked, because the next morning I felt much better. *Thank God!*

October 23, 2012 FB Post

My precious sister went with me on my first road trip since April. I could not have done it without her. She helped me drive, shlep, and set up. We sang together, I rested, she sold CDs. Because she was there and willing, I was allowed to be right where I was, at the tail end of Chemo/Dreamo. The Gathering of SHE is a celebration and elevation of the Divine Feminine. It was a sacred and playful space. I loved seeing so many friends from last year and from other venues out of context. I want to thank Carole Ammond Truelove for driving up to meet us on our way out. I feel so honored and loved. And again and again and again I thank Kristen.

SUE: Congrats on your working adventure and bless you on your journey dear Sister

JANIS: What lovely words. I feel your love in them.

KRISTEN: Love you fully too! What a wonderful, fun time we had!

October 28, 2012 FB Post

Hooray! I just received the preliminary CT scan results and it looks good! No new spots of concern and no metastases. The only worrisome result is an older blood clot in my left leg/hip, so I need to start on Lovenox again...that lovely daily shot in my tummy that is so incredibly expensive. A gal's gotta do what a gal's gotta do!

JIM: Lauren, you are a rare gift to this world I really love your outlook. You, my good friend, inspire me.

ERIC: May all the powers of our great and vast universe conspire to assist you in your healing

JEANNE: Seeing you healed and living health. The light of Love shines bright within you.

GEORGE: Let's pray that you will not have to have the shot for long

KALAR: And you do it sooooo well.

GRACE: I've had those shots in my tummy and they are very painful! I send you prayers of full recovery and complete health and the strength to get through everything that is needed! Namaste

DOUGLAS: Hooray Hooray, God blessed you today!

PAULA: Thinking of you and wishing you few and easy sticks! Love & Light.

CINDY: Minor—compared to what you've already been through!! excitement in your victory. You are a true overcomer!

"Singing and smiling! Smiling and singing!" I sang this to myself in a high voice every day as I shot myself in the gut. It burned and stung for ten to fifteen minutes afterwards. I thought I was finished with all of this. To learn that this kind of medical stuff could go on indefinitely felt very sobering, bordering on depressing.

Okay, another kick in the already painful stomach. I wanted to believe the worst was over. I had to believe that. But there I was, shooting myself in the tummy every morning, again.

The Tide is Turning

October 29, 2012 FB Post

Back in May or June, I received this beautiful T-shirt anonymously. My sister suggested I put it on FB to thank whoever sent it to me.

I am displaying this photo for many reasons. I and the world get to see how scrawny, skinny, and bony I look.

In the final stretches of treatment, I realized that there was nothing final about it. The dance with cAnswer is ongoing. Even in the face of healing, the word "cure" was never uttered. Having to give myself shots every day for three months took the wind out of my sails.

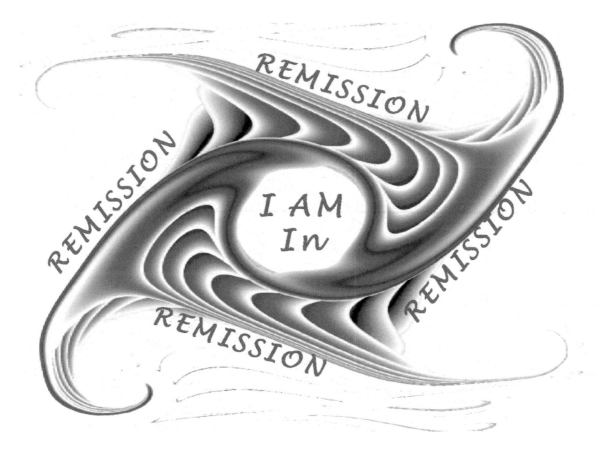

October 30, 2012 FB Post

What a beautiful word! It is official. The Doctor said it herself. I AM IN REMISSION! The tests are all conclusive. Thank you all for your ongoing prayers. I am so blessed and honored to have healed so beautifully, feeling your love for me all the way through it. I am in awe and gratitude and IN REMISSION!

KAY: Praise God, from whom all blessings flow. I am so happy to read ur healing words. Yay, Lauren!

SOPHIA: Yeah, Lauren, we are all so grateful for your healing

SHARRON: Gratitude abounds!

LISA: I knew it. I just knew it! LOVE you! Keeping you as I have, in my spiritual practice. My crew and I will bang the drums for you.

DIANE: So glad you are singing your song! Thanks for blessing us with your life!

MARTI: Thank God, Beautiful word, "remission". Much love to you

LIZ: Amazing, this is a blessed day, Lauren, I am so happy for you!

MICHAEL: WONDERFUL NEWS! IT WILL BE A MUCH MERRIER CHRISTMAS, KNOWING LAUREN LANE POWELL IS STRONG AND HEALTHY!! GOD BLESS YOU, SWEETIE!!

COCO: Remission? That sounds like re–mission. Meaning, time to re–commit to your mission of blessing the world with your awesome and loving consciousness. PRAISE GOD

CAROLYN: Congrats on such great news...keep bringing smiles to those happy cells with in...so they keep telling all the cells around them...we are happy, healthy and whole.

LYTE: Hooray! Does Re–mission mean you can REinvent your life with a new MISSION?

JOANNA: Praise God! Re–mission. Re–group. Re–new. Amazing prayer. Amazing healing. Amazing you!

ERICA: Wow. Envious. For some reason—the type of cancer that I'm dealing with—there is no official "remission"— there's five years of "watching" to make sure we got it all.

ME: Erica, call that stage "pre–mission" then! The whole idea, for me, is to feel about where I am at every step. If I have to make up words to do it, then I do!

LISA: Atta woman!!! So happy for yo,u sweet Lauren. May the blessings continue!

LINDA: Congratulations, Lauren. You are powerful and beautiful and in remission.

ELAINE: YAY YAY YAY!!!! and more YAY!

KAREN: Way to go Lauren! We are so excited for you.

SUSAN: WOW, WOW, WOW!

WANITA: Woooohoooooooo

ALMA: Thanks Giving!

JODY: YES!!!! YES!!!! I am dancing for you!!!

CHRYSSI: The best news ever! The world is blessed!

CINDY: Wow! What a fabulous expression of love and light you are!!!

CAT: WooHooo...doing the happy dance and singing!

JUNE: This is fabulous.

OLIVIA: I KNEW you would do it! Amen!

MARILEE: Bless your beautiful heart! We carry you with us always!

GIEO: You are such an inspiration in all ways! So glad to hear the good news

SUE: Congratulations! What sweet news!

JERILYNNE: Hot diggety dog darlin. What wonderful news... wow!!!!!!!!!!!

SCOTT: Perfect! You are.

SUE: How are you feeling? The shaved head is a flattering look for you, although I know it's not something you'd planned. I think so often of you & your lovely voice & your teaching people to speak more fully. Can't tell you how often I want to suggest to people that they lower their voice by a few octaves, esp when they go up into the squeaky higher registers or use that awful little girl voice! Keep up the good work!

Chapter Fifteen
It's Over! Isn't it Over?

November 5, 2012 FB Post

This may be all in my imagination, but it's been three weeks today since my last Chemo/Dreamo treatment and I swear I can feel my body coming back. I mean, my arms and legs kind of itch where the neuropathy used to be. I'm gaining a bit more energy and strength every day. I'm wide awake after eight hours of sleep, no matter what time I go to bed. I am anticipatory of awesome things happening and I am thinking more clearly. Whatever this is, I welcome it. I feel I am coming alive again!

HOLLY: I am a breast cancer "survivor" but I don't like to use that word because it does not describe who I AM at all. I like this way better, and it is so true. Cancer motivated me to redefine my mission and my life is so much better now (8 years later)! P.S. My hair is also back to the middle of my back, just the same as it was before, and I donated my adorable scarf collection to the local ACS.

DONNA: What joy! What awareness! Good for you!

JONATHAN: Wonderful report, Lauren. You are blessed that the neuropathy is leaving so soon.

GLENDA: YOU ARE COMING ALIVE AGAIN! And blessing all of us, too! GOD IS GOOD!!

ART: This is exactly what happened to Denise. Her strength grew a little more each day, and her hair came back in thicker than it was before the chemo. Her face filled back in with that healthy look, and I pray God has all the same plans for you.

ALISA: You were always ALIVE.... Maybe just a little bit sleepy... LOVE JOY PEACE GRATITUDE T.Y. GOD !!! For everything. Be well, stay well. Holy Spirit has a Divine calling waiting for you.

ELLEN: Lauren, You are a walking testimony of God's love & grace! You are in a unique position. You are given the opportunity to choose, once again, how you live your life & what you live for.

LAURA: May love and light be the transforming power that brings you healing, peace and joy.

GIEO: So glad to hear. You have a lot of people sending positive healing energy!

CHERYL: Praise the Powers that be!

LYNN: Imagination is where it all begins - First there was a thought... Love to you, Lauren!

JOHN: Yes, you're a living, breathing, healing body!!

LLOYD: You still receive a lot of healing.

KIRA: You are an inspiration and a joy!

KRISTEN/SISTER: You are my love, like a Phoenix!

LARRY/DAD: That is not ringing in your ears but echoes of the multitudes cheering you on every day.

MARY ANN/STEPMOM: Metamorphosis!

November 6, 2012 FB Post

More prayer please! I just learned that Dad's heart rate was up to 154 all last night and his doctor told him to get to the ER this morning. That's all I know. Please pray for his speedy healing. I hold him in the light of God and send him and my stepmother, Mary Ann, peace and serenity. So it is! Amen!

MICHELLE: All of you are in my prayers!! hugs!

JEAN: Seeing him surrounded by his angels.

JENNIFER: Prayers!!! Your dad and MaryAnn need a break!

MADELINE: He is held in White Light and filled with the Spirit.

AMY: Sending prayers and loving thoughts for strength and good health.

MARIA: Have been right here with you. Claiming. Sending. Done. Love.

GRETA: Lauren—sending prayers, light and love to you and family...

ELLA: Prayers are winging your way. Sending love and support.

November 7, 2012 FB Post

Dad seems to be doing better. He was in bed asleep by 5:00 PM last night. Heart rate has normalized. I do not know what is next, but I will keep you posted. Thank you so much for your prayers. I feel a lot of love pour out of my Macbook each time I ask for prayer, and I am moved and grateful! You all bless me and my family to no end!

TERRI: Brings tears to my eyes.Wish I had something similar with my Dad.

OLIVIA: Love will see you through this, as always. Prayers of healing pour out continuously to you and your sweet Dad

SOPHIA: We'll keep sending as long as you keep asking. Love you!

JODY: Lauren, this pic is beyond words, I just love it. I can feel the connection you two have so deeply in my heart. I can almost close my eyes and imagine that beautiful child placing a tender kiss on my lips. Thanks for sharing such an inspiring, beautiful, adorable, fuzzy love pic. Praying for you and your Dad!

ROBYN: Father God, Your heart and Love pour out of all fathers as this beautiful photo so poignantly shows. Thank You for this relationship! Pour out Your love and Your peace on Lauren's dad today, and on Lauren and her family. Bring healing and peace that only You can bring to them all. In the name of Jesus we ask this!

RENEE': Beautiful Picture, outstanding memory. Love and blessings to you and your family

Healing has Happened!

November 8, 2012 FB Post

OMG! Yesterday I had my first massage since March. Laying face down on the table with Lucy was the first challenge. Blanket under my chest lessened the pressure on the incision and on Lucy. Next challenge was holding back the tears. Who'da thunk that I would turn into a blubbering idiot! That lasted for about 10 minutes, when something shifted. I realized I missed my old life, again. Some more. I remembered that I used to get a massage as part of my self-care every other week. I wallowed in "woe is me, nothing will ever be the same" for awhile, then...HOLY SHIFT! I got it (again) I was *not* in the now moment. I was *not* enjoying what *is* because I was mourning what *was*. I took a deep breath and fell into deep appreciation for the moment and for all of my life right now. This is where I wish to stay...but I am still human, so I give myself permission once again to feel the feelings, then to get back to the now of life and embrace what is. God, I love my life! I am so grateful to be alive, healing, loving, sharing, crying, laughing. So grateful! What a great massage!

REV. LAUREN: You're doing just fine. You've had the ultimate trauma and traumas require as much recovery time as surgeries. Allow the emotions to flow without resisting them Lauren . They're all part of your process.

SANDRA: Thank you for sharing all of the ... HOLY SHIFTS ...in your life Angel and IN the moment.... You are an energy field of LOVE...and in this energy of I AM space....everything becomes Heaven ON Earth....I AM WITH YOU, still..HOLY KISSES, Divine Love. Sandra.

ROBIN: A great gift for your body, mind, and spirit, Lauren. Keep loving yourself.

JIM: Good Morning You are so Beloved You ARE Holy. You Are Now. And We Love Our Sister Lauren. Namaste'.

MARY: God morning, sister. Your body is blessed by the hands and hearts of So many. So keep on the holy shift train. Love you sweetly and deeply.

JEANNE: Peaks and valleys occur in everyone's life. Keep the eye on the peaks and do what you are doing: climb out if the valleys as quickly as you are able and don't look back. Blessings and many thanks for sharing your experiences. They help so many.

JOHNIEBETH: We have to grieve in order to live well. I know it is an awful feeling of loss, but one cannot open to the Good to come unless we shed more tears. I've been doing that myself lately and came down w/ a cold. I had more tears to shed. Remember Rev. Rainbow Johnson used to say there are more free radicals shed in tears from emotional crying than tears from an onion. It has been scientifically proven.

LEAH: I'm glad I'm not the only one who has to periodically relearn this one!

RAMONA: How courageous of you to share your journey with us. What love you share in exposing your challenges and victories. It encourages us on our path also. Thank you for the special treasure you are. HUGE (gentle) hugs this glorious day!

PAT: Beautiful! Thank you - such wisdom and awareness!

DOROTHEE': Having tears in my eyes while reading this. You are doing so well .... Thanks for sharing all of your story!

UNITY: Thank you for sharing. You are a very brave woman! We love you. Namaste

JOHN: Love you always Lauren…You are an Angel and a most beautiful and inspiring inner self, that you are. We must adapt to accomplish our life goals and contracts through the rough and the thicket through the streams, the valleys and the forests…Don't change the inner self who you are! Namaste!

DEANA: How beautiful to share the pure essence of your healing experience. ♥

MARIANNE: What a beautiful message for us all Lauren. You have such an amazing way to inspire us all!! Seeing only the best for you, my love!

GLENDA: You bless and uplift us all!

CHRISTINA: Thanks for the reminder. We are often so hard on ourselves when we notice that we are off course.

CHARLOTTE: Thank you for the reminder that I need to be pampered!

CLAUDELL: Ah yes. Thank you for raising the consciousness of the planet by your beautiful self–awareness. Come to ministerial school!

ALLEN: That's exactly what I needed to hear for today. Thank you for helping me pull my head out of the past and coming back to now.

TERRI: You continue to amaze me! I aspire to get to your vibrational level. Lots of love and I look forward to seeing you in 10 days!

KEITH: Feel what comes up; let go of what you can. Enjoy the gift of touch. It is the best healing thing there is. Glad you are my friend. Love the way you are.

JANE: Lauren, thank you for giving yourself permission to be human. Some people seem to try to surgically remove the "human" from us so we are just positive–thinking automatons. I prefer being fully human.

CAROL: How wonderful that a whole new life is now on your horizon, with all the amazing lessons that you have been through, all the astounding awarenesses you are continually experiencing, all the priceless actions of love and support you are receiving and have been continuing to give to others, even in this difficult "graduate degree work" of healing.

MARCIA: God Bless Lauren. Yes, I cry, too. It's a cleaning of the soul. What you say is so true: "Cry for what was, but we need to rejoice in the now." As I cry for my sister Mazz (for what was and how it uses to be), I cry now for what she is. She is alive, but the old Mazz is gone and there is a new person now in return. I have to love all over again. Grief takes on many forms.

ELLEN: Massage frequently allows the cells in your body to let go of the emotions they have been holding.

MARIAN: WOW - you are an inspiration!!

MARYLOU: Thank you for sharing your process with the rest of us! As you heal and breathe through the trauma, you allow us to access that life-giving thought/feeling and heal our own traumas as well. Celebrating Health and Wholeness!

November 8, 2012 FB Post

This is what my Chemo/Dreamo nurse sent to me a few weeks ago.

"*The CT looked great.* Keep in mind, they were comparing it to your last CT scan done at Bloomington, which was in April, prior to surgery, etc. When you bring the disc to your appointment on Monday, we may have our radiologists look it over and compare it to your CT that we did just prior to starting your chemotherapy in May. There are no new areas of any metastatic disease, and all of the previously seen spots and lymph nodes identified back in April show improvement and resolution. From a cancer perspective, things look as good as we hoped they would". Jamie (my oncology nurse)

Yeeha! *This* is what I choose to focus on. REMISSION!

CAROLYN: Awesome news..thank you for all your uplifting posts!

JOHN: Sending more love. You could not do anything but get back to helping us. Love you.

LINDA: Love the part about the chemo/dreamo nurse. :)

JANE: I see the cancer leaving your body and returning to perfect, glorious, excellent health. My cancer left in 1990. I learned many valuable lessons about forgiveness, love, gratitude and living each moment to the fullest. All is well in my world and will be in your world, too.

Still Celebrating Remission
Reinventing Myself and My Life's New Mission

EVE: Good work!!!! Nice insight. Thanks for sharing

JAMIE: You are a true inspiration....watching/observing you go thru this process and have aha moments like this is truly amazing! Thank you for sharing yourself with me and others!

LILLIE: I had to have those shots in my belly, too, recently. They DO hurt. I am sending you a belly shield of Love so the medicine glides in effortlessly. YOU are LOVED.

MARY: I feel your pain Lauren. I have type 1 Diabetes and have been sticking my stomach for over 25 years. Hang in there, it gets easier. Remember, it's on your path to healthy, happy living....

CAT: You are so inspiring. I try so hard to see things the way you do and turn situations around the way you do and it isn't easy. More power to you! You are AWESOME!

JONATHON: Thinking about you and praying for you in this matter. I know exactly how you feel. And I hurt for you.

CAROL: I think it is because we get frustrated with the process. I know I felt that way with intravenous antibiotics. Yet I knew that they were saving my life. Amazing—tearing just thinking about it, so I thank you.

MAUREEN: Hi Lauren, we are thinking about you. Mitch is on a blood thinner as well. He takes a pill every day and does his levels every week. I am sure it is a pain but, I love your thinking.

JODY: Had to give myself those shots. I could not do it the first time, it was like pinching yourself on purpose. Just went against my natural instincts. So I devised a plan to look in the mirror, and pretend I was giving it to someone else.

TERRI: Wow! I will have to try that! I have been injecting myself nightly for four years now; recently the pain has increased exponentially, to the point I have been noncompliant most nights.

SUSAN: Lauren, your very real and human journey through this ordeal AND your intentional spiritual work to reframe all of it is quite a testimony. I'm grateful to you for keeping it REAL, as opposed to only writing the fluffy feel–good spiritual insights (what I call a 'spiritual bypass'). You're owning your feelings and then allowing yourself to be transformed. Bless you and know you are well prayed for on this journey.

ELLEN: How beautiful your consciousness is. Every time you inject yourself, remember, you are giving yourself Love, the greatest love of all. Thank you for continuing to share your journey.

I administered those nasty pain–in–my–gut shots every day for three solid months. The shots were paused in January for a colonoscopy and the takedown surgery. Undergoing a colonoscopy with a colostomy fascinated me. Instead of going through the rectum, the doctors went through my stoma, my Lucy hole. When everything checked out okay, they scheduled me for the final surgery. Lucy was going home. My colostomy was to be reversed. (I never learned why in the world a colostomy homecoming is called a "takedown.") No more Lucy! Nine months was long enough.

During this journey on social media I have met many people with colostomies that will never be reversed. Facebook pages dedicated to "Stoma Buddies" or "Ostomates" are raising awareness about colon cAnswer and early detection with colonoscopies. These pages offer support to people with colostomies along with their loved ones. I consider myself extremely lucky that mine could be reversed.

That time, the doctor kept me for two weeks. Nine days passed before my body knew what to do with a resectioned colon. The entire second floor heard my whoop when I pooped. I promise, no pictures, but really! Imagine *not* being able to go. And when you do, it's into a bag affixed to your tummy and through a hole in your gut? Amazing!

Modern medicine and Lucy saved my life and earned my eternal gratitude. I'll never take a functioning digestive system and bowel for granted again. However, after nine months of cAnswer, colostomy, recovery, and healing, I didn't feel close to complete until Lucy went home. My tummy still felt weird, but I no longer experienced pain and therefore easily weaned myself off of the morphine. They opened and closed my smiley face incision once again and Dad said they ought to put in a zipper.

I weighed a healthy 120 pounds at the time of the surgery, so I had a bit more to work with than the time I weighed in at only 89 pounds. But the skin had been cut so much and the muscles moved so often that I had to doctor the wound for months. I learned about different types of gauze, wicks, and other packing material. While this medical stuff never seemed to end, I reminded myself that *Healing Has Happened* every time that grumpiness or impatience surfaced.

As I worked to mend the incision in my belly and the aftermath of Lucy's reversal, I remembered— *I'm Alive!* I used the same tools during the healing process as I had with the diagnosis, the emergency surgery, the Chemo/Dreamo treatments, the colostomy, and the surgery to fix Lucy. I expertly employed the tools of embracing what is, having fun with it, reframing it, being the observer, forgiving, and expressing love and gratitude. When I found myself moaning and complaining about ongoing issues, I thought about how far I'd come. Then I would ask Spirit to "Show me a Different Way to See This." I would breathe deeply, exhale, and listen. Guidance would come for the next step to lift up the experience.

As I come closer to the end of this chapter in my life called cAnswer, my job description becomes clearer. Now it is to lift up each experience life offers me. I haven't always risen to the occasion in the past. CAnswer made me an expert. Embracing each experience allows me to reframe them to see the bigger picture, rather than candy–coating life in a Pollyanna manner.

Embracing what is allows deep understanding and compassion to occur. When we embrace it all and focus on love in the midst of each Holy Shift, we emit measurable and far–reaching vibrations. This practice becomes a mindful, playful exercise until we graduate from practice to application when the Shift hits the fan. And Holy Shift *will* hit the fan!

How can we embrace each Holy Shift? What tools can we use this time? Sweet Spirit, we are willing! Show us how!

This journey through healing has taken five years to now, April 2017, my cAnswer–versary. Holy Shift! In 2017 I'm still here. I wish I could say it took that long because I was busy getting back to my life, but the truth is that, nine months after Lucy went home, one more surgery was required to repair the grand incision. After a year–and–a–half of remission, the tumor marker numbers of the CA–125 test started rising.

In July of 2014, when I was back in chemo, I went within and asked, "What?" I heard/felt, "Graduate School. Your Masters Degree." Holy Shift! In 2016 I'm still here, so cAnswer Dance #2 didn't kill me. The second dance offered no unknowns so I did it better. But that's in the next book, coming soon! "Holy Shift! Here We Grow Again!"

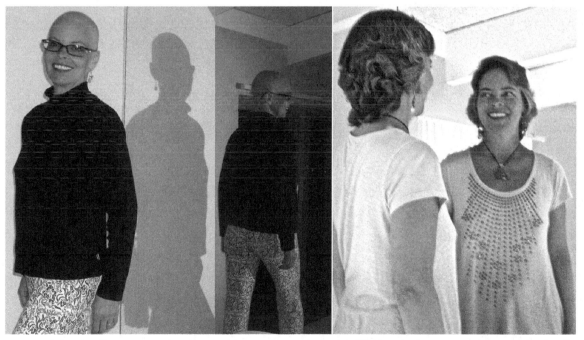

2012, in Chemo, sporting Lucy and in pain *2014, colostomy reversed, pain-free and*
LOOK AT THAT HAIR!

LOVING THE CONTRAST

Embracing impermanence means letting go. All things change.
Thank you God.

AFTERWARD

In August of 2013, seven months after my colostomy reversal, the incision had not healed. A mass had formed close to the surface of my belly. The surgeon told me the cAnswer must be back. I hadn't been in remission for a year. I went cold. I could barely make it across the hospital to my OB/GYN's office. By the time I arrived, I was shaking and weeping uncontrollably. Immediately she started talking about chemo again. I heard nothing after that until she finally examined me.

'Wait a minute," she said. "I don't feel cancer."

She ordered a CAT scan, the results of which I wouldn't see for a week. The white fluffy stuff I pulled from my wound every day made the colostomy surgeon pass me off to his partner for surgery number five to remove a *foreign substance.* Holy Shift!

I realised I did not handle well hearing the news of a recurrance. In a deep meditation I asked "How do I do *this* better?"

I heard, "Die. Go there. Practice. Embrace it."

For the last three months of 2013, I did just that. I grieved my own death. I picked out a room at hospice. I wrote music around my passing. I wrote more threshold songs than I ever knew were in me.

I put myself in Mom and Dad's place regarding possibly losing me. I grieved for them over and over again. At some level, I knew that my dying before them would be easier for me. Selfishly I knew I wouldn't have to grieve their passing if I went first.

Songs poured out of me: *When my Healing Comes in the Form of Dying, I Wonder What it Looks Like on the Other Side?, If You Should Outlive Me,* and *All Things Beautiful.* This is a *small* sampling of the songs that emerged during this time.

I decided at that time in December 2013, if I only had one year to live, I would get my music out there however that looked. So I began 2014 by posting a song a day on Facebook.

In July of 2014, the ovarian cAnswer recurred. This time I knew what to do and how to do it. I didn't know then, that I would stop short of three final treatments to walk my beloved mom home to God. She received a diagnosis of pancreatic cAswer the day before Thanksgiving and died in April 2015. While my family waited at Mom's beside, my dad sent us word regarding his diagnosis of MSA, Multiple Systems Atrophy, a rare subset of Parkinson's disease. He also passed the following April. Wow!

In 2016 the cAnswer came back to me a third time. Without Mom or Dad's support, I had to call upon my community for strength and music. I invited friends to accompany me and *sing* with and to me during each Chemo/Dreamo treatment round. My Chemo–Sabe was born!

I took so many exciting new journeys and learned so many new lessons that each cAnswer adventure deserves its own book. *Holy Shift! Here We Grow Again!* will detail the second cAnswer Dance and also Mom and Dad's passing.

Holy Shift! Third Time's the Charm will teach a new and better way to dance. This period inspired the birth of two new CDs.

From this last experience, I can see cAnswer centers across the country employing a new way of doing treatment filled with love, laughter, and *song.*

Holy Shift! Everything's a Gift!

ADDENDUM

Throughout my dance with cAnswer I received many letters from people who followed me to let me know how my journey affected them. With their permission, I share them in this section.

We've known each other since we were eleven years old! We met in sixth grade at The Stanley Clark School in South Bend, IN. I was frightened and concerned when I learned of your diagnosis, but confident that you would bring yourself and others through it in a way that no one else could. You have taught me to look for the blessings in every obstacle. There is always one there, even if it doesn't reveal itself for a long time. Whenever I have told anyone about you, I have always said that you're the happiest person I know, and that was true before, during, and after your experience with cAnswer.

~Francesca Bowling Kemper

Met you at Unity of Harrisburg, PA not so long ago (6–7 years?). You were so instrumental in helping me find my voice...and the self I was hiding. I had just begun delving into the therapeutic power of music and sound (by way of books) and the teacher (you) showed up! You helped me validate myself, just as you do for all who meet you. I am blessed.

~Robert Felton

Well, as it often happens in my life, I listened to my guidance, intuition and inner voice one day in the spring of 2010. It so happened Lauren had been invited to Unity of Ocala to do the message that morning. I was not going, but something told me I was going to attend and have an open mind. Well, attend I did, and was so impressed. I also invited some of my friends to the workshops she had after that Sunday morning. One was a dear friend who was planning a spiritual retreat that fall, but had not yet chosen a keynote speaker.

I called her right after the service and she came with me to one of the workshops. Well, the rest is history. We had our wonderful retreat that fall and many lasting friendships evolved from that one meeting in the spring. Lauren has such a powerful message for everyone! Thank you Lauren, for being you and for helping so many people through your voice and singing bowls.

~ Barbara Thomas

WOW! We first met in Clearwater, FL, where you sang at the International New Thought Alliance conference in 1997. Then we invited you to the Ignite Your Light Symposiums at the Spiritual Mind Center in Richmond, Va. We ALL LOVE YOU!! God Bless.

~Dwight and Thelma Smith

I first heard her sound at a Coptic Conference at Unity Church of Sarasota many years ago. I asked, "Who is that woman?" They said, "Oh, that's Lauren Lane Powell!" as though I'd been living under a rock. Perhaps it was her infectious personality, her ease with the audience, and her melodic voice accompanied by Crystal Bowls that brought me out from under the rock and into her angelic realm of healing sounds. Later, she taught a class on finding your voice, bringing dozens of women into the realization that by opening their hearts from the bottom up, a sound would emerge that could not be silenced by others. And she made them believe that to be their Truth.

In time, our relationship grew. I invited her to lead the Sarasota Women's Meditation Circle whenever she visited in winter. She was always a success, with women crowding her after the meditation. But the last time she led the women's meditation, I noticed how thin she was. She said she'd been working out and dieting, which was always a mantra for Lauren. I remarked, "Well, don't lose any more weight!"

Not long after that, we all learned she'd been diagnosed with Ovarian Cancer. It was a shock. But, like all the things she does in life, she took it on in a straightforward way, designating it as 'cAnswer.'

When I saw that, I knew Lauren would use her spiritual background and the power of her sound and music as a healing tool. Surely, with this diagnosis, there is always fear and emotion. But this sound–sister would lead the way with humor, familiarity, and by bringing together a community of followers, letting us share in the journey.

You see, most think the spiritual path is filled with hearts, roses, and airy fairy feel–good affirmations. The opposite is true. It's filled with obstacles and challenges and it's up to the Spiritual Warrior to rise up with determination and use every tool in their esoteric training to overcome what is in front of them. Lauren Lane Powell is one of those Spiritual Warriors. Using her voice, her music and the ethereal sound that makes her, *her*, she shows us the way when adversity strikes. What a lesson she's chosen to teach! Sing, Lauren. Sing For the Soul that we love!

~Jo Mooy

We met on www.blogtalkradio.com/ggmradio, on my show *Namaste Nutrition*. Lauren, you are such a wonderful inspiration, and to this day remain one of my favorite radio guests. Your magic, ethereal beauty, and journey was such an inspiration to me and to my audience.

Namaste
~ Claudia Cleary

Lauren,

We first met at Unity of Pensacola, maybe eight or nine years ago. It was not long after the release of *Natural Affirmations* (CD). I bought your CD and it's still my "go to" music when I begin to have thoughts of lack. We renewed acquaintaince this year in April when you returned to Unity of Pensacola. You gave the message and held a three–day workshop within days of diagnosis. How brave you are!!

~Hennie Hopkins

Hello From My Heart Sweet Lauren,

We met about 15 years ago at Port Richey, Unity. I've had a feeling of closeness with you since then, and that feeling has only expanded as time has gone on. Within that feeling has always been the knowledge that everything is perfect and that you have experienced this as an aid to assist in your teaching and singing. As I am sure everyone will concur, Lauren Lane you are LOVED!

~Gary Schineller

We met at Unity Church for Creative Living in Jacksonville, FL. I was in a few workshops in the past maybe ten years ago. I got a crystal singing bowl from you. You have a picture of me on your computer. The last time you were here, I just found out the cAnswer had taken hold of you…Holy Shift! You let it go! Praise to the great Physician within!!! LOVE JOY PEACE GRATITUDE!

~Alisa Pearl

Lauren!
We have never met! I live in Connecticut, and I've no recollection of how we are on each other's facebook pages. Further we have no mutual friends, far as I know. But your journey has moved me, and like Louise Hay in her book, "You Can Heal Your Life." You are amazing. God has entrusted you with continuing life, and you won't let Him down. I love you.

Your sister in Christ,
~Judith Marilyn Kaplowc

Lauren,

We met you in the summer of 2010 at Unity of Plano, Tx. You came to present your workshop with the quartz crystal bowls. Your vocal workshops, and your playing the bowls brought about a healing presence we had not recognized before. Your gift of that week has changed our lives. We continue to present workshops with the bowls in three locations monthly, spreading your message of Love! Your message of hope inspired us then, now, and will live on for generations to come! We love you so much!

~Pat and Charles Mawson

The first time I met you, you made me cry, but in a good way. You were singing "Once upon a time I used to fly with angels" and it stirred a remembrance in me. That was in Oklahoma City in 2007.

-Dee Dee Powell (no relation that I'm aware of.

I see you and your essence through other dear ones on Facebook and wanted to know you...peace...unity...whole health....Loads of Love!!

-Dawn Perryman

You are a Facebook friend and I have followed closely your journey, which has been brave and bold. You have inspired me and made me grateful for my wellness. I don't know how we came to be FB friends, but I am so happy we "met." Blessings upon Blessings to you as your creative journey unfolds.

-Diana Bludworth

I first saw your beautiful face at the Circle of Love Gathering where we spent the week together several years in a row. I have a singing bowl. You've been to my Spiritual Communities as a speaker, musician, and workshop presenter; I have been to your home and you have been to mine. You know my husband and I know yours. I spent time with your family on a Mexican retreat, and I love you!

-Rev. Pat Powers

I first met you in the late 1990s at Unity of Greater Cleveland, when you presented workshops and private lessons. I attended your workshop and loved it! You sang for both Sunday morning services. So wonderful! I didn't see you for a few years but then I had the opportunity to hear you sing and give the morning message at Unity of Medina, Ohio in 2008, I think. I bought a CD and listen to it often. I love your beautiful voice and positive inspiration!

- Ruth Yoder Barnes

We met at Unity in Jupiter, Fl about two years ago. I loved your angelic singing, your message and the crystal bowls. We didn't really talk at the time, but I feel like I got to know you on Facebook, before and during your cAnswer journey. You have been such an inspiration and a blessing. I am so happy we connected.

-Debbie Davis

I met Lauren at a Reiki Retreat. My initial reaction to her was one of awe. She is so warm and loving and fun. She introduced me to her amazing crystal bowls. We all fell in love with her from the get go. Her energy then and now is amazing. Hearing of her cancer was a blow to everyone she met. We felt a reverberation throughout our loving spiritual community. There had been a time that I didn't get to see her much. Yet I knew all of her journey. She would come to stay with me on her visits to Knoxville on occasion. We got to share with each other personal life challenges and how she has met hers head–on. I heard she was doing a program up in Sevierville, TN. I was unable to attend the program, but I asked if I could see her afterward. We met for a bite to eat. Her wonderful and amazing sister was with her. I was shocked to see Lauren. The toll taken on her body from the treatments she was undergoing was a bit overwhelming. Yet, Lauren shone through, her smile, her pushing forward. She took my breath away with her beautiful soul. The love and support of her sister brought tears to me. I loved seeing her. I could see her healthy and whole. Her body just had to catch up with that.

Some time had passed and Lauren was once again heading to Knoxville. We met for lunch again. The woman across the table from me was healthy and striking. She had come away from all her treatments with a blazing spirit! She continues to be an amazing inspiration to my very being.

~ Carole Ammond Truelove

I met Lauren four years ago at Unity Church of Ocala. She had come to do a weekend workshop and after hearing her speak during the Sunday service, I was drawn to her energy and her healing work. She also attended my Yoga class at Unity while she was visiting.

The Unity Minister asked if Lauren could stay with my husband and myself while she was here in Ocala. We graciously obliged, and it was one of the best gifts I could ever ask for. We became good friends and shared our life's journey. She did some of her magic healing techniques with me and I learned about purging my past hurts and regrets. Something happened that week we were together. I felt a shift in my energy and growth on my personal journey thanks to Lauren. She left me with a CD of her personal songs and I played it for months singing along in my car and feeling so happy and free.

Another one of her visits to Florida before her illness, she filmed a yoga video for me. I had never done this before and I was so appreciated to have something to share with my clients. Lauren also enjoyed it because it was a first for her too.

When I first heard of Lauren's diagnosis, I thought to myself "The Universe is using her as an example to heal so she can understand all that she has been teaching others for years." And I never had a doubt in my mind that she wouldn't heal from the cAnswer. I watched and followed her blogs and posts on how she researched and meticulously chose her treatment options, often reaching out to me for advice. I quietly stood back and knew she was being lead to all the right treatments for her. All the while she was optimistic and happy and grateful.

I'll be honest, there were times when I wanted to ask, "Why are you choosing that treatment?" Especially when I would see pictures of her looking very frail and weak. But my inner guidance told me to be still and know. Lauren has the same inner wisdom and she knew how to get the answers that are right and perfect for her. So I watched in total awe as she healed and got stronger every day!

Since my work is in Holistic Nutrition, I was able to offer Lauren an amazing nutritional system to strengthen her immunity and alkalize her body. I knew this would truly help her to regain her strength, especially when eating conventional food was not so much fun. I am glad she listened. It made me feel good to think I somehow was involved in her healing, although I know it was a power greater than both of us.

Seeing Lauren on Facebook and You Tube videos was hilarious. She would be dancing and singing in the halls of the hospitals and helping everyone around her, and herself, shift their energy to one of happiness and gratitude—just what it takes to heal. She knew what she was doing! As far as Lucy, I am a Nurse, so seeing Lucy did not affect me at all. I knew it was just a part of the process.

I am so proud and grateful to know Lauren Lane Powell. She shows the world that nothing is impossible. If she can do it, so can so many others who feel hopeless and in fear of dying from cAnswer. She is given a second lease on life so she can help the world heal, one person at a time. Thank–you Lauren for your strength and transparencies through the biggest challenge of your life. I Love You!

-Maryann Holden CHHC LPN AADP

For more information about Lauren and her music or to book her for your next conference, keynote concert or vocal coach, visit
www.harmoniesofhealing.com

To order featured CD visit
www.chantstoheal.com